LAFAYETTE OF THE SOUTH

TEXAS A&M UNIVERSITY MILITARY HISTORY SERIES

70

Lafayette of the South

Prince Camille de Polignac
and the American Civil War

Jeff Kinard

Texas A&M University Press
College Station

The paper used in this book meets the minimum requirements
of the American National Standard for Permanence
of Paper for Printed Library Materials, z39.48-1984.
Binding materials have been chosen for durability.
∞

Library of Congress Cataloging-in-Publication Data

Kinard, Jeff, 1954–
Lafayette of the South : Prince Camille de Polignac and the American
Civil War / Jeff Kinard.—1st ed.
p. cm. — (Texas A&M University military history series ; 70)
Includes bibliographical references (p.   ) and index.
ISBN 1-58544-103-1 (alk. paper)
1. Polignac, Camille de, b. 1832.   2. Generals—Confederate States of
America—Biography.   3. Confederate States of America. Army—Biography.
4. French—Confederate States of America—Biography.   5. Princes—France—
Biography.   6. Southwest, Old—History—Civil War, 1861–1865—
Campaigns.   7. Texas —History—Civil War, 1861–1865—Campaigns.   8. Red
River Expedition, 1864.   9. United States—History—Civil War, 1861–1865—
Campaigns.   I. Title.   II. Series.

E467.1.P66 K56 2001
973.7′13′092—dc21
00-010346

For Frances and Kelly

Contents

———•—♦—•———

Contents

Illustrations

—•◆•—

Acknowledgments

I will be forever grateful to my wife, Kelly L. B. Kinard, who played a key role in the completion of this book. She spent countless hours typing the manuscript, helping in its organization, and serving as its initial proofreader and editor. I am also indeed fortunate that Dr. Donald Worcester consented to proofread my chapters. His subtle corrections profoundly improved my final drafts. Dr. Grady McWhiney provided the spark to my investigations by suggesting the fascinating Camille de Polignac as my subject. Dr. McWhiney's infinite patience and insights were invaluable during each step of this project.

The staffs of many research facilities also contributed to my research. I am especially grateful to the cordial and helpful archivists of Northwestern Louisiana State University, Louisiana State University, Tulane University, the Southern Historical Collection at the University of North Carolina at Chapel Hill, and the National Archives in Washington, D.C. Ms. Peggy Fox of the Hill College Harold B. Simpson History Complex was particularly tireless in her help, as were Steve Bounds of the Mansfield State Historic Site, Ken Tilley of the Alabama State Archives, and Judy Bolton of the Hill Memorial Library at Louisiana State University.

I am also indebted to Mr. Daniel Frankignoul, a devoted student of Polignac's career, for his generous insights into the prince's life, Scott Burnett for his photographic expertise, Quentin Cline for his cartographic assistance, and W. P. B. Kinard for her organizational contributions.

Introduction

Near the small village of Mansfield in remote northwestern Louisiana stands an obelisk of Georgia granite. Since 1925 it has proudly proclaimed to those few visitors who pass by, "The LaFayette of the South," and just below, within a carved wreath, are the name and achievements of this singular yet largely forgotten Southern hero: "Prince Camille de Polignac, Lieutenant Colonel, July, 1861; Colonel, 5th Tennessee Infantry, August, 1862; Brigadier General, February, 1863; Major General, April, 1864. Twice promoted for gallantry on the field of Richmond, Ky., and Mansfield, La., U.S.A." During his lifetime, many had drawn the obvious comparison between the French nobleman in Confederate gray and his more famous predecessor, the Marquise de Lafayette, hero of the American Revolution. Yet only Lafayette gained the level of lasting fame to which both men aspired. Few took note when this last surviving Confederate major general died November 15, 1913. In the years since, his name—Camille Armand Jules Marie, Prince de Polignac—has appeared only incidentally in the literature of the Civil War.

Yet Camille de Polignac's current obscurity belies this aristocratic French adventurer's remarkable career. He had already won distinction in the Crimean War and had explored Central America before volunteering for Confederate service in 1861. A primary reason for Polignac's relegation to the realm of the footnote has been that the majority of his service was in the Confederate Trans-Mississippi Department. Only recently has the Trans-Mississippi been viewed as more than a backwater of the conflict. It is true that its history boasts no epic battles on the scale of Gettysburg or such charismatic leaders as Robert E. Lee or J. E. B. Stuart. Yet the war west of the Mississippi River was no less brutal than that of the East and no less critical to the war's outcome. Although almost always outnumbered and poorly equipped, the soldiers of the Trans-Mississippi consistently held their own and inflicted significant damage to their enemy. More importantly, they tied up huge numbers of Federal troops who otherwise would have been available in the East.

Fortunately, Polignac kept a detailed diary during his Confederate service. In it he dutifully recorded combat narratives as well as his daily experiences and impressions of everyday Southern life. These revealing entries incidentally provide a lively Gallic counterpart to Sir James Arthur Lyon Fremantle's famous observations. Also, from his unique vantage as a foreigner struggling to rise within its ranks, Polignac provides a little-seen and revealing aspect of the inner workings of the Confederate Army. Even during his lifetime, many of Polignac's contemporaries faulted the Southerners' distrust of foreigners for his lack of recognition. Despite his proven abilities, Polignac found that winning advancement required the careful cultivation of influential friends in the Confederate hierarchy. His resultant campaign thus led to his contact with a veritable who's who of the Confederacy, including Judah Benjamin, Jefferson and Varina Davis, Mary Chesnut, Edmund Kirby Smith, Braxton Bragg, P. G. T. Beauregard, and Richard Taylor.

Polignac subsequently came to command a surly brigade of Texas misfits who, unable to pronounce his name, promptly dubbed him "General Polecat." To the surprise of all concerned, the French prince eventually transformed his wild Texans into one of the most dependable brigades in the Trans-Mississippi. Having won promotion to major general for his pivotal roles at Mansfield and Pleasant Hill, Louisiana—key battles in the defeat of Union general Nathaniel Banks's Red River Campaign—Polignac next rose to divisional command. Later, confronted by Union admiral David Porter's gunboat fleet, Polignac countered with hit-and-run tactics that effectively neutralized the most technologically advanced naval force of his time. During the waning days of the Confederacy, Polignac made a final attempt to save his adopted country by running the blockade on a secret mission to his homeland. Charged with gaining Napoleon III's aid, he arrived shortly after Lee's surrender and, seeing no reason to return to America, remained in Europe for the remainder of his long life. Although he again served France as a general during the Franco-Prussian War and won honors as a mathematician, till the end of his days Polignac looked back to his Confederate service as the apex of his career.

LAFAYETTE OF THE SOUTH

CHAPTER 1

"Lieutenant Colonel, C.S.A., 'Thru Courtesy'"

W hen Camille de Polignac died peacefully in Paris on November 15, 1913, *Le Figaro* reported he was "working on a
[mathematical] problem that had occupied his leisure hours
for ten years." It was a fitting end for a renowned mathematician. During his eighty-one years, though, Camille de Polignac had
done much more than puzzle over difficult equations. He had also gained
recognition as a talented musician, engineer, journalist, political econo-
mist, and scientist. But above all, Camille de Polignac was a soldier. Of
the French nobility, he had served his country in both the Crimean and
Franco-Prussian Wars. Yet for four years—between 1861 and 1865—he
had fought for another flag. When he returned to Paris on a secret mission in the spring of 1865, he did so as Camille Armand Jules Marie,
Prince de Polignac, major general, Confederate States of America.[1]

Polignac's own writings tend to obscure his true reasons for throwing
in his lot with the Confederacy. That a scion of a wealthy royalist family
should commit himself to the cause of Southern states' rights seems to
defy logic. If anything, Polignac was an opportunist and opportunity presented itself in 1861. An intensely ambitious man, he was driven to win
fame and glory—military fame and glory. In 1861, with his native France
at relative peace, the unfolding American conflict presented the most vi-
able avenue to his goal. Polignac the opportunist did not see himself as a
mere soldier-of-fortune or mercenary, but rather as more of a chivalric
knight-errant with an almost mystical sense of his own destiny—a destiny that must be linked to a suitably romantic and noble cause.

It was, as he would have viewed it, fate that initially drew Polignac to
the Southern cause. His first American acquaintances, whom he met in
New York City shortly before the war, were all Southerners—Southerners who, for the most part, also spoke French. These men, including
such future luminaries as P. G. T. Beauregard, John Slidell, and Judah P.

Benjamin, were quite aware that the South would require foreign assistance should it secede from the Union. They, especially the canny Benjamin, began cultivating the politically naïve young nobleman as a possible future ally and liaison with the French government. It was through Benjamin and the others that Polignac developed his own ethical reasons based on the defense of "constitutional liberties" for joining the South.[2]

At first he gave little, if any, thought to the slavery issue. As a European aristocrat he had rarely bothered himself with the plight of any laborers, slave or free. After all, European landowners viewed peasant workers much the same as many of their Southern counterparts viewed their slaves: for their economic value and little more. As the war progressed, however, Polignac found it necessary to at least rationalize slavery's continued existence to both himself and his European friends. By early 1864 Polignac realized that the moral issue of human servitude had become a major impediment to the South's winning significant foreign aid. His subsequent defense of the "peculiar institution" was neither particularly original nor convincing. Borrowing heavily from ponderous proslavery editorials and various other partisan sources, he concluded that the South was blameless in both the introduction and continuance of slavery in the Southern states. Profit-hungry Yankee and English slavers, he wrote, had exploited the labor-starved South's needs and forced the first slaves on the unwilling Southern planters. It was only when the international slave trade had become unprofitable to them that these hypocritical outsiders had declared the practice immoral. Polignac was not opposed to gradual emancipation, but immediate abolition, as he saw it, would have been disastrous to both the unprepared freed slaves and their former masters.[3]

Polignac's upbringing contributed immeasurably to his unique outlook. He was born February 16, 1832, in Millemont, France. His mother, Mary Charlotte Parkyns, was of an aristocratic English family. She was the second wife of Jules Armand August Marie, Prince de Polignac. At the time of Camille's birth, his father was imprisoned at the Fortress of Hamm in the Somme Valley for his role in the failed royalist coup d'état of 1830. Former ambassador to England and prime minister under Charles X, the elder Polignac was unswerving as an ardent proponent of the restoration of the monarchy. He was also something of a religious fanatic, supporting his views by claiming personal visitations from the Virgin Mary. His passionate defense of the Catholic Church after the French Revolution earned him and his descendants the title "prince," bestowed by Pope Pius VII in 1822.[4]

Camille de Polignac in Confederate uniform. In poor condition, this *carte de visite* is probably a copy of an original print made during or soon after the war. Although most of his contemporaries described Polignac as wearing a beard and mustache, this, the only known portrait of him during the Civil War, depicts a youthful, clean-shaven man in the uniform of a brigadier general. *Courtesy Alabama Department of Archives and History, Montgomery.*

The Polignac family carried on a tradition as political and social out-siders and expatriates. Although of noble blood, they were originally relatively unknown and considered upstarts by the established French aristocracy. Camille's grandmother, the beautiful Comtesse Jules de Po-lignac (Yolande Gabrielle Martine de Polastron, 1749–93), rose from obscurity to notoriety in the 1770s as Queen Marie Antoinette's favorite and most trusted confidante. Critics within the royal circle noted that the comtesse quickly gained a controlling influence over the queen—many rumored that the two were lovers. In 1780 the ambitious comtesse gained her husband the title of duke, and two years later she became the royal children's governess. With the coming of the French Revolution, the Polignacs fled France for Italy. In December, 1793, following Marie Antoinette's execution, the duchess fell ill with grief and soon died.[5]

After his wife's death, the Duke de Polignac shepherded his large ex-tended family through a life of exile. From Italy they traveled to Russia, where the duke's son Jules, Camille's father, served in Catherine the Great and, after her death, Paul I's army. Jules eventually resigned his commission and in 1800 traveled to London as aide-de-camp to Count d'Artois, later Charles X. From London Jules made a number of forays into France, where he actively worked to undermine Napoleon's regime. He was twice arrested and, although he escaped once, he spent ten years in prison before he was released during the Bourbon Restoration. The rise of Charles X to the throne in 1824 seemed to Polignac to vindicate all of his own sacrifices.[6] In turn, Charles unwisely made Polignac his most trusted advisor. His decision proved a grave mistake. Bending to the fanatical prince's advice, Charles rashly moved to suppress the grow-ing democratic spirit in France by attempting to oust the newly elected Chamber of Deputies. The Chamber, however, backed by popular sup-port, resisted and Charles's coup failed. On August 2, 1830, he abdicated his throne to his cousin Louis Philippe, the Duke d'Orléans. Jules de Po-lignac was subsequently arrested for his role in the affair and condemned to life in prison. He was thus a prisoner in the Fortress of Hamm when his son Camille was born. In 1836 Louis Philippe commuted the sen-tences of a number of Royalist prisoners, among them Jules de Polignac. Banished from France, Jules moved his family back to England and later to Bavaria, where he purchased an estate. It was not until 1845 that he could return to live in France. He died March 30, 1847.[7]

Jules de Polignac's first marriage, to Barbara Campbell of the Scot-tish House of Royaume-Uni, produced a son, Armand (1817–90). Ar-mand, a cavalry officer, later became the Duke de Polignac. Barbara died in 1819 shortly after giving birth to their daughter, Seyna, who soon followed her mother in death. Camille de Polignac was the second youngest child born to Jules and his second wife, Mary. Their oldest son, Alphonse (1826–63), was a talented man who attended l'Ecole Polytechnique and l'Ecole d'Artillerie, later serving in the Crimean War. Ludovic (1827–1904), also a soldier, attended l'Ecole Polytechnique as well as l'Ecole d'Application. He spent the majority of his career with the Arab Bureau of Algiers. Their only daughter, Yolande (1830–55), died at the young age of twenty-five. Edmond (1834–1901), the youngest child, devoted his life to music and became an accomplished composer.[8]

From an early age Camille de Polignac yearned to become a soldier. While a boy in Bavaria, he listened raptly as his father discussed military matters with his close friend, the famous Swiss strategist Henri Jomini. Polignac later credited his "passion" for strategy, which he asserted "has always occupied my mind," to "having in my childhood played at the feet of Jomini, who became a great friend of my father's and during my father's exile, faithfully visited our estate."[9]

Camille graduated with honors in mathematics from College Stanislaus in 1852 and, as had his brothers Alphonse and Ludovic, applied to the French military academy, l'Ecole Polytechnique. Unlike his brothers he failed the entrance examination. Although devastated, he was determined to win distinction as an officer. In the spring of 1853, he enlisted in the 3rd Chasseurs, 2nd Escadron, 1st Peloton as a private. By proving himself as an enlisted man, he firmly believed that he could work his way up through the ranks into the officer corps. It was the sort of move that would characterize Polignac's career. Convinced in a very real sense that he was fated for greatness, he stubbornly refused to allow any obstacle to deter his destiny.[10]

The outbreak of the Crimean War in March, 1854, proved a godsend to Camille. He obtained a transfer to the trenches before Sevastopol, firmly convinced that he would prove himself in battle and clear the barriers to his promotion. Polignac indeed impressed his superiors with his bravery and leadership during the heavy fighting in June, 1855. He was nominated for promotion to 2nd lieutenant in the 4th Regiment, Chasseurs d'Afrique, on July 24, 1855. After the fall of Sevastopol on September 8, Polignac took leave to recover from what he described as "a nervous state rather than an illness."[11] Polignac suffered bouts of depression and what he termed "sick headaches" throughout his life — most often during moments of intense stress. He refused, however, to allow the episodes to interfere with his activities for long and usually overcame them with rest. By midsummer of 1856 2nd Lt. Camille de Polignac, holder of the Medal of the Crimean War, had returned to France. Yet garrison duty in the French capital proved tedious after the excitement of battle. Soon after his return home, Polignac applied for a discharge from the army in which he had tried so hard to rise.[12] The 2nd lieutenant received his discharge from the French Army on February 15, 1859. More than anything else he was desperate for a change of scenery. Garrison duty in Paris had certain advantages, for Paris was, after all, the most exciting city in the world and his family was nearby. Yet for an ambitious junior officer it was a dead end. There was little glory to be won from behind a desk, and for nearly four years he had languished without recognition or hope of promotion. Within days of his release from service, he prepared to leave for Central America. The region was attractive for a number of reasons. Its exotic plant and animal life as well as its geography appealed to Polignac's keen scientific curiosity. More importantly he, like many ambitious Europeans and Americans, viewed the region as ripe with opportunity. Polignac was well connected and most probably obtained letters of introduction from a member of the famous Erlanger family. Prominent in international banking and finance, the Erlangers would have been able to open a number of doors in the region. Polignac's efforts were apparently rewarded, smoothly paving his way into the upper echelons of Central American society and government. In March, 1859, he arrived in San José, capital of Costa Rica. Warmly received by Pres. Don Juan Maro and "all the authorities of the country," Polignac exploited his title to its full extent in seeking influential connections. He remained in the capital a number of weeks while enjoying its social offerings and exploring opportunities.[13]

After many inquiries Polignac settled on Nicaragua as his most likely avenue to success. Beset by filibusters such as the Tennessean William Walker, the largest Central American country was in desperate need of improving its defenses. Although the recently discharged 2nd lieutenant had little formal training in the field, he boldly presented himself to the Nicaraguan government as a military engineer. He must have been a very convincing applicant for, as he later wrote, "the government . . . placed all its forces at my disposition."[14] The details of Polignac's Nicaraguan sojourn remain obscure. His own later explanations, especially those concerning his motives and ultimate aims, seem self-serving and almost to defy credibility. If he is to be believed, however, and if his activities had been successful, they would have had profound diplomatic implications. For roughly four months Polignac, by his own account in an 1861 letter to P. G. T. Beauregard, personally supervised the construction and organization of both Nicaragua's coastal and transit defenses. Such a project alone would have held great appeal to Polignac's ego, yet with his new position, he meant to accomplish much more. In an obvious attempt to curry favor, Polignac alleged that he meant to help establish a strong United States presence in Nicaragua to offset British interests in the region. As he put it to Beauregard, he "intended offering the United States Government . . . a sort of military consulate . . . which would have been useful in counterbalancing the influence of the English."[15]

For some reason Polignac found it necessary to abandon his ambitious project and return to Costa Rica in midsummer. He remained in San José for another four months contemplating his next move. In a number of letters to his brother Alphonse back in France, he discussed the possibility of returning to military service. Unrest in both Italy and China was creating the possibility of French intervention and with it the opportunity for adventure. But his recent acquaintance with Alexander Dimitri, the U.S. minister to Nicaragua and Costa Rica, soon turned his attention northward.[16]

In late 1859, hoping "to sow seeds that will bear fruit in the future," Polignac sailed for New York City. Dimitri, a native of Louisiana, was encouraging and provided him with letters of introduction to influential friends from his home state. In November Polignac returned to Nicaragua, where he boarded ship at the port of Greytown. Among his belongings he carried Dimitri's introduction to U.S. senator John Slidell.[17] Polignac sought out Slidell and his law partner Sen. Judah P. Benjamin within days of arriving in New York, where they were attending to business. Although neither was a native Louisianan or even Southern-born, they had become an inseparable and immensely powerful political team in their adopted New Orleans. Born in New York, Slidell, eighteen years Benjamin's senior, was tall, polished, and politically ruthless. He had just recently returned from a posting as ambassador to Mexico. Within months he would create diplomatic headaches for the new and hated Republican administration with his role in the Trent Affair and as Confederate representative to France.[18]

Benjamin, described by Stephen Vincent Benét as "the dark prince . . . with the slight perpetual smile," provided a more amicable counterpart to his somewhat dour friend. He was also Slidell's physical opposite. A description of him in his later years by an English lady is revealing as to both Benjamin's appearance and why he and Polignac were to become lifelong friends: "I had not met Benjamin and had pictured to myself an American of the Jefferson Davis type. To my surprise, when he entered the room I saw a short, stout, genial man, of decidedly Jewish descent with bright, dark eyes, and all the politeness and bonhomie of a French-

Judah Benjamin befriended Polignac in New York City in 1859. The urbane
cabinet member profoundly influenced the impressionable Frenchman's decision
to join the Confederate cause. Although the two became lifelong friends,
Benjamin, the shrewd politician, initially valued Polignac's political connections
more than his camaraderie. *Courtesy Alabama Department of Archives
and History, Montgomery.*

man, looking as if he had never had a care in his life." Another Southern lady described him as "Hebrew in blood, English in tenacity of grasp and purpose, . . . French in taste."[19] Benjamin was one of the most complex men of his times. A descendant of Sephardic Jews, the future Confederate cabinet member, later known as the "brains of the Confederacy," was born on the island of Saint Croix in the British West Indies. His parents soon moved the family to Fayetteville, North Carolina, before settling in Charleston, South Carolina. After a two-year stint at Yale, ending under mysterious circumstances in 1827, he moved to New Orleans, studied law, and married a wealthy Creole girl. By the time he met Polignac, his estranged wife and daughter had lived in Paris for fifteen years—not far from the Polignac residence. He, like Slidell, spoke fluent French and like both Polignac and Slidell was something of a wanderer. All three men were cultured, cosmopolitan, and aristocratic. They became friends.[20]

At their first meeting in New York, Polignac eagerly took the opportunity to lay out his plan for U.S. intervention in Nicaragua. The two men listened politely to their guest and apparently showed some interest in his proposal. Central America and the Caribbean had, after all, long held the fascination of Southerners as a new frontier for national expansion. If successfully carried out, the proposition would have been a major coup for Southern interests. Owing to what Polignac referred to as a "lack of funds," however, his idea never went beyond the preliminary planning stage. Still, Polignac's newfound acquaintances would prove to be a "seed" that would later "bear fruit" of the most interesting sort.[21]

Another Louisianan as well as future ally who Polignac met during his stay in New York was Maj. Pierre Gustave Toutant Beauregard. John Slidell's French Creole son-in-law, Beauregard had much in common with Polignac, including a similarity in appearance. Although the Creole was somewhat older, the two men were of similar height and aristocratic bearing. They also affected the Napoleon III beard and mustache so popular among Gallic military types of the day. Conversing in their preferred French, they discussed Polignac's Nicaraguan project. As an army engineer Beauregard found the technical aspects of interest but would also have noticed the irony of the situation. Only four years earlier, following a dispute with his superiors, he had nearly resigned his commission and gone to Nicaragua himself. He would not, however, have gone as an engineer but as second in command to William Walker, the notorious filibuster.[22] Upon parting, the Creole invited Polignac along as his guest on an inspection tour of his own latest engineering projects in New Orleans. Polignac had to decline with "great regret" because of urgent

A major in the U.S. Army when Polignac met him in New York in 1859, Pierre
Gustave Toutant Beauregard cultivated the politically naïve Frenchman's
friendship. At the outbreak of hostilities Polignac immediately volunteered
directly to Beauregard, then a general in the Confederate Army, and was
soon assigned as assistant inspector general to Beauregard's staff. *Courtesy
Alabama Department of Archives and History, Montgomery.*

business in France. For the next few months he continued his connections with his new Southern friends via the transatlantic mails.[23]

There is no evidence that Polignac was particularly concerned or even aware of the deepening American political crisis before meeting Dimitri and the other Louisianans. They were, however, obviously convincing proponents of states' rights—upon his return to France Polignac thought of little else. He regularly scanned the newspapers for recent developments in America and sought out expatriate Southerners for political discussions.[24] He maintained an increasing correspondence with Judah Benjamin, who continued to cultivate Polignac's interest. As the Union began to unravel, Polignac sensed in the American situation a new opportunity to further his ambitions. His new friendships naturally drew him to the cause of Southern independence. The Southern, soon to be Confederate, statesman saw in the French aristocrat a kindred spirit. Benjamin also saw him as a potential conduit to the crucial European aid and recognition his new nation would need. In March, 1861, he wrote Polignac asking his help in making introductions to key French officials for Confederate commissioners Pierre A. Rost and William A. Yancey. Yearning not for a political but a military career, Polignac put little effort into the project.[25]

By the end of the month, Prince Camille de Polignac had offered himself body and soul to the Confederacy. Written from his Paris home March 22, 1861, to Beauregard, then commanding Confederate forces in Charleston, Polignac's application for Confederate service was a strange and revealing document. In many ways it read like any typical job application—a rather creative mix of fact combined with an attempt to offer what the applicant thinks the employer wants to hear. Thus in Polignac's attempt to prove his sincerity, hyperbole reigned supreme.[26] In regard to recent events, he was perfectly candid when he wrote: "I have followed with deepest interest the great events which have taken place in your country, & all my sympathies have been with the democratic party whose rights seemed to me incontestable." He was also reasonably forthright as he continued, "I have always had a profound admiration for your country." But he quickly shifted to wild exaggeration: "I have always considered [the United States] as an adopted fatherland, where I should be happy some day to settle. I had even left the French Army for the sole purpose of making a beginning of the project." He finally assured Beauregard that he "perpetuated the traditions which make of our two nations, two sisters, & that I shall be happy to come & offer the tribute of my person to your cause."[27]

Polignac's letter also reveals a profound difference between the European military outlook of his day and that of America. The difference would also prove his most difficult obstacle while in Confederate service. Extreme poverty in mid-nineteenth-century Europe was a fact of life for millions. Many found the military their only opportunity for a livelihood, and thus most European armies were predominately composed of dispossessed peasants. Under the threat of brutal discipline, these professional soldiers were trained to obey orders with the unquestioning precision of automatons. As a wealthy product of the French military, Polignac expected no less from all enlisted men. In his letter he also made it clear that he considered common soldiers—in other words, peasants—as tradable commodities. Prompted by conversations with Southern agents in Paris concerning the formation of a new national army, Polignac hit on a typically grandiose scheme. In order to ingratiate himself with the fledgling Confederate government, Polignac advanced the possibility of providing the South with Irish and French mercenaries. As later events proved, it was the North, with its open ports, and not the blockaded South that would benefit the most from the influx of European immigrant-soldiers. Often lured by cash bounties and a chance to escape crushing poverty, many foreigners, especially Irishmen, did swell U.S. ranks during the Civil War as recruits, not mercenaries. Cut off by the blockade and increasingly impoverished, the South simply could not compete and, for the most part, relied on native-born troops. Ironically, Polignac himself disdainfully came to view foreign-born Federal soldiers as mere mercenaries fighting for money rather than conviction.[28]

Polignac returned to New York City, probably sailing on the *Glascow* from Liverpool on Wednesday, June 12, 1861. Only four days earlier, Tennessee had completed the Confederate States of America by finally seceding from the Union. Still, war had not yet robbed Americans of their innocence. Other than some skirmishing, there had so far been only one significant military action—the Confederate bombardment resulting in the Union evacuation of an unfinished fort in Charleston Harbor. On that Sunday, April 14, Brig. Gen. P. G. T. Beauregard had propelled both himself and the fort's commander, his old artillery instructor Maj. Robert Anderson, to instant celebrity as respective "heroes of Sumter."[29] Viewed by Charlestonians from their rooftops and delighting both Northern and Southern newspapermen, the drama had resulted in relatively little bloodshed. Anderson's few casualties were the result of a single unfortunate accident, not the roughly four thousand projectiles fired by the Confederate batteries. All in all, the thirty-four-hour weekend fireworks extravaganza seemed glorious. Both sides took pride in the valor of their gallant soldiers. Thousands of naive young men flocked to either Old Glory or the Stars and Bars, anticipating a short but exciting adventure. War fever gripped the land.[30]

The arrival of the French aristocrat attracted only minor attention among the distracted New Yorkers. Although he generated some excitement in acknowledging to local reporters his intention of joining the Confederate Army, no attempt was made to detain him. He calmly made arrangements with the French consul for the forwarding of his mail and visited friends. It was a strange spring. Polignac had no difficulty in the largest of Northern cities preparing for his journey to the new Confederate capital, Richmond, Virginia, where he would report for duty. His progress southward was largely uneventful. Wartime travel restrictions had yet to be firmly established, and he passed into the Confederacy by way of Cincinnati, Ohio, without incident. Self-appointed Virginian authorities proved somewhat more suspicious of the foreigner in their midst. While Polignac was resting overnight at the Cabal House, a Lynchburg hotel, three local men took it upon themselves to investigate his intentions. Shaken from his bed by loud knocks at his door, he underwent an impromptu interrogation. The rough Virginians were somewhat mystified by Polignac's strange accent, but he sleepily managed to assure them of his Southern loyalties. The next morning he continued on to Richmond.[31]

In the early summer of 1861, Virginia's once staid and close-knit capital took on many of the characteristics of a frontier boomtown. The recent transfer of the Confederate government from Montgomery, Alabama, to the city on the James River had sparked an unprecedented population explosion. Thousands of volunteers as well as government officials and political opportunists swelled the city's peacetime population of some forty thousand souls by the hour. With the influx of outsiders came soaring prices, vice, crime, and shortages. Above all, the city's new status and the atmosphere of crisis brought its citizens a sense of fevered excitement and expectation. Even the heavens seemed to promise great and fearful things to come. On June 28 John B. Jones, a clerk in the Confederate War Department, recorded in his diary the appearance of "a flaming comet in the sky."[32]

As the weather grew warmer, Richmond prepared for war. Jones also noted that "Marshal [*sic*] music is heard everywhere, day and night, and all the trappings and paraphernalia of war's decorations are in great demand." A Richmond matron remembered "soldiers singly, soldiers in pairs, in squads, in files. Drums and fifes and crowds of soldiers, and nothing more." Most of the "soldiers," however, were actually untrained and unequipped farm boys. For all the confident saber rattling, experienced, trained officers were in woefully short supply. Beardless cadets from Lexington's Virginia Military Institute drilled recruits on Richmond's fairgrounds, much to the scornful amusement of retired veterans and the entertainment of Richmond's belles.[33]

Polignac had every reason to expect that he would find his destiny in Richmond. French tactics and theory dominated the military mind of the nineteenth century; American military manuals were essentially translations directly from the French. In the South even the Marseillaise had been adapted by Confederate musicians as a Southern battle song. Not only was Polignac a veteran of the French officer corps, but as a child he had literally sat at the very feet of the revered theorist Jomini. Only a fool could fail to see the young prince, "a knight errant" as one woman called him, as a godsend. By now he also had some extremely well-placed friends in the capital. Among them, Judah P. Benjamin was now attorney general of the Confederacy and, owing to his triumph over Fort Sumter, P. G. T. Beauregard was the most famous general in the South. A skilled courtier, Polignac was certain he could exploit his connections and title to win a lofty appointment in the infant Confederate Army.[34]

The Spottswood Hotel on Main Street was the political heart of the Confederacy. A "miniature world," as a senator's wife observed, the Spottswood served as the temporary residence of Pres. Jefferson Davis and his cabinet while they awaited the completion of more permanent accommodations. Rooms in the fashionable hostelry witnessed high-level conferences as politicians and generals plotted the course of the new nation. Inevitably, below them the hotel's lobby bulged at all hours with petitioners of every stripe seeking various political favors.[35] As a wealthy titled aristocrat and friend of Benjamin and Beauregard, Polignac expected a warm reception at the Spottswood. He was not disappointed. Polignac obtained an interview with the president soon after his arrival in Richmond. At nearly six feet, the dignified, almost gaunt Davis stood nearly a head taller than the diminutive Frenchman. The president would have had little time for an extended interview—politicians and landed gentry were virtually mobbing his office under the presumption that wealth and social status were proper qualifications for military command. Unfortunately for the Confederacy, such prerequisites were all too often sufficient for appointments. Noting the relative disparity in numbers between enlisted man and the "embryo heroes" who clamored to lead them, Jones wryly commented: "The President is appointing generals enough, one would suppose. I hope we shall have men for them." Although Polignac's military credentials were far better than those of many of the new brigadiers, he failed to gain his three stars and wreath that day at the Spottswood. Davis compromised.[36]

On July 6, 1861, Prince Camille de Polignac obtained his commission as a lieutenant colonel in the Confederate States Army. On his official records, a clerk added under the heading "Remarks" the notation "Thru courtesy." Polignac's petition had posed a ticklish dilemma for the overworked Davis. The president was keenly aware of his new nation's urgent need for European recognition and economic aid. It also needed good officers. But, as Jones had noted, he had a surplus of potential generals. Davis, like Lincoln, had to walk a fine line appointing generals for either their perceived military talents or as political favors. Polignac was something of an unknown factor.[37] On the one hand, his title carried the cachet of Napoleon III's inner circle, and his military experience appeared greater than that of many applicants. On the other, his true political influence was unclear, and his military performance had been unexceptional. Davis played it safe. As a lieutenant colonel, Polignac could console himself with a rank much higher than he would have held in the French Army. However, it did not quite carry the authority for an important command. The simple fact was that Davis did not want to offend a potentially influential connection with Napoleon but neither did he need another high officer. As a lieutenant colonel the cocky aristocrat could not cause too much trouble, and should he prove himself capable, he could be elevated quickly. As the perceptive Jones sardonically put it, "Well, Washington had his Lafayette."[38]

It came as no surprise to anyone that Davis's potential Lafayette should find his first assignment on the staff of the "Napoleon in Gray." His new position as assistant inspector general was, as he later admitted, usually reserved "as an outlet for troublesome & worthless officers," although he quickly added that this was not the case. His were essentially watchdog duties—inspecting troops and overseeing the compliance with orders from the Adjutant's and Inspector General's Offices. Although wielding little real authority, he was in a position to get a hands-on feel for the workings of Beauregard's Army of the Potomac.[39] Lieutenant Colonel Polignac was like no officer the troops had seen. Auburn haired with deep blue eyes, he strove to set an example of European military efficiency. His meticulous manner and dress, however, often served only to amuse the casual sensibilities of the rough farmers he was attempting to turn into trained soldiers. One, observing Polignac drilling more experienced troops at the Richmond fairgrounds, entertained his friends by quipping, "that there furriner he calls out er lot er gibberish, and therm there Dagoes jes maneuvers up like hell-beatin-tanbark. Jes like he was talking sense."[40]

As a true professional soldier, Polignac would have also stood out in stark contrast to many of the glittering incompetents of Beauregard's staff. Even the least association with the "hero of Sumter" had become a social necessity among Richmond's elite. As a result, the Creole's head-quarters were constantly jammed with fashionable young heroes and celebrity-worshiping young ladies as well as visiting dignitaries. The many distractions greatly hindered any attempts at establishing an effi-cient staff organization. In this surreal combination of military nerve center and mint julep–fueled salon, Polignac did his best to assimilate.[41] He actually did quite well. Anything having to do with the French mili-tary was considered superior to all else. And, while Beauregard was very Gallic, Polignac was actually French. Consequently, Polignac could be assured that the more enlightened officers of Beauregard's staff would look to him for the most up-to-date military theory. They would soon find he had theories to spare. Polignac also found his title and wit gained him instant admission to Richmond society. Although many a hostess could never quite remember whether he was a count, a duke, or a prince, it made no difference. To them he was very nearly royalty.[42]

But the most pressing matter of mid-July, 1861, was the massing of Brig. Gen. Irvin McDowell's Union forces above Bull Run. McDowell's troops had already occupied Alexandria, Virginia, and, determined to deny them the vital railroad junction of Manassas, Beauregard had be-gun massing his own forces in the nondescript little town. Although in-creasing in numbers daily, Beauregard's recruits were still little more than civilians in uniforms. The vast majority of their officers were little better, and their commanding general had never held an assignment of such complexity. Fortunately, their opponents were just as ill-prepared.[43]

The Battle of First Manassas took place on July 21, 1861. There is no information as to what if any role Polignac played in this first major battle of the Civil War. Most probably, he attended to mundane rear-echelon staff duties during the fighting. His mentor, however, won even greater glory on that hot summer day. Although the Confederates made numerous potentially fatal errors at Manassas, the unlucky Federals made even more. Despite later controversies concerning the roles of the vari-ous generals involved and the failure to pursue the routed Union Army, Beauregard received the lion's share of credit for the victory. The next morning, at the suggestion of Brig. Gen. Joseph E. Johnston (soon a full general himself), Beauregard's nominal superior during the battle, President Davis promoted him to the rank of full general. As John B.

Jones observed, "Beauregard is, to-day, the most popular general in the service."[44]

Significantly, the fighting at Manassas made it obvious that neither the Northern nor Southern armies were prepared for a major war. In the North, in an effort to avert future disasters, Lincoln called for a major overhaul of his army's command. Davis was less fortunate. His victory at Manassas only confirmed the egotistical Beauregard's conviction of his own infallibility. Idolized by the public and press, the general quickly gained confidence and boldly criticized the president and his administration. He was indeed justified in his alarm over the amateurish state of Confederate logistics. Among Beauregard's many complaints to the administration, those concerning his army's supply services were among the most bitter. For the rest of the year his battles were to be fought not against Washington but with Richmond.[45]

Beauregard directed much of his wrath against Commissary General Lucius B. Northrop. In an administration infamous for its inefficiency and red tape, Northrop reigned supreme. Even before the blockade this bureaucrat among bureaucrats failed to keep Southern troops adequately supplied and fed. In the months following Manassas, Beauregard's feud with Northrop escalated to the point where Davis felt it necessary to defend the embattled functionary. The president's efforts only served to widen the rift between himself and his most popular general.[46]

Polignac played at least a small role in the controversy. In October, during the height of Beauregard's heated exchanges with Richmond, Polignac submitted the equivalent of an efficiency report on the state of the Confederate Army. Predictably, his findings agreed with the general's dire assessments—after all, the two men shared many personality traits, viewpoints, and even reading habits. Beauregard apparently instigated the report with the view that Polignac's previous service qualified him as an expert in the field. Polignac threw himself into the project with energy and not a little eccentric creativity. Confident in his ability and with an eye on making his name known, he urged that his recommendations be submitted directly to Congress. He diplomatically acknowledged the basic quality of the Confederate soldiers but found defects in supply, uniforms, and the method of choosing field officers. Polignac was especially critical of the practice of electing company officers. As a strict disciplinarian, he correctly viewed the procedure as at best little more than a popularity contest. At its worst it placed men of questionable talent into positions of grave responsibility. Polignac was adamant that the practice could be disastrous in the long run. He backed his point by citing a number of instances in which officers and men manipulated the election system to their own ends. In one case, "a first lieutenant acting captain ordered the second lieutenant of his company to turn out with their regiment on the day of a review, to which he received a peremptory refusal. The delinquent, however, by dint of entreating, escaped being brought before a courtmartial, & a few days afterward, he was selected a captain over the head of the officer whom he had refused to obey." Although he admired the theory of democracy, Polignac felt there was no place for it in the military.[47]

Polignac had a vested interest in changing the system. Unless it was reformed, he had little hope of winning the field command he had come to covet above all else. In a repetition of his experience with the French Army, he had initially failed in his attempt to win his goal. Nine years earlier he had sought an officer's commission by applying for admission to l'Ecole Polytechnique and had been rejected. He had then swallowed his pride and enlisted as a private. Through sheer persistence he rose through the ranks to enter the officer corps. A continent away he had set himself a higher goal and again failed.[48] When Polignac arrived in Richmond, he had fully expected an important command with an appropriately high rank. When he found himself buried in an insignificant staff job, he again overcame his disappointment and pragmatically set out to rise above the situation. He took a two-prong approach. First, he made it a point to make the acquaintance of as many influential people as possible. By demonstrating his zeal for the cause and his abilities to those in power, Polignac knew he could better his chances for advancement. He was not a sycophant like so many of those hovering around the Davis circle, merely a realist who understood how the game was played and played it. His report, although apparently never acted upon, was part of the game. He meant it as a work of conscientious skill to be appreciated by those above him in the Confederate hierarchy.[49]

The report itself contained an even more direct assault on his greatest obstacle. The elective system of selecting officers virtually guaranteed he would never win a command. Regiments, especially on the company level, were self-contained units composed of men from the same locality. When a man voted for an officer, he was casting a ballot for a man he most probably had known all his life. In addition to the reasons Polignac cited, many officers were often the same men who brokered power back home. As politicians, landowners, and major employers, they held considerable power within their home counties. The privates were quite cognizant of the fact that when they returned from the war, they would still be answerable to these same men. They too had to play their own version of the game.[50] In the close-knit and rural antebellum South, many farmers rarely traveled more than the short distance from their homes to the closest market town. They often looked upon their neighbors in the next counties with a degree of suspicion—almost as foreigners. It takes very little imagination to picture their reactions to Camille Armand Jules Marie, Prince de Polignac. The Frenchman, whose English was rapidly improving, became increasingly aware of the jibes often directed at him by the rustic soldiers as he rode past. Officers and men alike seemed to take endless delight in lampooning his accent, manners, dress, and even his mustache. One officer likened his appearance to a "French peddler."[51]

Predictably, even his name afforded his comrades no little degree of hilarity—a nuisance that would annoy Polignac throughout his Confederate service. He soon began signing his reports "Camillus Julius Polignac," or simply "C. J. Polignac"—not exactly Anglicizations of his name but at least more masculine sounding to his rough-hewn fellows. In another attempt to gain acceptance, he began perfecting his vocabulary of American profanity. The lieutenant colonel was brilliantly successful in the endeavor, causing another officer to recall with admiration that when appropriately angry Polignac "swore like a trooper." Despite his efforts, though, he would continue to find the Southern soldier's distrust of outsiders a formidable barrier to his advancement.[52] Polignac also criticized what he observed as "the enormous quantity of baggage in the army." The Southern Army had not yet learned to travel light. Polignac reported, "I find, on examination, that the number of wagons required by the army of the Potomac to move with 15 days' rations is between *4000* & *5000* not including the ambulances." He predicted "dangerous consequences" should future campaigns hinge on speed and timing. His solution was to replace the army's heavy wagons with pack mules or horses. His recommendation did hold a certain logic. Still, he did not explore the unique problems of obtaining, feeding, and handling the vast numbers of animals his plan would have entailed. Also, supply officers were already set in the traditional ways of their branch of service, any semblance of innovation would have been anathema. In any case the question soon became moot as the South exhausted its reserves of supplies and draft animals.[53]

Polignac's final remarks addressed one of Beauregard's pet projects. During the Manassas fighting the general had become concerned over the lack of consistency in his troops' uniforms and battle flags. The wide variety of both had led to considerable confusion during the smoke and chaos of battle. He solved the problem of the similarity between the South's "Stars and Bars" and the Union's "Old Glory" by designing an entirely new banner. Even in the thick of heavy fighting, there would be no mistaking the sympathies of troops carrying the blue cross and red field of Beauregard's Confederate battle flag.[54]

Many Northern and Southern units also wore uniforms that were essentially interchangeable, other than minor accoutrements. At First Manassas, therefore, Southern troops were just as likely to wear blue as gray, and many Yankees wore gray as well; the Zouaves' gaudy uniforms posed their own unique problems. A considerable number of men lost their lives at Manassas simply because of mistaken identity. Beauregard and, most likely at the general's suggestion, Polignac each proposed inventive yet impractical solutions to the problem. That neither proposal was acted upon probably saved many a private from embarrassment and a number of generals from sure death. Beauregard submitted a proposal that Southern troops be issued two bright red-and-yellow strips of cloth. Gaily attached to either side of the men's coats from shoulder to belt, Beauregard predicted the ribbons would end identification problems. Although Beauregard's attempt at *haute couture* would have considerably enlivened his men's drab wardrobes, Davis vetoed his suggestion.[55]

Polignac was more concerned with the uniform specified for Confederate generals. An advocate of martial splendor, he found the regulation "uniform given to generals . . . not entirely suitable to their rank." Although citing a few weak practical reasons for a change in the relatively unadorned general's coat, Polignac was in fact attempting to insert a bit of the French system into the Confederacy. His view of military regalia was typically Continental: "in military matters prestige is necessary to create among subordinates of all ranks that sense of deference & respect to their superiors which alone insures discipline & makes armies strong & efficient." He urged the adoption of new insignia to aid in distinguishing the numerous grades of staff and field officers. For generals he suggested "a coat different in color" to make commanders more easily identifiable on the battlefield.[56] Polignac's ideas were still predicated on his own French training, which stressed that officers should lead by example and be especially conspicuous on the battlefield to hearten their troops. The old manuals, however, did not yet grasp the implications of new military technology. The invention of the minié bullet and telescope-equipped sniper rifles were in the process of revolutionizing long-range accuracy.[57] Polignac simply did not consider the fact that very conspicuous officers were also very conspicuous targets. Commanders on earlier battlefields were rarely victims of deliberately aimed fire from the inaccurate smoothbore muskets of their day. Civil War sharpshooters were destined to empty many a high-officer's saddle at extreme ranges.

Had his new insignias and uniforms been issued, Polignac would only have aided snipers in their deadly business.[58]

The government did not act on any of Polignac's proposals. Most probably his report was scanned quickly at the War Department or in Adjutant General Samuel Cooper's office and filed away as impractical. The system was already in place and functioning, and Polignac's ideas would have shaken it to its core. His main concern, the election of officers, was already part of the army's framework. To have changed the process would have invited chaos. Alterations in the transportation system would have been equally as disruptive. His ideas on uniforms were probably simply too foreign, too French.

For Polignac and the Army of the Potomac, the remainder of 1861 was relatively uneventful. As winter approached, the men occupied their time building log huts in the vicinity of Centreville and learning the fundamentals of soldiering. There was little worry of a major offensive by either side. Chastened by the lessons of Manassas, both Northern and Southern commanders bided their time training their new armies. While Polignac attended to his staff duties, enlisted men, many without winter clothing, shivered in their crude log huts and drilled in nearby fields. On occasion they engaged in spirited snowball fights.[59] They were, after all, very young.

CHAPTER 2

"Time Will Tell"

January 1, 1862–May 12, 1862

———•◆•———

Richmond's citizens greeted the new year with uneasy anticipation. The stalemate along the Potomac belied the preparations being made for the expected decisive battle to end the war. Rumors abounded of Union armies of fantastic size poised to overwhelm the thin defensive lines to the north. Other reports told of massive fleets set to strike the South's port cities. Matters seemed even more precarious in the far-off western states. Still, many younger officers complained of the "dullness of the war," while their elders nervously predicted that 1862 would be far different from its predecessor.[1]

Several of Polignac's new acquaintances figured prominently in the newspapers that New Year's Day. On November 8, 1861, crewmen of the U.S.S. *San Jacinto* forcibly removed John Slidell and his colleague James M. Mason from the British packet *Trent*. Their seizure interrupted the two men's diplomatic missions to Europe to garner support and recognition for the Confederacy. Charles Wilkes, the *San Jacinto*'s captain, very nearly accomplished the mission in which the two Confederates later failed. The incident sparked an international crisis that threatened to bring Great Britain into war with the United States. Secretary of State William H. Seward finally defused the situation by ordering the two commissioners released. Clerk John B. Jones celebrated New Year's Day by crowing: "Seward has cowered beneath the roar of the British Lion, and surrendered Mason and Slidell, who have been permitted to go on their errand to England. Now we must depend upon our own strong arms and stout hearts for defense."[2] Despite the Confederacy's strong arms and stout hearts, its leadership was divided and contentious. Clashes of ego and will between high officials and military officers severely tested the country's stability. This internecine feuding soon turned two of Polignac's most prominent friends into bitter enemies.

On September 17, 1861, President Davis had replaced Leroy Pope

Walker with Judah Benjamin as his secretary of war. His new post inevitably set Benjamin on a collision course with Polignac's commanding
officer. That a lawyer and politician with absolutely no military training
held authority over him particularly rankled Beauregard, but the general
was no match for the politicians. In the months after Manassas, the two
clashed repeatedly—Benjamin invariably besting the politically naïve
soldier. Their power struggle was widely publicized. As a war hero Beauregard could count on wide popular support against the often reviled and
distrusted "Dark Prince," as Benjamin was often called. Many even
spoke of a Beauregard presidential candidacy. Such talk and his own
growing reliance on his brilliant secretary of war inevitably alienated
Davis from Beauregard. The president eventually decided the opinionated Creole was more a liability than an asset.[3]

The petty politics of the high and mighty placed Polignac in an un-
enviable position. Taking an overtly partisan stance either way exposed
the ambitious young officer to the danger of attaching his star to the
losing side. Turning against his commander was unthinkable since that
would have branded Polignac as disloyal and violated his personal sense
of honor. Yet he was also a personal friend of Benjamin. Moreover, he
was aware that his best chances for advancement lay within the authority of the secretary of war and the president. Fortunately, raised in the
traditions of the *ancien régime,* he had been prepared from birth to navi-
gate such intrigues as those of the evolving Davis court. On February 2,
1862, Beauregard left Centreville to report as second-in-command to
Gen. Albert Sidney Johnston in Bowling Green, Kentucky. His transfer
was the result of months of bitter exchanges between himself and the
Davis administration. Both the president and Benjamin as well as innumerable other Richmond officials were relieved to see him go. It seemed
a good compromise.[4]

The Creole could assuage his ego with the knowledge that despite his
new subordinate position the defense of the West was of critical strategic importance. The administration comforted itself that the popular
and respected Johnston would keep a sharp eye on the mercurial Beauregard. Also, their troublesome gadfly would be on the other side of
the Appalachians. Many saw the general's transfer as a flagrant hatchet
job. John B. Jones, from his vantage in the War Department, observed:
"Beauregard has been ordered to the West. I knew the doom was upon
him."[5] Polignac did not immediately follow his commander. He lin-
gered in Virginia two months touring the Tredegar Iron Works, attending to administrative loose ends, and especially establishing useful political connections. He astutely realized that Beauregard's influence had

waned and his new posting could very easily mean exile. Richmond's holiday rounds of parties, dances, and receptions conveniently provided Polignac with the means to avert obscurity. That season the dashing aristocrat was a fixture at the most elite functions. He soon gained a minor celebrity status.[6]

Polignac was a particular favorite among the ladies. An accomplished courtier, he carefully cultivated the friendship of two women who had accompanied their prominent husbands to Richmond. Both Mary Boykin Chesnut and Varina Howell Davis were intelligent, perceptive participants in Richmond's social and political circles. The young Frenchman shrewdly noted that both Mrs. Chesnut and Mrs. Davis wielded considerable influence over their powerful husbands. The wife of James Chesnut of South Carolina, a Confederate congressman and aide to Jefferson Davis, Mary Boykin Chesnut was eleven years Polignac's senior. Although not a beauty she was an attractive woman known for her "delightful sense of humor" and gift for conversation. She was worldly, having traveled abroad, and an intellectual—she read history as well as French literature, often in the original. Chesnut's famous diary also revealed her often acidic judgments of her contemporaries. Her assessment of Beauregard, whom she dismissed as a man who "never had much brains," was typical.[7] Mrs. Chesnut's initial impression of Polignac was little better than her opinion of his general. She amused herself for months chuckling over Polignac's humiliating introduction to the Davis family. Invited to dine with the president and his wife, the unfortunate newcomer mistook the wife of a newspaper editor for the First Lady. The congressman's wife wryly observed, "May he prove of clearer vision on the field of battle."[8]

The incident was apparently rather traumatic for Polignac. At a July 4 dinner with the Davises, Mrs. Chesnut observed he was notably "triste and silent" and "cautious in his approaches." She attributed his reticence to not only his earlier "gaucherie" but to "his English not being too ready."[9] Conversational difficulties plagued Polignac, but not for the reasons assumed by Mrs. Chesnut. He was multilingual and his English was excellent—his mother was British and much of his correspondence and home conversation was in that language. His English, though, was of the proper British variety (with a pronounced French accent) and thus a far cry from the American vernacular. The endless variety of American accents, dialects, and slang often frustrated Polignac's best attempts to hold meaningful conversations and, as Mrs. Chesnut observed, reduced him to uncomfortable silence. He doggedly practiced his polite Southern English, however, and at last won over even the doughty diarist. He

A born courtier, Polignac quickly noted that the intelligent and charming First Lady of the Confederacy, Varina Davis, held considerable political influence in her own right. Although the ambitious officer initially cultivated her as his personal advocate to her husband, the two became close friends and confidants. *Courtesy Alabama Department of Archives and History, Montgomery.*

eventually became a welcome guest at the Chesnut residence, and the lady of the house even stopped sniping at him in her private writings.[10]

Varina Howell Davis, the First Lady of the Confederacy, was thirty-five when the war began. In contrast to the childless Mrs. Chesnut, Mrs. Davis was pregnant with her fifth child when she met Polignac. Although her inevitable enemies among the Richmond society ladies snobbishly referred to her as "a coarse western woman," English journalist William H. Russell was more typical in his assessment. To him she was "a comely, sprightly woman, verging on matronhood, ladylike and clever . . . , and she seemed a great favorite with those around her."[11]

Mrs. Davis became Polignac's friend and confidant. He was a frequent guest at the Brockenbrough mansion, the three-story brick building in which the Davises set up housekeeping after moving from the Spottswood. Known as the Confederate White House, the mansion featured a large garden in which the lieutenant colonel and Mrs. Davis spent many pleasant hours. He apparently truly enjoyed the First Lady's company yet he sheltered ulterior motives, for he knew that her husband valued her opinions. Because his own access to President Davis was often tenuous, he counted heavily on Mrs. Davis as his advocate before the Confederacy's leader.[12]

On April 10 Polignac departed the capital to rejoin Beauregard's staff. The abysmal Southern railway system and Federal incursions into northern Alabama necessitated a week-long circuitous journey through the Deep South. After reaching Chattanooga in southeastern Tennessee via Lynchburg, Virginia, he learned that the usual route was cut by the capture of Huntsville, Alabama, only days earlier by troops under Union general Ormsby Mitchel. Detouring south to Atlanta, Georgia, Polignac next passed through Montgomery, Alabama, and crossed Mobile Bay by ferry. In Mobile he at last boarded a Mobile and Ohio Railroad car that reached Beauregard's new headquarters at Corinth, Mississippi, on the seventeenth.[13] Beauregard had chosen Corinth, a northeastern Mississippi rail junction, for his new headquarters after recent reverses made Bowling Green untenable. It was a good choice. The town's rail connections and central location offered rapid transportation and communication across the Confederate defensive line as far west as Memphis. Extensive defensive works discouraged attack.[14]

The Confederate Army at Corinth was like none Polignac could have imagined. From its commanders down it was a complete shambles. The bloody yet indecisive fighting at Shiloh only ten days earlier had claimed 10,697 Confederate casualties, including 1,726 killed. Gen. Albert Sidney Johnston was among the dead. A Yankee bullet severed an artery in the commander's right leg and he bled to death while his staff looked on helplessly; no one thought to apply a tourniquet.[15] The Tishomingo Hotel faced the railroad tracks near the station where Polignac detrained. It had no vacancies. Nearly all public buildings and many private homes in Corinth were filled with wounded survivors of Shiloh. Inside the Tishomingo surgeons bent to the grisly task of amputation. For days townspeople and soldiers alike shuddered at the mountain of amputated arms and legs that arose outside the hotel's door. Of every ten of the amputations performed inside, only two patients survived. Medicines were scarce, scores died each day of gangrene, tetanus, and simple bad doc-

Railway Station and Tishomingo Hotel, Corinth. Polignac arrived here April 17, 1862, shortly after the Battle of Shiloh. This drawing, made by Harry Finn from a photograph taken in 1862, depicts the rail depot and Tishomingo Hotel, used at the time of Polignac's arrival as a hospital. *From Johnson and Buel, eds.,* Battles and Leaders of the Civil War, *2:742.*

toring. Polignac found the streets of Corinth filled not with confident veterans but with cripples hobbling slowly on their new crutches. Hundreds of others had decided they were not cut out to be soldiers and had gone home.[16]

After Johnston's death Beauregard had assumed command of the survivors, a "mob," as his second-in-command, Gen. Braxton Bragg, aptly referred to the nearly fifty thousand troops. Reorganization was crucial, yet both generals were plagued by their own poor health. Beauregard, suffering from the lingering effects of an earlier throat operation and plagued with recurrent colds, was often incapacitated. Despite a personal rivalry with Bragg, Beauregard appreciated his administrative abilities and welcomed his transfer to the Army of Mississippi.[17] Although Bragg's administrative and organizational talents were formidable, his unfortunate deficiencies were legion. Tactless, often arrogant, he regularly alienated fellow officers and terrorized his own troops with draconian disciplinary measures. His mood at Corinth was hardly brightened by a painful flare-up of carbuncles. Nevertheless, his presence helped stabilize the Confederates' situation after Shiloh even with the liabilities.[18]

Shown in this photograph wearing a pre–Civil War U.S. Army uniform, the unpopular Braxton Bragg was second-in-command of the Confederate forces under Beauregard when Polignac arrived in Corinth. Although Polignac appreciated Bragg's organizational abilities, he, like so many other officers and men, considered him a timid combat officer. *Courtesy Alabama Department of Archives and History, Montgomery.*

Although promoted to full general on April 12 for his contributions at Shiloh, Bragg considered the battle a defeat. The disorganized retreat coupled with the Confederates' inability to follow up their success of the first day's fighting convinced him of the necessity of tighter control. As he put it, "Our failure is due entirely to a want of discipline and a want of officers." To remedy the situation he instituted a series of measures designed to rein in the independence of his volunteer citizen-soldiers. Bragg's efforts to instill professionalism in his army of amateurs were largely successful. His soldiers, however, would never follow him out of personal loyalty and affection such as those of the beloved Robert E. Lee: they would follow Braxton Bragg out of fear.[19] Tennessean Sam Watkins aired the consensus of many of his fellow enlisted men: "None of General Bragg's soldiers ever loved him. They had no faith in his ability as a general. He was looked upon as a merciless tyrant." Shiloh had also coincided with the expiration of many of the volunteers' twelve-month enlistments. Polignac observed that, having served their obligations dutifully, the men felt betrayed when the Confederate government authorized conscription and arbitrarily extended their enlistments. According to Watkins it was Bragg's strict enforcement of the new regulations after Shiloh that made his name "a terror."[20] The morale of the Confederate soldiers at Corinth, especially those of certain Tennessee regiments singled out by Bragg, was abysmal. Desertion became epidemic. Private Watkins (often prone to exaggeration) recorded that as punishment, "men were shot by scores." To Watkins and his fellow volunteers, compulsory service removed their free choice and insulted their sense of personal honor and patriotism. He declared: "it was mighty rough on rebels. We cursed the Southern Confederacy. All our pride and valor had gone, and we were sick of war and the Southern Confederacy."[21]

Unlike the European armies of Polignac's experience, the army at Corinth was composed of amateur citizen-volunteers who had overnight been coerced into serving as conscript soldiers—an action that totally outraged their innate sense of democracy and fair play. Many of their elected line officers too often undermined the controls necessary for an effective military force. By pandering to their men's baser instincts in order to win elections, they purposely relaxed official protocol and discipline. Bragg's heavy-handed efforts to restore order added focus to his soldiers' disillusionment with army life. Nothing could have prepared a veteran of the rigid French military system for Corinth, Mississippi.

Polignac spent his first week in Corinth reacquainting himself with old friends, meeting newly assigned staff officers, and attending to such mundane necessities as acquiring a saddle. Brig. Gen. Thomas Jordan,

Beauregard's aide, solved Polignac's most immediate problem by graciously inviting him to share his quarters. Beauregard had sprinkled his staff with relatives and fellow Creoles, and Polignac enjoyed conversations in fluent French with the general's brother about gold mining in California and with his quartermaster officer about acquiring proper servants. The latter, Capt. E. A. Deslonde, promised to provide Polignac with "a tip top negro who can cook, attend to a horse, & behave in company, in short who will make a stylish footman." The new arrival found it rather easy assimilating into the culture of the aristocratic Creoles of Beauregard's staff, but above all he wanted a field command.[22] His prospects seemed promising; Shiloh had claimed dozens of field officers. Both Beauregard and Bragg recognized the need for competent replacements, and Polignac was unquestionably a professional. On April 22 Polignac confidently wrote, "Tomorrow I will get from Gen. Jordan my orders to report to Gen. Bragg in order to be assigned the command of a regiment." The regiment in question, the 18th Louisiana, had not yet been consulted.[23]

Two days later Polignac glumly penned, "It appears that I cannot get the command of the 18th Louisiana Regt." The Confederate command assignment process mystified Polignac. His superiors had chosen him to command the regiment but its men refused to accept him. He did not even get to meet with the unit. The process, as Polignac described it, required an intermediary who "went to see the officers of the 18th Louisiana of which I am to be the Colonel, in order to feel their pulses about this assignment, & to pave the way for me. This is an indispensable step (strange as it may appear & inconsistent with the rules of discipline as established in the European armies) with a regiment of volunteers & is a consequence of the elective system & of the whole organization." Beauregard and his chief of staff scrambled to find Polignac a suitable consolation assignment. Within hours of his rejection Polignac exulted: "I am going to be assigned to a brigade. The order has been issued. This is still better. Confidence! Confidence! 'Macte animo' [glorious spirit]."[24] Polignac eagerly set out to equip himself with the trappings fitting a brigade commander. He obtained a promise from Captain Deslonde of a handsome mount, and a visit to the ordnance officer secured a more stylish English saddle. Assigned a brigade, well mounted, and confident, Polignac noted with satisfaction, "another unexpected turn of fortune—either 'feast or famine' as the proverb says. I now only want a servant to feel comfortable."[25]

His new command was the 2nd Brigade of Brig. Gen. Daniel Ruggles's division. Polignac found the general, a West Point graduate and distinguished Mexican War veteran, "a fine old gentleman" but added that many considered Ruggles "not much of a soldier." The general's best days were behind him. He had led his men bravely at Shiloh but could not control them between battles. A general consensus held that his age prevented him from paying "but little attention to [his troops'] comfort & drilling." His neglected volunteers routinely foraged among local civilians to obtain basic needs. Complaints inundated the chief of staff's headquarters. Bragg, Ruggles's immediate superior, found it necessary to admonish him to "preserve the best discipline possible with our men, preventing the plundering of our people, which is now too common."[26] Polignac shared Bragg's views regarding professional military standards. It is quite possible Bragg thought the French veteran would exert a steadying influence within Ruggles's command. The lieutenant colonel quickly set about selecting a more efficient location for his brigade as well as better encampments for the entire division. Two days later his plans collapsed.[27] The 2nd Brigade, as had the 18th Louisiana, simply refused to accept an outsider. Veterans of Shiloh, they demanded the return of their familiar and trusted leader in that battle, Col. Preston Pond, Jr. As a foreigner, an avowed disciplinarian, and a "yeller dog" staff officer, Polignac as a proposed replacement "raised a bristle" among the officers and men of the regiment. The return of Pond on April 29 ended any hopes of reconsideration. Once again the would-be field officer besieged Beauregard's headquarters.[28]

The general, harried, ill, and distracted by the grim military situation, must have groaned at Polignac's return. He quickly rid himself of his by now annoying petitioner by agreeing on a course to bypass the uncooperative lower echelons. He promised to go over their heads and write directly to the secretary of war recommending his promotion to brigadier general, then promptly forgot the matter. Polignac, however, took Beauregard at his word and observed that by dispatching his request directly to Richmond, he would "settle the matter at once & in a way much more profitable & gratifying to myself."[29]

A few days later during dinner, one of Polignac's fellow officers casually commented that Polignac's hair "was of a colour of Caesar's." The colonel could not have known that the young Frenchman harbored a secret conviction that he was destined to follow in that ancient general's footsteps. His simple observation prompted Polignac to muse later, "Why is it that the mere mention of that slight similitude sounded as sweet to my ears as the sweetest compliment." Alone that evening he reflected on the great Caesar's fame in relation to his own obscurity. He concluded that to achieve his own place in history "every nerve must be strained . . . every pleasure, every desire, every love must bend . . . to work reality out of this flattering dream." However intense Polignac's ambition, it was no match for army red tape. By May 6 he was again buried in the inspection department.[30]

Heightening his frustration, a crucial showdown with the approaching Union Army seemed imminent. Although the Confederates in and around Corinth numbered some fifty thousand, the enemy fielded over twice their strength. Maj. Gen. Henry W. Halleck, overall commander of all Union forces in the West, arrived from his headquarters in St. Louis to lead the huge Federal juggernaut in person. Combining Maj. Gens. Ulysses S. Grant's and Don Carlos Buell's armies at Pittsburg Landing with still more troops, Halleck started his advance in late April. The twenty-two-mile march proceeded at a snail's pace. Fearing a surprise attack such as had opened the Shiloh fight, Halleck ordered his troops to dig entrenchments at the end of each day. Beauregard, as a consequence, had nearly a month to prepare for their arrival.[31]

Yet he needed much more than time. Even as his engineers completed Corinth's formidable defenses, Beauregard realized the futility of their labor. As the days became warmer water grew scarce. Troops dug shallow pits to obtain ground water. Owing to typically deplorable camp sanitation, their improvised wells were soon contaminated with sewage and refuse. Having no alternatives, the men held their noses and drank. Thousands fell ill as typhoid fever and dysentery swept through their camps.[32] On May 17 Polignac recorded that "sickness prevails." As Pvt. Sam Watkins remembered: "We became starved skeletons; naked and ragged rebels. The chronic diarrhea became the scourge of the army. Corinth became one vast hospital. Almost the whole army attended the sick call every morning." A later estimate held that as many men succumbed to disease at Corinth as from wounds at Shiloh. Beauregard's army was dying.[33]

The Creole general still hoped somehow to repel the Union advance. By drawing off or isolating smaller, more vulnerable elements from Halleck's main force, Beauregard felt he might reduce his enemy piecemeal. However, diversionary cavalry raids on Halleck's communication lines in Kentucky and Tennessee failed.[34] Polignac, although unfamiliar with American cavalry innovations, was certain he knew the reason for their lack of success. As an infantryman he was traditionally skeptical of the cavalry's innate worth and considered the raids "silly." As a Frenchman he saw the Americans as violating every tenet of proper warfare. Polignac dismissed the Confederate cavalry as ineffective and "of no account" because "they are all armed with fire arms & I believe that measure to be a great extent to the cause of their inefficiency." In his view only the lance and saber were suitable arms for mounted troops. In reality, Beauregard simply did not have enough men and horses to pose a significant threat to Halleck's rear. On two occasions, however, Union general John Pope seemed willing to help advance Confederate strategy.[35]

Pope had a knack for making enemies. Bragg, who had known him during the Mexican War, detested him. "Accused of kidnapping two Mexican women, one 14 years old . . . for carnal purposes," Pope had forever disgusted his puritanical future opponent. Late in the summer of 1862, he would alienate his entire command in Virginia before leading it to humiliating defeat at Second Manassas.[36] In May, 1862, however, Pope was still a hero. Two months earlier he had opened a vast stretch of the Mississippi by forcing the surrender of the strategic fortress Island No. 10. By late April he commanded Halleck's left wing. Emboldened by his earlier success and frustrated by his commander's slowness, Pope pushed ahead of the rest of the army. On May 3 his division arrived in the vicinity of Farmington, "a little village," according to Polignac, "which lies on a hill" four miles east of Corinth. Without waiting for Halleck to catch up, Pope tested the Confederate defenses.[37]

Despite the Federals' ponderous approach, Pope caught Brig. Gen. John Sappington Marmaduke, the Rebel commander at Farmington, off guard. "At 4:30, right after dinner . . . a heavy firing" alerted Polignac to Pope's attack. Polignac later blamed the confusion that crippled the Confederate response to Marmaduke's incompetence. As Polignac viewed it, "on being attacked unawares . . . (Marmaduke lost) all his presence of mind & all control of his command & (gave) the untimely order to retreat."[38] Embarrassed by his rout, Marmaduke reported that a vast force of as many as fifteen thousand Yankees had nearly overwhelmed his single brigade. According to Polignac, however, "no enemy could be seen" in the dense woods. Sure that he would have acted more coolly had he commanded, he wryly observed, "The booming sound of their artillery was all that betrayed [the enemy's] presence & that very much frightened our men." Polignac was convinced that he could have prevented the panic— that while he and his talents went unappreciated, others less capable were losing the war.[39]

According to Polignac, Beauregard's entire army responded to Pope's initial attack with "considerable slowness." Despite the magnitude of Shiloh, many of the men had never been in battle and their officers had yet to learn the martial profession. Polignac singled out Ruggles's division, whose 2nd Brigade had so recently rejected him, for its inefficiency. Inspecting the lines long after Pope's opening shots, he noted "the long roll was not yet beaten when we rode by."[40] Fortunately, Pope withdrew without exploiting the Southerners' confusion. Unaware that the aggressive general had been acting on his own, Beauregard and Bragg expected an all-out attack the next day. That night Polignac reported, "All the troops are held in readiness." At five the next morning, he satisfied himself that the men were in their positions and "ready for a fight." Yet under a thickening overcast, the woods and fields before them remained eerily silent. Scouts soon reported that Pope and his troops were gone. At two in the afternoon, soaked by a steady rain, the men returned to their camps.[41]

Pope, described as typically "aggressive and sometimes rash" in battle, was not rash enough to risk a major engagement. Now separated by a marsh from his closest reinforcements, he was dangerously vulnerable but nevertheless refused to retreat. Beauregard was certain Pope had played into his hands.[42] At his melodramatic best, Beauregard exhorted his troops that the time had come to "drive back into Tennessee the presumptuous mercenaries" threatening their "subjugation." Bragg, who was to lead the frontal attack, was even more florid than his commander. He promised his men that "at one blow" they would not only "redeem Tennessee, Kentucky, and Missouri . . . but open the portals of the whole Northwest."[43]

At eleven in the morning of May 8, Pope's and Bragg's advance pickets met between the two roads linking Corinth and Farmington. As the fighting intensified along Bragg's front, scouts reported an unguarded crossroads north of Corinth. To guard against a possible flank attack, Bragg ordered Polignac to detach three companies of Maj. Gen. Benjamin F. Cheatham's division to guard the intersection. Confident in his own position, Beauregard waited for the sound of firing on Pope's left that would announce his own flanking maneuver.[44] Maj. Gen. Earl Van Dorn was to command the decisive attack. Rarely punctual, Van Dorn, according to Polignac, finally succeeded in "get[ting] his troops in position but the setting in of the night prevent[ed] his attacking the enemy."[45] Van Dorn vowed to redeem himself the next day but, as Polignac observed: "At daybreak Genl. Van Dorn finds that the enemy here retreated from the positions they occupied the evening before."[46]

Although he had failed to crush Pope, Beauregard congratulated both himself and his troops for having forced a Union retreat. Also, as Polignac observed, the day's relatively bloodless action had raised morale and served as a much-needed training exercise. As Halleck continued his slow advance, both men still held hopes of a Confederate success. On May 12

Polignac noted: "The enemy are said to have marched their whole army to within 2 miles or 3 from our lines of entrenchments. I believe that we shall attack them which I consider a good policy particularly if we can succeed in crushing separately their different columns which they are marching upon us—I believe not adequately supporting one another—Time will tell."[47]

CHAPTER 3

"Was Not Caesar, Caesar at Twenty?"

May 13, 1862–August 10, 1862

————•—•————

As the opposing armies' commanders pondered their next moves, Polignac polished his vocabulary and social skills. He knew from painful experience that his greatest obstacle to advancement was his foreignness. In order to learn the many nuances of Southern speech and manners, he took every opportunity to join his fellow officers' camaraderie. They, in turn, apparently enjoyed his company during their often raucous evening gatherings. Despite his desire to fit in, Polignac found certain habits common to Southern gentlemen too repulsive to adopt himself. Accustomed to fine French wines, he politely declined to join his comrades in rounds of local corn liquor and cigars. He also noted that he was quite "remarkable" for not affecting the universal habit of tobacco chewing and spitting.[1]

He delighted, however, in joining his fellow soldiers' occasionally ribald discourses, as he put it, "to get my ear & tongue broken to the english [*sic*] idioms." He at times recorded what he considered rough but amusing anecdotes for possible repetition during future fireside banters. One story particularly invited his analysis. It "alleged as the cause of the death of some vain & overconceited fellow that he had a peacock feather stuck into his *asshole* & strutted himself to death!!" Somewhat tongue-in-cheek, he observed that the yarn was "a sample of Western witticism & refinement which all being considered is perhaps not devoid of wit," adding "but only relatively not absolutely."[2]

Polignac's interests, however, went far beyond recording risqué stories. He was determined to understand the people whose cause he had joined. His investigations were somewhat limited—his rigid, class-conscious upbringing prevented him from close association with common soldiers and citizens. Yet he eagerly engaged other officers and those he considered gentlemen in spirited conversations. On one occasion, a "beautiful starlight night—deliciously cool," Polignac listened raptly for hours as a South Carolinian described plantation life. To improve his English further, he attended sermons delivered by a Reverend Palmer, reputedly "among the best preachers in the country." Although Palmer's command of language impressed Polignac as "excellent," he confessed to being "somewhat disappointed" in his lack of modern scientific enlightenment. As an educated Christian, Polignac believed one could reconcile scientific logic and Biblical interpretation. He found the minister's literal interpretations "shallow," complaining that: "[he] speaks of the covenant God made with man after the deluge & of the *rainbow*, which *he bent over* the earth as a solemn pledge of this covenant. That quotation is indeed too antiquated: to point out a direct interference of God in a simple & material fact in nature, an unavoidable consequence of any heavy rain is rather inconsistent with the state & progress of science nowadays, it jars & falls short of the object intended."[3]

Polignac was also unprepared for the exuberant animation that Palmer, like so many country preachers, used during his sermons. Accustomed to stately, dignified discourses from the pulpit, he was taken aback by Palmer's wildly expressive fire and brimstone performances. As Polignac observed, "He had certainly overlooked the first precept of Demosthenes with reference to orators." It particularly disturbed Polignac that Palmer "moved his arms & legs in the most awkward way." He explained: "I think it is well for an orator to speak from the pulpit so that his legs be hidden; the gesticulation of the arms is all that is wanted. I do not know what gesticulation of the legs could be graceful & add to the effect of the speech." Despite Palmer's theatrics, Polignac conceded, "he speaks fine & good English" and regularly sought him out for "long head to head conversation."[4]

As his English improved Polignac gained the reputation of being something of a wit. In one instance a naïve young aide expressed the desire to obtain a bottle of brandy from an old colonel renowned for his portable liquor stores. His messmates, with barely contained glee, advised him that if the aide sent an empty bottle to the colonel, he would obligingly return a full one. To complete the transaction they insisted he include a note stating, "A nod is as good as a wink to a blind horse."[5] As the credulous victim searched for pen and paper, Polignac wryly observed that their gruff superior officer "might return the bottle with the answer: 'An empty bottle is as good as a full one to an ass.'" Delighted, the other officers put Polignac's witticism to paper and had it delivered to the mortified youth as having come from the colonel. The aide, once let in on the joke, took the whole affair good naturedly, and "at dinner the case was taken up and enlarged upon in a very boisterous conversation in which what was 'wanting in wit was made up in laughter.'"[6]

Despite such interludes grim realities overshadowed the month of May. News of Confederate reverses from New Orleans to Norfolk cast a pall over Corinth's defenders. As his health continued to decline, Beauregard's despair mounted. Even Polignac, who considered the general his mentor, noted the commander's indecision.[7] Polignac was mystified that Beauregard allowed the Federals "undisputed possession of the Tennessee River." Although he repeatedly attempted to convince the general to take action, he drearily reported: "Nothing has been done much as I urged it on Genl. B[eauregard] ever since I have been here to prevent the transports carrying troops & supplies to run up the river to [illegible] or Pittsburg Landing which object might be effected with a few batteries of flying or horse artillery supported by cavalry."[8]

Polignac's pessimism deepened when he was assigned to investigate a local telegraph company's claims against the army. He was convinced his talents were being wasted in the drudgery of settling insignificant accounting issues. As he labored to balance the army's outstanding financial obligations, he privately reflected on the failings of the Confederacy's highest leaders. In his view the Confederacy's military setbacks were the direct result of the timid policies of Pres. Jefferson Davis and Gen. Joseph Johnston.[9] Polignac, who believed "of all policies the worst is to wait," advocated a vigorously aggressive policy. Union general John Pope shared his sentiments. He too was frustrated by the lethargy apparently gripping the two armies' commanders. Barely a week after his first abortive attempt to break the stalemate he tried again.[10]

Pope's unsupported advance came as something of a reprieve to Beauregard. As both his health and military situation deteriorated, his greatest enemy had become his own despair. Personally, he must also have felt particularly alone. Gen. Thomas Jordan, his chief of staff and closest confidant, had become incapacitated by an attack of typhoid fever. On the nineteenth Beauregard wrote Adjutant General Samuel Cooper advising him of the possibility of Corinth's evacuation, and yet he seemed incapable of making even that decision. Pope provided Beauregard the opportunity to, if not initiate action, at least to counteract his own.[11] Polignac's spirits lifted on the nineteenth. Despite his defeatist letter to Cooper, Beauregard called "a long meeting of all the Generals & Major Generals" to plan another trap for Pope. Afterward Polignac noted with satisfaction, "From some hints I believe that an attack has been decided upon on our part—so much the better."[12] As the division commanders readied their troops, Jordan, in need of more expert care, was placed on an outbound train. Beauregard, already missing his counsel and support, wished his friend a sad farewell. Polignac shared in the commander's loss—Jordan left town owing him two hundred fifty dollars.[13]

Beauregard planned to attack by 10:00 in the morning of May 21. In a carbon-copy of the previous action, Bragg would attack Pope's front while Van Dorn struck his left flank. Polignac had immediate misgivings, writing, "I fear the time selected is too late to take the enemy by surprise & follow up what advantage we may gain." He needn't have worried about early-rising Yankees. During the night heavy rains and "a perfect gale" prompted Beauregard to postpone the attack until the following day.[14] On the twenty-second Beauregard's entire command must have felt a sense of déjà vu when, as Polignac reported: "The contemplated attack did not take place owing to some misunderstanding which I have not been able to trace to its source—arising partly from the guides used by Genl Van Dorn whose troops never got into position & were ordered back at 2 of PM." Van Dorn's failure doomed Beauregard's last hope of gaining the initiative.[15]

May 23 "dragged along," as Polignac gloomily observed, "darkened . . . by a heavy succession of showers from morning till night." A melancholic mood pervaded the camp as Beauregard ordered trusted staff officers to begin exploring escape routes. Polignac, who remained at headquarters, burned with curiosity as the commander called a private conference with his generals. The meeting's length, as Polignac anxiously observed, "seem[ed] to indicate that there [were] conflicting opinions as to the policy of the men among them." Whatever decision the generals settled upon they kept to themselves. Their only hint to their staffs was a pointed order to expel from the camp a particularly obnoxious newspaper correspondent.[16]

Corinth was infested with Union spies and Southern newspapermen. Throughout the campaign both regularly provided Halleck with timely intelligence of Confederate plans. Union agents had infuriated Beauregard by intercepting a telegram containing his troop strengths, which were later published in a New York paper. Southern war correspondents proved equally damaging. The reporter singled out by the generals had just recently published a complete itinerary of the Confederate movements before a subsequently unsuccessful attack.[17] Polignac particularly found humor in observing an oft-frustrated, unnamed New Orleans correspondent who would often "prowl about the camps" in search of news and, more importantly, free corn liquor.[18] Beauregard too was keenly aware that there were persistent eyes and ears about his camps. His clever manipulation of them led to his only, albeit Fabian, success of the entire campaign. On May 25 he and his corps commanders reluctantly agreed to abandon Corinth. To conceal their decision they encouraged rumors of a fresh offensive to circulate among the camps. Even Polignac, one of Beauregard's most inquisitive subordinates, was taken in by the ruse. The generals put on a good front, leading him to declare confidently that "no evacuation can now be contemplated." [19]

Beauregard's caution was well founded. During the retreat his army would be at its most vulnerable. Any perceived chink in Corinth's defenses would serve Halleck as an invitation to attack. Beauregard also feared that the enemy's numerically superior cavalry could easily circle the town and sever his escape route. The crux of his scheme depended on maintaining the facade of an impregnable fortress while emptying it of its defenders and equipment. Secrecy was critical. [20] It was not until the twenty-eighth that Polignac, confirming the effectiveness of the generals' deception, could report "we are decidedly to retreat." Far from resenting his exclusion from his mentor's confidence, he wholeheartedly agreed that the gravity of the situation demanded extraordinary measures. His description of the day's events revealed his grasp of the generals' concerns as well as, incidentally, his own prejudice: "All tents have been struck in the camps & are being sent to the rear. The troops have been issued 3 days rations & ordered to be ready for a forward move so as to prevent the enemy (who has numerous spies among us) from finding out our real object or being informed of it by deserters who are equally numerous, particularly from some of the Louisiana regiments composed mostly of Irishmen." [21]

On the twenty-ninth Polignac tersely reported: "Retreat effected in good order"—a remarkable understatement. Beauregard's evacuation of Corinth was, as one scholar noted, "a masterpiece of trickery." The general masked his exodus by feigning what Halleck feared most. The near disaster of Shiloh's first day still haunted the Union general, manifested in his hesitant, crawling advance on the Confederate base, and Beauregard played on his dread of another surprise attack. Despite his superior numbers, Halleck was now paradoxically moving his army as if he and not his Confederate counterpart was on the defensive. Beauregard's safe withdrawal depended on his adversary's continued caution. [22]

For good measure Beauregard created the illusion he was receiving massive reinforcements. As the last troops shuffled out of town, empty railroad trains chugged noisily back and forth as if delivering reinforcements. At intervals men chosen for their vocal powers cheered lustily as thousands of fierce, phantom Rebels detrained. The members of one regimental band, left behind to provide musical accompaniment, must have wondered at their departing comrades' opinion of their talents. They all, however, played their roles to perfection. When Union scouts gingerly investigated the abruptly silent stronghold on May 30, they discovered a virtual ghost town. The Rebel Army was miles to the south, pressing deeper into Mississippi.[23]

The Confederate evacuation was indeed a total success. The retreat south, however, degenerated into a near debacle "as fatal," Polignac bitterly observed, "as a battle." Thousands of tired and disillusioned Rebels took advantage of the relative freedom of the road to make for home. As a professional, Polignac deplored deserters yet believed he understood their motives. Musing on the mass desertion of an entire company, he faulted the government's haphazard recruiting and conscription policies. "The whole system of recruiting," he complained, "is so inefficient, defective, & preposterous that the rules . . . have to be broken through in order to keep up the army which naturally brings about a great deal of dissatisfaction: hence desertions. The administration first allures the men into service with the bait of a small term—attempts to keep them & does so by compulsion when their time is out."[24]

At all levels during the retreat, Polignac observed "confusion & mismanagement." He blamed Beauregard for allowing himself to become overly distracted by minor issues. The general, observed Polignac, became "much ruffled" over an inaccurate report of sick troops abandoned at a rail intersection. According to Polignac, Beauregard failed to grasp "how necessary it is that a Gen[eral] commanding in chief should confine himself to giving general orders, entrusting their execution to the Gen[erals] under him without looking too much into the particulars & details." Although his concern was commendable, Beauregard put off all other plans for hours as he personally directed an investigation of the report. Commenting on the potentially disastrous delay, Polignac pointed out that "a mere misapprehension of a comparatively insignificant circumstance arising out of an inaccurate investigation came very near checking the whole move."[25]

Garbled and misdirected orders coupled with inept officers contributed to delays and confusion. One cavalry officer named Claibourne, whom Polignac considered if not competent at least consistent, reaffirmed the Frenchman's assessment. Neglecting to confirm whether the last Confederate rolling stock had made it safely across, he burned the Tuscumbia River bridge. When six late-running trains arrived soon after, the cavalryman burned them as well. Although Claibourne denied the Federals their use, his pyromaniacal zeal cost the Confederates six irreplaceable locomotives and tons of vital supplies.[26]

Despite Gen. Braxton Bragg's appraisal of the march as a "moral and physical" benefit to the troops, both he and Polignac were appalled at the widespread straggling. On the thirty-first Polignac counted "immense numbers of stragglers left behind & half-starved in the woods." Others were "lying about in farms, trespassing on the hospitality of the country people." He wryly added, "elsewhere they would be called deserters." Many were indeed determined never to return to their regiments. Pvt. William Watson commented that one group of several hundred stragglers were "quite indifferent and defiant" at the prospect of rejoining their units. On June 1 Polignac observed, "The demoralization is great—a complete disorganization prevails."[27]

Union cavalry nipped at the Rebels' heels as they struggled south. Although lacking the strength to pose a significant threat, the troopers repeatedly harassed the Confederate rear guard. In the hamlet of Boonsville, they surprised a detachment of Confederate horsemen resulting in what Polignac disdainfully reported as "panic among our cavalry—as usual." With the town to themselves, the Federals put torches to "a train & building with three sick in it"; Polignac grimly added, their "remains have been found since."[28]

During the first week of June, Beauregard maintained temporary headquarters at Baldwyn, some twenty miles south of Corinth. He desperately needed to reassemble his scattered command and reorganize it. As the general considered his next move, patrols combed the countryside gathering soldiers discharged from service on their personal authority.[29] On June 2 Polignac recorded, "The functions of Insp[ector] Gen[eral] devolve on me on account of the departure of Gen[eral] Slaughter for Saltilo." As acting inspector general, Polignac busied himself investigating the tragedy at Boonsville and the desertion of the "military superintendent of the telegraph" at Corinth. He also supervised the redistribution of artillery batteries among the various commands. On June 7 the army continued its retreat to Tupelo, Mississippi.[30]

The Southerners managed the thirty-two-mile march from Baldwyn to Tupelo in one day. All in all, the town was a better location for Beauregard's purposes than either Corinth or Baldwyn. Most importantly, it was well supplied with fresh water—a near luxury to the parched Rebels.[31] The disheartened Confederates, however, had little else to cheer them. On the eleventh Polignac reflected on the recent string of Southern disasters: "The enemy is at Memphis. Fort Pillow has been evacuated. If we don't maneuver we shall be defeated, & if we do not move, our army will dwindle down to nothing through sickness & desertion. Our troops . . . are almost too undisciplined to be organized—nothing but a successful campaign will bring them up to the required standard." Polignac placed much of the blame for the troops' low morale on Gen. Braxton Bragg.[32]

According to Polignac, Bragg had created "a great deal of dissatisfaction" through his heavy-handed attempts to restore order and establish discipline. Polignac fully supported the general's goals but faulted him for his total lack of diplomacy in what had become an extremely delicate situation. As he put it, "Gen[eral] Br[agg] is a good officer, & wants to reform the army, but I am afraid he undertakes too many changes at once, & does not possess the discriminating qualities required to carry out such a task."[33] As a man who had spent much of his adult life as a regular army officer, Bragg simply could not fathom the minds of his now essentially civilian soldiers. Polignac, as a fellow professional, sympathized with his dilemma. "The men, whom our troops are made up with, have been accustomed for . . . years to have no check put on their proclivities—the system under which they are mustered in & kept together tends to keep up their former independent ways, for want of impressing them with a sense of deference for their officers & making them sensible to the necessity for themselves of enforcing discipline."[34]

To as rigid a man as Bragg, the whole concept of such an army was alien and contradictory. Polignac, who had been in the country little more than a year and with the western command less than two months, believed he understood the problem perfectly. He prided himself as a close observer of human nature. As he saw it, a Confederate officer must be half soldier and half diplomat, for "any attempt to break over the old plodding course at once & not gradually may be attended with dangerous consequences—those men have been so much accustomed to being 'talked up' by politicians that some talking may well be necessary to 'screw them up' to something like an army. Evils in this army have to be corrected partly by persuasion, partly by compulsion."[35]

An editorial published exactly one month earlier in the May 13 issue of the London *Times* prompted Polignac to ponder his own quandary. The correspondent's position perfectly harmonized with his own observations and touched upon his deepest ambitions. Stating, "If at any moment the genius of a great general were developed . . . the whole fortune of the war might, no doubt, be reversed," the author declared, "but there is no decisive genius on either side. Beauregard came near to it, but he was a day too late at Corinth." Polignac could not restrain himself from musing that if only given the chance he could prove himself the military genius the South so desperately needed.[36] Amidst the "dull & plodding multitude" of the Confederate officer corps, he privately raged that his own "progress [was] checked because he [had] not yet been found out." He partially blamed his own relative youth, asking "Was not Caesar, Caesar at twenty?" Despite his continuing obscurity, however, Polignac was reasonably confident, declaring the next day, "I don't despair as I am here & believe in my luck & have faith in my destiny."[37]

Gen. P. G. T. Beauregard, however, had lost his faith. The seemingly endless string of Confederate defeats along the Mississippi Valley coupled with his own humbling retreats had sapped the general's self-confidence. Moreover, the Creole's health had continued to deteriorate and his critics seemed to multiply by the hour. As he battled his own depression, Beauregard focused his wrath not on the Yankees but his own president.[38] From late May to mid-June, Pres. Jefferson Davis had repeatedly demanded that Beauregard keep him informed of his intentions. The general had consistently ignored him. Seething, Davis eventually determined to remove his insubordinate lieutenant, and on June 17 Beauregard provided him with grounds for his dismissal. Abruptly leaving Tupelo to take the healing waters at Bladen Springs, Alabama, Beauregard opened himself to the charge of deserting his post. His "sudden departure," as Polignac put it, left his staff in disarray. On the nineteenth Polignac noted that only he and one other of the general's staff were left in Tupelo. The next day President Davis officially relieved Beauregard of command of the Western Department. In his place he appointed an old and trusted friend—Gen. Braxton Bragg.[39]

Polignac was somewhat dubious of Davis's choice, commenting, "This news will have at first a demoralizing effect on our army." The selection was at least a temporary reversal for himself as well. In order to secure a command, he had taken great pains to convince Beauregard of his talents. Now, on the verge of success, the general himself had fallen from grace. But Polignac, convinced of his own destiny, took the latest setback in stride.[40] On the twenty-third Polignac dispatched a note to the new commander outlining his proposal for a renewed offensive. Typically, he did not consider such an action overly presumptuous. He was confident his contribution would be appreciated for, as he stated, "I know now, that my opinion in military matters is regarded . . . in a very gratifying way." He came to view Bragg's appointment as "an opportunity [that] will soon offer for me to ascend higher."[41]

Bragg indeed shared Polignac's opinion that the Western Department was crippled by incompetent officers. He considered eight of the highest generals under his command as so much "dead-weight" yet their political influence frustrated attempts to replace them. From the brigade level down he counted dozens of unfit field officers. He targeted Polignac's old nemesis, the elective provision of the conscript law, as the culprit. It was, as he put it, a system "where the officers were made subservient to the men." Although he set up brigade promotion boards to certify the competency of elected officers, Bragg was frustrated by the politicians. Each time he tried to impose military efficiency upon a politically inspired regulation, the new commander found it rejected as "not in accordance with the law." [42]

Bragg consoled himself by assembling a staff of his own choosing. Having declared, "I had no use for fawning sycophants on my staff," he paid Polignac something of a compliment by retaining his services. Bragg also kept on brilliant, doomed Col. John Pegram as chief engineer. (Destined to rise to the rank of general after transfer to the East, in 1865 the handsome Pegram was killed only weeks after his marriage to a beautiful Richmond socialite.) Polignac found the thirty-year-old Virginian delightful company, and the two men became close friends. [43] Pegram was "a man of sense and intellect and . . . very religious." In "some respects" Polignac considered him "peculiar," for "he never drinks wine nor indulges himself with any other drink—strange for an American." During their off hours the two friends fought boredom by reading to one another, playing chess, and discussing strategy. [44] They, as had Beauregard, advocated a grand strategy of aggressive concentrated movements at the expense of "protecting small & unimportant points." Bragg also favored an offensive, and the time seemed ripe. Halleck had divided his forces, sending Maj. Gen. Don Carlos Buell's Army of the Ohio through northern Alabama following the tracks of the Memphis and Chattanooga Railroad. No one held any doubts as to his objective. Chattanooga, Tennessee, was the most important rail hub between Atlanta, Georgia, and Richmond, Virginia. Its loss could ultimately sever Bragg's supply lines and worse, divide the Confederacy. [45]

This move presented Bragg with a dilemma. He could not allow Buell to take Chattanooga, yet he could not abandon central Mississippi to almost certain invasion. On June 23 Polignac and Pegram urged an attack on the divided Federals either at Corinth, where Halleck remained, or as Buell crossed the Tennessee River. Although Polignac endorsed the latter course "as teeming with more fruitful consequences," he correctly predicted Bragg would settle on "a sort of compromise." [46]

Handsome and popular, John Pegram served as Bragg's chief engineer in Tennessee and Kentucky. Polignac and Pegram remained close friends until Pegram's tragic death in the last weeks of the war. *Courtesy Alabama Department of Archives and History, Montgomery.*

It took Bragg a month to make his decision. After much soul searching, he settled on leaving Maj. Gen. Sterling Price's sixteen-thousand-man army at Tupelo. Price's divisions would thus be in position to defend northern Mississippi and, if necessary, reinforce Maj. Gen. Earl Van Dorn's sixteen thousand men now defending Vicksburg, Mississippi. In the meantime, Bragg and thirty thousand troops would join Maj. Gen. Edmund Kirby Smith's force holding Chattanooga. Once he was united with Kirby Smith, Bragg envisioned a two-pronged Confederate invasion of Tennessee. The invasion, as he reported to General Cooper in Richmond, would entail his and Kirby Smith's force cutting off and defeating Buell in East Tennessee. As Price's and Van Dorn's forces combined and concurrently invaded the western counties, the remaining Federal units would find themselves isolated and trapped in a huge pincer movement.[47]

Polignac first came under the command of Gen. Edmund Kirby Smith during
Bragg's unsuccessful invasion of Kentucky. He would again come under Smith's
command upon his transfer to the Trans-Mississippi Department. *Courtesy
Alabama Department of Archives and History, Montgomery.*

On the morning of July 21, Bragg called Polignac and Pegram aside to explain his scheme. Polignac later outlined the initial move: "Part of the troops to go across the country with the baggage train & artillery, part by rail. Troops from Mobile to go at once." Although he held "some misgivings" as to whether the Confederates could reach Chattanooga before the Federals, he pronounced it a plan "likely . . . to secure success." On July 22 Polignac recorded, "The movement has begun."[48]

Polignac remained with Bragg's staff in Tupelo for two more days. As the army headed east "by land & by rail," he addressed such routine matters as paroling prisoners and attending a review of General Price's army. Polignac noted an improvement in the army since Bragg's takeover and subsequent disciplinary measures. He noted that the troops who would be left to defend Tupelo "presented a very creditable appearance" with many regiments "any regular army might be proud of." One of Price's brigades amused Polignac with its new battle cry. Maj. Gen. Benjamin F. Butler, commander of New Orleans's Union occupation force, had recently outraged the South by issuing his infamous Order No. 28, unanimously considered by Southerners as a grievous insult to Southern womanhood. The brigade, commanded by Brig. Gen. William L. Cabell, had registered its displeasure by replacing the command "charge bayonet" with "Butler! damn Butler!" Polignac observed, "This is called here an interpolation of Hardee's tactics."[49]

On the evening of July 24, Polignac accompanied Bragg and his staff as they boarded a southbound train. Owing to the disruption of the Confederate rail system, Bragg was forced to transport his command to Chattanooga by two widely separated routes. His cavalry and horse-drawn elements took the most direct route across northern Alabama. Bragg, his staff, and the infantry took the painfully indirect rail route already familiar to Polignac. They arrived in Chattanooga early in the morning of July 30.[50]

Polignac did not immediately realize that Bragg had made military history. Despite Buell's head start and much more direct route, Bragg beat the Union forces to Chattanooga. Moreover, he had accomplished the feat despite the meandering 776-mile course that carried his army through four states over inferior Southern rails. In the face of such obstacles, Gen. Braxton Bragg, for the first time, had proven the feasibility and effectiveness of fast large-scale, long-distance strategic maneuvers by train. Bragg's innovative use of the railroads thus enabled him not only to outrace Buell but to outflank him as well. More importantly, it placed all Union forces in Tennessee in jeopardy.[51]

Sinking into another depression, Polignac was too occupied battling his "internal foes" to appreciate Bragg's coup. Frustrated by his own professional stagnation, he gloomily focused on the shortcomings of the commanders of either side. Upon his arrival in Chattanooga, Polignac immediately announced that his "apprehensions about Buell" had been "exaggerated." He was especially baffled by the Union general's failure to exploit his now lost advantage: "I have overrated [Buell's] military capacity. He is still on the right bank of the Tennessee river, somewhere about Bridgeport, & moving slowly up it is said. What in the world prevented him from crossing the river? I find that slowness in action & want of purpose in councils are the prevalent features of this war on either side."[52]

He faulted the Confederate bureaucracy's inefficiency and snail-like pace for his own stagnation. Although he had barraged Richmond for weeks with requests for promotion, Polignac had heard nothing in reply. His frustration increasingly manifested itself in protracted "sick headaches" and frequent bouts of depression. As each day "dragged along with a dullness to none comparable but to that of London on a Sunday," he often pondered "to what purpose have I lived during its progress[?]" Polignac's answer to his own question was his own sense of destiny. In spite of his "low spirits," he declared, "I must call in all my strength for a new onset through life."[53]

Less than a week after arriving in Chattanooga, Polignac decided the Fates would not reward his service with Braxton Bragg. He had learned that staff officers tended to remain staff officers; that the advantage of the relative safety of a general's retinue was more than offset by the remoteness of promotion. His best hope of advancement, he believed, lay in an army that was actively engaged with the enemy. Only by dramatically proving himself in combat could he convince his superiors of his abilities. Polignac craved action and yet, as he wrote on August 6, "nothing, as I believe is the case, is going to be undertaken here."[54] Events seemed to be moving much faster in Knoxville. While Bragg waited for his wagons and artillery to arrive in Chattanooga, Edmund Kirby Smith, commanding in Knoxville, planned to attack a Federal force holding Cumberland Gap. His intended move was part of a grand strategy he and Bragg had agreed upon on August 1. Once Kirby Smith had captured the strategic mountain pass and Bragg's transportation had come up, they would then join forces for a concerted move against the plodding Buell. With Buell out of the way they would then invade Kentucky.[55]

The plan's greatest defect lay in the command relationship between Bragg and Kirby Smith. Owing to a recent restructuring of the Western Department, Bragg had been surprised to learn that Kirby Smith was not his subordinate, as he had expected, but his equal in the eyes of their superiors in Richmond. The new arrangement had thus created a ticklish situation in which Confederate forces in Tennessee were under two generals who could coordinate their moves only through mutually agreed upon cooperation. Although the new system seemed perfectly logical to the Richmond bureaucracy, it invited disaster.[56]

With Bragg's arrival in eastern Tennessee, Kirby Smith dropped all pretenses of coordination. In the first week of August he seized the initiative and, in effect, the command. He would, he made known, move into the Bluegrass State as soon as he had neutralized the Federals at Cumberland Gap. In Kirby Smith's view, Bragg could—when or if he could overcome his indecisiveness—follow his lead. It took Polignac less than a day to make his own decision.[57]

CHAPTER 4

"I Stood with You–I Marched with You– I Charged with You"

August 10, 1862–August 31, 1862

———————

Polignac arrived at Knoxville in the early afternoon of Sunday, August 10, 1862. Clutching his baggage amidst the milling soldiers and townspeople at the rail platform, he pushed through the crowded streets to department headquarters. Although deeply absorbed in the planning of the upcoming campaign, Maj. Gen. Edmund Kirby Smith graciously found time to receive his new lieutenant colonel's orders personally.[1] At thirty-eight, tall, with slightly graying hair and beard, Kirby Smith was described by one of his aides as possessing no "remarkable intellectual endowments" but nevertheless gave the impression of "uncommon quickness of perception and rapid mental movements." The general greeted the young Frenchman "with great affability & courtesy," for the two men had much in common. While at West Point, where he was known as "Seminole" for his swarthy complexion and Florida birth, Kirby Smith had excelled in Polignac's favorite pursuits—mathematics and botany. The two had little time to discuss mutual interests, however, and while Kirby Smith returned to his maps, Polignac introduced himself to the headquarters staff.[2]

Kirby Smith's chief of staff was Polignac's old friend Col. John Pegram. Polignac's pleasure in seeing a familiar face was tempered, however, by his all too familiar assignment of duties. Despite his transfer he was not to receive his coveted field command but continued in his old staff capacity as assistant inspector general. Furthermore, he had no place to spend the night. Owing to the overwhelming influx of troops in the small town, all of Knoxville's hotels and boarding houses were bursting at the seams. After many unsuccessful attempts at finding a bed and with night closing in, the tired Frenchman struck a deal for a room in the home of a Mr. Cruise. Polignac's temporary landlord, although reportedly a staunch Unionist, could apparently see no reason why politics should interfere with profits.[3] As Polignac settled into his new surround-ings, Kirby Smith returned to the thorny problem posed by the Union position astride Cumberland Gap. Located on the far eastern Tennessee-Kentucky border, the gap had served as the primary gateway through the rugged Cumberland Mountains since the days of Daniel Boone. Union general George W. Morgan's capture of the gap the previous June se-verely restricted Confederate movements through the Cumberlands, and his eight-thousand-man division threatened Southern operations throughout the region, greatly complicating all aspects of Bragg and Kirby Smith's already shaky equation for the invasion of Kentucky. By the time of Polignac's arrival, Cumberland Gap had become the sole focus of Kirby Smith's attention.[4]

According to Polignac, by August 11 already privy to the comman-der's plans, Kirby Smith considered Morgan's position "impregnable." As Polignac described it, the gap was "a narrow defile, four or five yards in width & bordered on each side by bluffs several hundred feet high." For nearly two months Morgan had reinforced the gap's already formi-dable natural defenses by constructing elaborate trenches and gun em-placements on its forward slopes and on the cliffs above the strategic gateway to the Bluegrass State. Yet Kirby Smith believed he had found his old friend's Achilles' heel. Morgan's stores of supplies and food were limited, and Kirby Smith reasoned that if he could cut the Federals off from their supply depot one hundred miles away in Richmond, Ken-tucky, he could perhaps starve them into surrender.[5]

Even though having arrived only a day earlier, Polignac found what he considered glaring flaws in Kirby Smith's grand scheme. Although un-recorded, it would have been well within Kirby Smith's opinionated new assistant inspector general's character to enlighten his commanding gen-eral as to his strategic oversights. Still Polignac was a trained military man, and his detailed critique of Kirby Smith's plan, as confided to his di-ary, has considerable merit. His primary objection, the splitting of Kirby Smith's meager forces into two smaller units "separated by an interven-ing range of mountains . . . & at several days march from each other" in hostile territory, was completely sound. He was also quite perceptive in observing that the Confederates were particularly vulnerable to such common camp illnesses as typhoid fever, then at almost epidemic levels, not to mention the constant bushwhacking on the army's fringes. De-spite Kirby Smith's optimism, his army was now deep within hostile ter-ritory.[6] The commander's confidence, however, must have been conta-gious, for within a day Polignac had at least come to accept the feasibility of the general's plan. He still had reservations concerning the vulnerability of the divided Confederate forces but comforted himself with the belief that of the opposing Union commanders, neither Morgan nor Maj. Gen. Don Carlos Buell were "equal to [their] opportunities." Although none of the decisions involved were his to make, Polignac at least reconciled himself with the knowledge that he would at last have a part in an offensive action.[7]

In the cool, half light before dawn of Thursday the fourteenth, Polignac joined his fellow staff officers as they saddled their mounts and set out for the Kentucky border. The main force, consisting of Brig. Gens. Henry Heth's, Patrick Cleburne's, and Thomas J. Churchill's divisions, nine thousand men in all, had already marched the previous day. That evening the staff caught up with the army as it bivouacked some twenty-four miles from Knoxville near the hamlet of Clinton on the Clinch River.[8] Three days later Kirby Smith and Maj. Gen. John P. McCown, with Cleburne's and Churchill's divisions, pitched their tents at the foot of the Cumberlands. Before them lay Rogers' Gap, a narrow, steep track into the heart of the forbidding mountains. In the meantime Kirby Smith had split his forces, directing Heth and Brig. Gen. Danville Leadbetter to pass through Big Creek Gap with three thousand men, the army's wagons, and its artillery trains.[9]

Polignac apparently grew bored with his mundane military duties during the crossing and indulged himself in his latest scientific interests. Using a somewhat dated geology book as his text, he spent much of the time jotting down notes concerning the various rock formations in the area. His attention soon returned to more martial matters, however, when he accepted an invitation to join Kirby Smith's chief of artillery on an inspection of one of his batteries. The captain of the battery, a recent veteran of the German Army, was only too happy to deliver a detailed lecture on recent ordnance developments to his French guest. For his part Polignac, fluent in German, was particularly impressed with the advanced Blakely rifling of two of the captain's four guns.[10]

The crossing of the Cumberlands proved a severe test of the endurance of Kirby Smith's troops. The men, many veterans of Belmont, Shiloh, and Elkhorn Tavern, "a rough wild ragged looking assembly," began the ascent at Rogers' Gap on August 17, much of the passage taking place at night. Polignac noted that at several places the path was so steep that their mules were useless. In such instances the men were forced to resort to their own sheer muscle power to pull and push their wagons up the mountains. Kirby Smith later declared rather melodramatically that the crossing was "a feat rivaling the passage of the Alps."[11] The exhausted troops filed out of Rogers' Gap before dawn. Ahead, cavalry scouts fanned out through the mostly pro-Union countryside, their orders to prevent any of the inhabitants from raising the alarm of invasion. The columns marched the entire August day over the mountainous Kentucky landscape, vainly searching for water. Finding nothing better, they finally pitched their tents in "a damp bottom on the banks of an almost dried up creek by the road." [12]

As their men scrounged for firewood and filled their canteens with the muddy creek water for their evening meal, Polignac and his fellow staff officers invited themselves for supper at a small farmhouse nearby. The impoverished and careworn mountain women who served the young officers could hardly offer what Polignac considered a "palatable experience." With all of their men away at war, they had to make do as best they could. Although noting their resourcefulness, Polignac was unimpressed with the results. With an odd mix of wonder and disdain he sniffed, "we had to sweeten our coffee with honey for want of sugar." [13]

At daybreak a restless Polignac fell in with Kirby Smith's aide-de-camp, Capt. John G. Meem, Jr., as he led the cavalry advance guard toward Barboursville some seventeen miles northwest. An important supply depot for Morgan's division at Cumberland Gap, the town was described as "a dilapidated village" but "the metropolis of this mountain region." To the Confederates Barboursville represented a bonanza of much needed food and supplies. As the weary troopers guided their horses toward the village, wildly inflated reports of as many as thirty-five thousand troops threatening his lifeline reached Morgan. Taking no chances, he ordered the evacuation of Barboursville, its garrison and supplies to be rushed back to his mountain stronghold. [14] Despite Morgan's precautions, when the Confederate cavalry galloped into town shortly before midnight, they caught the Union rear guard by complete surprise. Meem personally garnered credit for capturing half of the fifty prisoners taken. When Kirby Smith learned of the exploit, he declared his aide-de-camp's "spirit worth a whole regiment." Polignac too was tasting at last the thrill of action if not official recognition. Most importantly, the troopers also captured between fifty and sixty heavily laden supply wagons. [15]

Kirby Smith's plan was apparently proceeding beautifully. By August 22 Generals Heth and Leadbetter had crossed their three thousand men through Big Creek Gap to bring Kirby Smith's strength at Barboursville up to nine thousand troops. As the Confederate forces converged on his doomed supply base, Morgan remained defiant in his mountain redoubt, declaring he would hold out so long as he had "a pound of meat and an ounce of powder." Kirby Smith was determined to ensure the Union general's belligerent inertia and placed the other half of his invasion force, the nine thousand men of Stevenson's, Rains's, and Barton's divisions, squarely in front of Cumberland Gap. With Morgan safely bottled up in the mountains, the Confederate commander was free to push on into the fertile bluegrass country.[16]

With the Southern infantry and artillery massing around Barboursville, Kirby Smith's cavalry prowled deep within Federal-held territory. The technically minded Polignac was particularly fascinated by the exploits of a skilled telegraph operator who accompanied Col. John Hunt Morgan's raiders. By tapping into the Federal Army's telegraph lines, Morgan was consistently able to stay one step ahead of his baffled opponents, striking at will in the vicinity of Paris, Kentucky. In the meantime, Col. John W. Scott led his Louisiana and Georgia troopers from their base in Kingston, Tennessee, across the border. During the night of August 16, his 896 riders reached the outskirts of London, Kentucky, a village about halfway between Barboursville and Lexington. They made their 160-mile trek in seventy hours, a respectable feat in rough and hostile territory. Scouts reported that five companies of the 3rd Tennessee Volunteers (U.S.) made up the post's garrison. The colonel quietly moved five hundred of his most seasoned men through the trees to wait in the darkness at the edge of town.[17]

The shock of five hundred shrieking gray horsemen completely unhinged the raw Unionists as Scott's cavalry crashed out of the woods shortly after dawn. A few Federals briefly held their ground, killing one Rebel officer and a private, but they soon gave way to panic. Within minutes the cavalrymen killed seventeen Tennesseans and rounded up some one hundred prisoners. Their booty also included several hundred muskets, forty supply wagons, and several teams of draft horses and mules. Scott's men spent the next few days scouring the roads leading out of London and gathering still more horses, mules, and wagons abandoned by the fleeing Union survivors. Well aware of Kirby Smith's urgent need for quartermaster and commissary stores, Scott hurried his prizes to Barboursville.[18]

Polignac noted that Kirby Smith's logistical problems were indeed mounting. Never particularly prosperous, the region around Barboursville had been stripped of whatever useful supplies that the retreating Federals could carry. Also, far from finding the new recruits they had counted on among the locals, the Confederates found themselves in enemy territory surrounded by a resentful population. As bushwhackers picked off unwary Rebels who strayed from their camps, Kirby Smith characterized Barboursville as "loaded with the most flaming demonstrations of bad taste of patriotism."[19] Despite their hostile reception Kirby Smith ordered his troops to respect the locals' property and stay on their best behavior. Although their commander's hopes of winning over the Kentuckians were fading fast, Confederate commissary and quartermaster officers took pains to compensate local farmers for what corn, beef, and other supplies they could obtain. That the officers paid for the goods with promissory notes or Confederate currency did little to impress the impoverished farmers, who faced a bleak winter with little food for themselves. Kirby Smith soon realized that he must move his army or it would starve. A retreat would destroy his troops' morale, so he called in his staff to make plans for an advance on Richmond. By the twenty-fourth Polignac had made his own decision about the future.[20]

On that day he confided to his diary: "I have resolved upon leaving the staff & volunteering into a regiment as a Lt. Col. there to take my chances, as I feel convinced that it must be—altho more dangerous—yet a surer way to distinction & preferment. Time will tell." After more than a year of unsuccessfully politicking for promotion and command, Polignac would now try to win his dream by force of arms. The next morning Polignac accompanied Irish-born Gen. Patrick Cleburne and his staff as Kirby Smith moved his divisions out of Barboursville. On the twenty-eighth he reported for duty to the commanding officer of the 5th Tennessee Regiment, 2nd Brigade, Cleburne's division. His own slightly superior rank to the regiment's ranking officer, Lt. Col. Joseph A. Smith, did not go unnoticed by the prickly Frenchman. Still, he viewed his new assignment as an opportunity to achieve the recognition and advancement he craved. As the 5th Tennessee marched along the Richmond Road, Polignac "Dismounted & walked with the men," as he put it, "to let them get used to seeing me & impress them favorably, from the first, being well aware that under such circumstances & (with the object I had in view) much depends on the first impression."[21]

Defying his earnest attempts to gain the acceptance of the veteran troops and his fellow officers, Polignac was greeted with hostility and derision. Many, such as Kirby Smith's aide Capt. Paul F. Hammond, found Polignac "anything but popular." Hammond, for reasons of his own, obviously detested him. He found Polignac "undeniably ugly" and even derided the prince's wardrobe, describing it as "neither tidy nor becoming ... and which helped to give him the mingled appearance of buffoon and Italian organ-grinder." Surrounded by such open animosity, it is little wonder that Hammond, like many of his fellows, found the sensitive interloper "morose, unsociable, silent, perhaps melancholy, and misunderstood for the most part, and seemingly inclined to be tyrannic."[22]

Simply put, Polignac was an outsider. Most Confederate regiments were composed of men drawn from the same locale. Both officers and men had grown up together, many shared family ties, and they all had trained and fought together. The vast majority of these soldiers were independent rural folk who distrusted authority as well as the unfamiliar. Polignac desperately wanted the acceptance of his fellow soldiers, but differences in language and culture continued to frustrate his efforts. Though he could now speak passable American-style English, the European soldier still had difficulty with the various Southern dialects and often found camp slang especially impenetrable. In many cases his attempts to converse led others to see him as a caricature of a Frenchman —a curiosity and the subject of countless, often apocryphal, camp stories. In one oft-told instance a young Creole soldier searching for his regiment after a two-week furlough saluted Polignac, inquiring: "I belong to Colonel Censer's 'lay-out' but don't know where it is. Will you please tell me where it is?" Responding, "eyes bulging with amazement," Polignac asked the boy to repeat himself. "To Colonel Censer's 'lay-out,'" he replied, " you know it, it belongs to your 'she bang.'" In his reaction, certainly embellished in its wide retelling, Polignac, losing most of his English and all his composure, exploded "well d——n my eyes to ze deep blue h——l, I have been militaire all my life. I was educated for ze army. I have heard of ze compagnie, ze battalion, ze regiment, ze brigade, ze division, and ze army corps, but ——, ——! my soul to ze —— if evair I hear of ze 'lay-out' or ze 'she bang' before."[23] Well aware of the circulation of such tales, Polignac at times seemed sullen and morose to observers, retiring to his tent to practice his English by writing in his diary, reading, and indulging in mathematics. Such solitary activities offered a refuge to a man sensitive to others' criticism and ridicule, yet it also accentuated his alienation. He was a lonely man seemingly shunned by his fellows "while," as Hammond remembered, "jest and laugh circled merrily all around and about him." Yet despite such resistance, Polignac was determined to become an effective and accepted officer.[24]

Arriving in the vicinity of Big Hill at the end of a second day of hard marching, the 5th Tennessee pitched their tents in what Polignac described as "a fine orchard." As the men gathered firewood in the fading light and commissary sergeants began passing out much anticipated evening rations, the twilight's quiet was suddenly shattered by distant firing and excited shouts. Word quickly passed around the campfires that Colonel Scott's cavalry pickets had been driven in by a powerful Union force and an attack was expected at any moment. Amidst the confusion, the brigade commander, Col. Benjamin J. Hill, rushed his men into a line of battle that Polignac considered "defective" because "both our flanks were very much exposed." The imminent attack, however, never materialized. After a few tense moments, the order passed down the line to return to camp. Within minutes, though, that order was countermanded.[25]

The Battle of Richmond, Kentucky, like so many battles, began by accident. Union major general Horatio G. Wright, commander of the Department of the Ohio, faced the necessity of stopping Kirby Smith's invasion even though his only available troops were hardly up to the task. Recently recruited from Ohio and the Unionist population of Kentucky, his men had little to distinguish them as soldiers other than their new uniforms. As Brig. Gen. Charles D. Cruft, commander of the 2nd Brigade, Army of Kentucky, reported, his men were nearly "all fresh recruits" and "knew nothing of the duties or habits of soldiers. Most of them had been less than a fortnight away from their homes. They could but indifferently execute some of the simplest movements in the manual of arms, but knew nothing whatever of company or battalion drill." The general sadly assessed his command not being a military force but rather "a mere collection of citizens, hastily assembled, armed, and thrown together without the least knowledge of military rules or discipline." He concluded, "It was a sad spectacle to a soldier to look at these raw levies and contemplate their fate in a trial at arms with experienced troops."[26]

On the twenty-fourth Wright issued orders that he desperately hoped would buy time to drill "Both officers and men . . . earnest and brave, but wholly inexperienced and untrained." He instructed the six-foot, two-inch-tall, three-hundred-pound Union commander at Lexington, Maj. Gen. William "Bull" Nelson, "If the enemy is in force get your troops together, and do not risk a general battle at Richmond unless you are sure of success. Better to fall back to a more defensible position, say the Kentucky River, than to risk much." Spread out through the Kentucky countryside, most of Nelson's subordinate commanders received the new orders. Two miles south of Richmond, in the vicinity of Big Hill, "a wild region almost uninhabited," Brig. Gen. Mahlon D. Manson of the 1st Brigade did not.[27]

Manson moved decisively. The possibility of retreat apparently never occurred to him. Instead he saw only two alternatives: either allow the Rebels to attack his troops in their camps around Richmond or seize the initiative and advance to meet them on more favorable ground. He chose the latter course. Scattering the elements of Scott's cavalry menacing his front, Manson hurried his most experienced regiments forward to an enviable position on a steep ridge straddling the Richmond Turnpike. The

Federal line of battle, with infantry in the center and two pieces of artillery anchoring each flank, commanded the road and open fields to the south of town. At about five o'clock, as soon as the Confederate advance guard came into range, the Union gunners pulled their lanyards. It was this initial cannonade that had disturbed Polignac's and the 5th Tennessee's supper in their "fine orchard" and alerted the far-flung officers of both armies that the battle had begun.[28]

Shortly after dark Scott and his men reached the safety of the Confederate lines at a pace that the 2nd Brigade's commander, Colonel Hill, diplomatically reported as "a brisk trot." Hot on Scott's heels, Colonel Hill continued, "a regiment of Federal cavalry, commanded by the notorious [Col. Leonidas] Metcalfe, came thundering down the road, crying 'charge, and shoot down the rebels.'" General Cleburne suspected that Metcalfe's men "were all excited with liquor." As "the musket balls began to whistle round," the Confederate line, including Polignac's 5th Tennessee to the right of the road, unleashed a volley that encouraged the Federals to "run off at full speed."[29]

Unable to see the approaching enemy in the darkness, Hill's forward skirmishers and sharpshooters on the left of the road did not shoot until the last minute. Finally making out their targets by sound alone, they fired, killing one Federal outright and wounding several others. The survivors wheeled their horses around and sped back down the road at a gallop. As their hoofbeats faded, pickets of the 48th Tennessee scrambled forward through the gloom to round up three dazed and unhorsed cavalrymen. To their delight they also recovered thirty modern breechloading Sharps carbines dropped on the road and in surrounding bushes by the stunned horsemen. Their division commander later reported a total of thirty prisoners taken as well as one hundred weapons at the cost of only one wounded Confederate. Polignac's assessment of the evening's proceedings, "So much for cavalry outpost service on both sides," was a fair representation of the opinions of his fellow infantrymen.[30]

Owing to the possibility of further Union reconnaissance, the brigade spent a tense and uncomfortable night under the stars. The next day Polignac recorded: "Our line remained in position. The men sleeping on their arms & having been ordered out before the rations which had been issued were cooked & consequently with empty stomachs & very light havresacks [*sic*]." Kirby Smith, for his part, was well pleased with the day's events. His fear that the Federals would fall back to make a concentrated stand high on the bluffs above the Kentucky River was apparently unfounded. He viewed the resistance of Manson's green troops at Rogersville and Big Hill as welcome proof of his enemy's willingness to meet his force in battle on equal ground. The general's staff shared his optimism. As Paul F. Hammond remembered, "raw levies were counted as nothing in the hands of our veterans."[31]

No one was more aware of the disparity in the two armies' battle readiness than the commander of the Army of Kentucky. "Bull" Nelson had assumed that Manson, like his other subordinates, had received his and Wright's orders to avoid engagement with the invaders and, as Kirby Smith had feared, pull back to the Kentucky River. When Manson's courier arrived at Nelson's Lexington headquarters at 2:30 A.M. on the thirtieth with news "that he anticipated an engagement," Nelson was dumbfounded. Recovering, he "immediately sent couriers, with orders . . . not to fight . . . but to retreat by way of the Lancaster Road." As his anxiety mounted over the fate of Manson's recruits in the hands of Kirby Smith's veterans, he decided that Manson's withdrawal demanded his personal attention. Shortly, he too was on the road to Richmond.[32] Polignac and the men of the 5th Tennessee awoke Saturday, August 30, after spending a night under the stars. Confederate Paul F. Hammond remembered the morning dawning "warm, clear and beautiful. No brighter sun ever scattered the mists of early day." Mahlon D. Manson was too concerned over the sight of gray-clad infantry emerging from the village of Kingston, less than a mile away, to notice nature's beauty. It was 7:00 A.M. From his vantage near a nondescript building called Mount Zion Church, the Union general could count the flags of the two Arkansas and three Tennessee regiments of Col. Benjamin H. Hill's 2nd Brigade. Hill's superior, General Cleburne, was also counting enemy flags. Riding ahead, the 4th Division's commander had confirmed earlier cavalry reports of a heavy Union concentration concealed in the woods to the right of the turnpike. Cleburne quickly ordered Hill to march his brigade to within less than six hundred yards of the Federal position before wheeling to the right behind the protection of a low rise in the open fields. As Cleburne ordered his 1st Brigade under Col. Preston Smith to take a supporting position to his rear, Manson began the battle—with a plainly visible little mountain howitzer captured from Colonel Scott the previous day.[33]

Manson's insult apparently carried more sting than the untrained artillery crew's efforts. The Irish-born Cleburne somewhat petulantly reported theirs as "a ridiculous fire" and responded with his own expert gunners. Polignac, with the 5th Tennessee directly behind the Confederate battery in the center of Hill's line, was squarely in the sights of the Federal artillerists. Although the first salvos of solid shot, shell, and spherical case passed safely overhead, the gunners quickly adjusted their aim to send a deadly storm of iron into the midst of the Tennesseans, wounding a number of Southerners. The Federals' "most accurate shot" killed the number one and two gunners of a fieldpiece, both of whom were struck through the body by a single solid shot, according to Polignac, who was standing close by.[34]

The Confederate gunners, however, had found their own range. After less than half an hour, General Manson became concerned over his mounting casualties and ordered sharpshooters out to neutralize the Rebel cannoneers. Cleburne countered by sending out his own marksmen. Polignac noted that both the 5th Tennessee's and adjacent 15th Arkansas's skirmishers scampered away into the woods, which soon erupted in "a brisk firing." The effectiveness of Hill's skirmishers allowed Cleburne to bring up another battery from Preston Smith's brigade while his marksmen to the left of the road protected that flank.[35] Neither side made a decisive move. Manson and his staff waited with the officers of the 55th Indiana behind a fence facing the Confederate right for reinforcements under Brig. Gen. Charles Cruft to arrive. Only a few hundred yards away, Pat Cleburne received orders from recently arrived Kirby Smith "to avoid a general battle until General Churchill's division could get up." In the meantime Cleburne directed his artillery "to fire very slowly and not waste a round." The lull, as the combative Cleburne put it, "a mere fight of artillery and skirmishers," lasted well over two hours. Still, the casualties mounted, victims of long-range, anonymous sniping and artillery fire.[36]

Cleburne's second battery on the field was in particular trouble. Owing to misunderstood orders, Captain Martin's artillery of Preston Smith's brigade had unlimbered on a low hill near Zion Church, perilously close to three companies of Union skirmishers. The exposed gunners were irresistible targets to the snipers hidden among the trees only yards away. Within minutes Martin, his senior lieutenant, and several of his men lay around their guns groaning from wounds as the reinforced Federals moved forward to capture the crippled battery. With remarkable coolness Martin's uninjured veterans rehitched their horses and lifted their wounded onto the caissons. Then under cover of advancing Confederate sharpshooters, they galloped to a more defensible position beyond the effective range of Yankee rifles. With the resolve of men bent on revenge, the battery continued the fight with canister and shell.[37]

By midmorning, reinforcements on both sides were reaching the field. Shortly after hearing the first distant artillery fire, Brigadier General Cruft, commanding the Union 2nd Brigade, had hurried his 3,085 men forward from their camps near Richmond. Five miles down the road, his lead columns encountered Manson's empty artillery wagons urgently rattling back to Richmond for more ammunition. Cruft ordered his own artillery ahead to protect Manson's position. His infantry arrived on the firing lines minutes later only to be greeted within "a few moments" by a chilling quiet as the Confederate artillery abruptly ceased firing. For their first time, for many their last, Cruft's raw recruits experienced the Rebel yell.³⁸ The Yankees had barely taken their positions when, out of the concealment of a too-close cornfield burst Col. T. H. McCray's shrieking Texas and Arkansas veterans. Kirby Smith's reinforcements, Brig. Gen. Thomas J. Churchill's 3rd Division, had arrived. Although Cruft's recruits "manfully resisted" the initial assault, they were no match for McCray's seasoned brigade. Cruft reported that his "raw troops went to work in earnest, and for some forty minutes the rattle of musketry was terrible." But, as the Union general admitted, "It was however, impossible, with the troops composing our lines, to stand against the impetuosity of [McCray's] charge." By 10:30 A.M. "the panic was well-nigh universal . . . , the whole thing was fast becoming shameful." McCray's assessment of the fight was succinct: "At the place designated the brigade was moved in line of battle directly on the right wing of the enemy's line, which was immediately turned, and they fled in confusion, leaving on the field a large number of killed, wounded, and prisoners." For the Confederates the fighting on their right would be costly.³⁹

With his own right flank collapsing, Manson adopted a near mirror image of Kirby Smith's strategy. The Confederate 154th Senior Tennessee Regiment of Col. Preston Smith's 1st Brigade had pushed ahead of its supporting regiments on the right and was heavily engaged. Manson, by moving three regiments through the woods and cornfields to the Tennesseans' extreme right, counted on cutting them off and collapsing the Rebel line. But his men had not yet gained the discipline to exploit their cover. Almost immediately aware of the threat, Preston Smith threw two regiments behind the advancing Federals, taking them by complete surprise. After "a few well-directed volleys," the Federals abandoned their cover and fled "in great confusion." They briefly rallied, but as Preston Smith reported, under the 1st Brigade's "steady advance and galling fire from Minie and Enfield rifles the enemy soon broke and fled for his rear, leaving the ground strewn thickly with his killed and wounded."⁴⁰

General Cleburne was convinced Manson had weakened his center and "staked everything" to turn the Confederate right. He therefore decided to attack the Federals with his own center, Hill's brigade, as soon as Preston Smith's regiments had fully anchored his flank. To coordinate the maneuvers Cleburne galloped off just as "Smith's brigade came up at double quick, taking its position on the right of the 15th Ark. (Hill's Brigade)." Retracing his route Cleburne paused briefly to offer words of encouragement to Col. Lucius E. Polk, who was being carried to the rear with a serious head wound. Within seconds the general too was down. A minié ball had struck him in the face, piercing his cheek and knocking out a number of teeth. Although not fatal, the wound was excruciating, forcing Cleburne to leave the field. "Thus," as Kirby Smith reported, "at a critical moment I was deprived of the services of one of the most gallant, zealous, and intelligent officers of my whole army."[41] The loss of Kirby Smith's most capable field commander was greatly mitigated, however, by the presence of Preston Smith's cool hand. Assuming divisional command the colonel, having allowed his men a short respite to refill cartridge boxes and send some five hundred prisoners to the rear, resumed the attack just as the last of Manson's reinforcements arrived.[42]

As one of their officers, Maj. Frederick G. Bracht, put it, the 18th Regiment Kentucky Volunteers (U.S.) were determined "to meet the invading foe in deadly conflict as ever inspired a veteran regiment." Jogging at the double-quick the Kentuckians brushed past the dazed survivors of earlier fighting to form their line of battle in an open field. Bordered on the left and front by Rebel-filled woods, cornfields, and brush, the 18th's exposed position became a killing ground. The raw recruits gamely attempted to demonstrate their newly learned maneuvers under "a terrible fire," but as Bracht reported, "Before we were yet formed considerable numbers of each company had bit the dust and many more were groaning with ghastly wounds." Despite ordering his men to drop and fire from the prone position "a la Zouave," Bracht's casualties mounted. Finally, his horse shot from under him and many of his company officers killed or wounded, the regimental commander, Col. William A. Warner, bowed to the inevitable and joined the Union retreat.[43]

The Confederates did not follow. Churchill's men poured a final volley into the fleeing Federals, but their ammunition was running low and soldiers all along the line were nearing collapse. Although Southern casualties were relatively light, insufficient sleep, fighting under a blazing sun with empty stomachs, and lack of water had taken their toll among the men. Kirby Smith had no choice but to allow his exhausted soldiers to find what shade they could and pass around the last swallows of muddy creek water left in their canteens. Polignac occupied his time during the hour or so lull musing over what he considered potentially "fatal" flaws in the commanding general's strategy.[44] The general, however, was confident. As he waited for his ammunition wagons to come up, Kirby Smith ordered Colonel Scott to take his cavalry around the Union flank to positions behind Richmond. By doing so he robbed himself of his ready reconnaissance capability but felt trapping his retreating enemy was the higher priority. It seemed a reasonable risk. At about 1:00 P.M., their cartridge boxes refilled, the entire Confederate line advanced through "open fields . . . intersected with fences overgrown with vines and bushes."[45]

Meanwhile, Manson's recruits were making the most of their natural cover. Screening his command with his artillery and Colonels Metcalfe's and Munday's cavalry, the general had turned a rout into a reasonably orderly retreat. It took nearly two miles to effect the transformation, but in the vicinity of White's Farm, the site of Friday night's skirmishes, he about faced. Concealed within the woods, lying behind vine-covered fences, and with Federal artillery placed in commanding positions, Manson's men were ready for the best the advancing veterans could offer. Their general too was counting on redeeming both himself and his fleet-footed command. Soon, as Manson later reported to "Bull" Nelson, "The enemy . . . began advancing in great force through the open fields in line of battle." Manson's entire being was focused on that gray line when, as he continued, suddenly "a courier rode upon the field and delivered to me your [Nelson's] written order, dated at Lexington, August 30, directing me to retire by the Lancaster Road if the enemy should advance in force." Before he could fully grasp the note's implications, the entire battlefront erupted.[46]

Churchill's division on the Confederate extreme left was somewhat ahead of Cleburne's division because of the uneven terrain. Paul F. Hammond, riding with John Pegram and Kirby Smith, observed the first volley: "[T]he enemy was perfectly concealed, and attempted an ambuscade, which nearly proved disastrous. Rising from their concealment, they delivered a terrible fire at short range, and moved to the charge. Our line wavered and destruction seemed inevitable." Churchill described the fire from Cruft's 18th Kentucky and 12th Indiana as "terrific." As he waited for Preston Smith to bring up Cleburne's brigades, he played for time and ordered his forward troops, commanded by Colonel McCray, to lie down under cover of a ditch and fence. The Rebels lay out of sight a "full five minutes" as the Yankees approached "in heavy force." When they had advanced to within less than fifty yards, "Churchill's voice rang out clear above the din . . . to rise, fire, and charge." McCray's brigade was irresistible. His division commander reported the enemy "gave way in every direction," and "The field was covered with the dead and wounded."[47]

Polignac, marching in line of battle with the 5th Tennessee on the Southern far right, was too far away to participate. His regiment sustained casualties, however, as they attempted a wheeling maneuver with the rest of Cleburne's division on open ground under Union artillery fire. Polignac barely escaped injury when a shell burst directly overhead and wounded eight men, including a Lieutenant Karl marching at his side. When the cheering division finally reached the Union positions, they found them nearly deserted. The second of the three phases constituting the Battle of Richmond had been fought and won essentially by a single brigade of Churchill's division—Colonel McCray's Texans and Arkansans.[48] The excitement sparked by the Federals' panic, however, was infectious. Kirby Smith himself was apparently the first to catch the fever, bolting suddenly from his coterie of staff officers in a one-man charge. Only the urgent pleading of the popular Pegram persuaded him to return, but by then the general's personal escort had sniffed the promise of nearly risk-free glory. As the firing faded, Capt. T. M. Nelson and his "cavalry company of eighty young gentlemen of the best families of Georgia" obtained permission to enter the fray. McCray's tired and bloodied brigade was soon treated to a stirring sight as "Nelson and his splendid fellows dashed forward in gallant style . . . and captured three hundred prisoners."[49]

Maj. Gen. William Nelson finally arrived at Manson's camp accompanied by a single staff officer at two o'clock that afternoon. Evading Scott's cavalry patrols on the Richmond Road, it had taken them four-and-a-half hours to make the last twenty miles from Lancaster. The strong enemy presence in his army's rear coupled with the constant far-off firing were the worst of omens. The general had no illusions as to what he would find in Richmond. He and Manson arrived in the Union camp within moments of each other. Nelson's presence did inspire a momentary burst of confidence, the beleaguered troops raising a loud cheer at his arrival. Their enthusiasm, however, attracted the attention of a Rebel gun crew whose reaction somewhat complicated Manson and Nelson's already strained reunion. Furious at Manson, whom he held personally responsible for the rapidly deteriorating situation, Nelson ordered the camp abandoned.[50]

The two generals managed to gather less than 2,500 men for a last stand on the outskirts of town. The Union line of battle stretched from the turnpike through the town cemetery and into the woods. Brigadier General Cruft, who had somehow managed to keep part of his 2nd Brigade reasonably intact, established a position in the cemetery and adjacent cornfield and woods. As the last man took his place in the line, skirmishers from the 5th and 48th Tennessee Regiments appeared on their front and opened a scattered fire. Cruft's skirmishers responded with a lively enough volley to force the Rebels to take cover behind a wood fence and some nearby haystacks. The Confederate attack stopped cold. The stout fence proved impossible to knock down and the troops were loathe to expose themselves by clambering over it. Both "officers and men huddled up and [were] dodging behind haystacks," none apparently eager to finish the day's work. "All day long," Polignac later recorded, "I had endeavored to observe more coolness & experience than their old officers, by standing up right under fire, not dodging, locating the skirmishers in front of the battery & had succeeded thus far so well that I was then virtually in command." Seeing that none of his fellow officers were inclined to take the initiative and "knowing the effect of personal valour on soldiers," Polignac continued, "I worked myself up to a degree which I did not think myself capable of, took the colors of the Reg. over the fence, waved my handkerchief from the top of a tombstone as we entered the cemetery, urged the men, [and] stood constantly by them." Polignac had read the situation perfectly. Stirred by his seemingly reckless bravery, the Tennesseans broke cover and with a wild yell stormed over the fence and into the cemetery. After a brief but furious firefight, the Union soldiers at last lost their nerve and broke for the rear, leaving the mossy headstones in the possession of the 5th Tennessee and its exhilarated new leader.[51]

The final phase of the Battle of Richmond lasted only thirty minutes. As the disgusted William Nelson later reported: "The enemy attacked in front and on both flanks simultaneously with vigor. Our troops stood about three rounds, when, struck by a panic, they fled in utter disorder. I was left with my staff almost alone. The enemy's cavalry was now in our rear, and the panic at such height that it was a sheer impossibility to do anything." As twilight settled in, the Rebels followed the stricken Federals through the town's streets. It had been a successful but exhausting day for the Southern infantrymen. Kirby Smith, "Bull" Nelson's Confederate counterpart, later reported with satisfaction that "our indomitable troops deliberately walked (they were too tired to run)."[52]

The rest of the fight belonged to Col. John S. Scott's cavalry. He and his 850 troopers had spent most of the day listening to the sound of the distant battle while patrolling between the Lexington and Lancaster Roads. The first stragglers began appearing at about 4:00 P.M., and their numbers grew steadily for two hours until the main Union force appeared on the road. Scott estimated their strength at about 5,000 men and also counted nine artillery pieces. The colonel and his men, lying in ambush, waited until the entire caravan was within carbine and shotgun range. Then, as Scott reported, "My forces, being well ambuscaded, poured a destructive fire into their ranks, killing about 60 and wounding a large number—the firing commenced in obedience to my orders on the extreme left, extending to the right, which was nearest Richmond— after which almost the entire force immediately surrendered." Scott's men captured all nine cannon, hundreds of muskets, a number of wagons "loaded with army supplies," and at least 3,500 prisoners. The colonel reported that he would have netted more Union troops, but his small force simply could not find them all in the darkness.[53]

The most determined escape attempt was by Brig. Gen. Mahlon D. Manson. He and several staff officers bolted the doomed column after Scott's first volley but made it only half a mile before running head-on into a Rebel cavalry patrol. If one can say anything for Manson's luck on August 30, it was consistent. The graycoats unleashed a volley at the approaching horsemen, killing the general's horse, which collapsed on top of him. The severely injured Manson and his surviving staff ended the day as prisoners.[54]

The disastrous defeat at Richmond left the Union command in Kentucky badly shaken. Recovering from a severe leg wound at his headquarters in Lexington the next day, William Nelson placed the blame squarely on Manson. In a report to Maj. Gen. Horatio G. Wright, commanding the Department of the Ohio, Nelson concluded, "What the motive of General Manson was in bringing on an action under the circumstances, and marching 5 miles to do so, I will leave him to explain to you." Although greatly exaggerating the Confederate strength, Charles Cruft summarized the general attitude of his fellow professionals: "It was an attack by at least 15,000 well disciplined troops, under experienced officers, upon 6,250 citizens, ignorant of war, without officers of experience."[55]

Polignac was elated. Writing in his tent after the battle, the de facto commander of the 5th Tennessee recorded: "After the fight, they all looked to me as a man, fit to command them as one who had escaped by a miracle: 'Oh! you will stay!' exclaimed one, as they gathered around me, 'I thought *you must* have been killed' said another! I shook my finger to him denyingly, & said: 'All is fate.' It was then the other exclaimed: 'You will stay!'" His spirits were still soaring the next day. "What a reward & how exultingly do I rejoice over the resolution I set up & carried out to join a regiment. Yesterday ignored & although after one year's service, not better known than when I first arrived. Untalked of, without distinction & not expected by the many ever to acquire any, to-day I am praised by my superior officers & looked upon as a man by all." Both Preston Smith and Benjamin Hill observed Polignac's performance and mentioned him prominently in their official reports, noting his "gallantry" and adding, "He deserves the thanks of this country." Polignac himself made a special effort to bring Hill's attention to the bravery of a fellow officer, a Captain Griffin of the 48th Tennessee. His motives were not, however, totally altruistic, for as he rather cynically noted, the praise was "both just & political, as this man seeing himself exalted by me will certainly vouch for my zeal."[56]

Polignac stayed with the 5th Tennessee as its acting commander for another two weeks. It was a difficult time for him. Frustrated at what he considered Kirby Smith's "indecision" and tactics, he also faced his own personal crisis. By mid-September his subordinates had had enough of their substitute colonel. Polignac was initially confident that he had won the allegiance of the enlisted men with his bravery at Richmond. The officers, however, were a different story. It was the contrast between Polignac's and their own performance in the battle that stung most deeply. Also, as their commander, Polignac at last had the opportunity to put his own rigid ideas of military discipline and procedure into practice. As he confided to his diary, several officers felt he "handled them rather severely." In their view he was an usurper—a foreigner with no right to command them.[57]

It was with this in mind that two of the 5th's officers, "intoxicated" according to Polignac, approached their brigade commander, Col. Benjamin Hill. Colonel Hill who, Polignac noted, was also heavily into his cups, listened sympathetically. The officers were old friends; Hill had previously led the regiment before assuming temporary brigade command. Despite his praise for Polignac's leadership only two weeks earlier, the colonel decided that he too preferred his departure. He advised the regiment's adjutant that he should organize an election to choose a new colonel.[58]

Disgusted, his authority undermined, Polignac decided to resign. As a professional military man of the European mold, he simply could not fathom the mind-set of democratically inclined citizen soldiers. He rationalized his decision somewhat by citing that the already understrength regiment, which had fielded a scant 295 men at Richmond, was rapidly dwindling away because of desertions. He accepted no personal blame for the defections, attributing them to the recent expirations of the soldiers' enlistments.[59]

He was nevertheless determined to depart with a flourish. Polignac had put a great deal of effort into making an impression at Richmond and did not want it to go to waste. Lieutenant Colonel Polignac's farewell address to the 5th Tennessee was a curious mix of pep talk, self-promotion, and sour grapes. That evening, as the regiment stood before him in a double column, he purposely remained mounted to convey his most martial impression. He began somewhat disingenuously by vowing that he had joined them not for "any personal motive" but from a sense of pure patriotism. He urged the men to remember that their shared combat had made them "blood relations," and he had always had their best interests in mind. As proof he reminded them that he alone had procured for them rations of sugar and coffee and the promise of new rifled muskets. He strongly hinted that had he been allowed to remain longer, he would have been able to accomplish more for the men—much more than their own officers. The speech had its desired effect for, as Polignac recorded, "After I had wound up, I was heartily greeted with three cheers & Capt. Large (an Irish man Comp A) & many noncommissioned officers & privates expressed their heartfelt sorrow at my leaving them." By the end of the month, Polignac was back with Kirby Smith's staff.[60]

CHAPTER 5

"One Will, One End,
One All Pervading Thought"

September 1, 1862–April 2, 1863

H aving tasted the excitement of battlefield command, Polignac found the drudgery of staff duty excruciating. He had proven himself in combat and yet the arbitrary nature of the elective system had robbed him of his opportunity to exercise his talents. Moreover, neither Kirby Smith nor Bragg seemed up to the task of defeating Buell and winning Kentucky over to the Confederacy. It appeared to Polignac that competence was something of a liability in the Confederate command structure. Prevailing military theory held that the key to winning battles lay in the timely concentration of offensive forces. To their critics, including Polignac, this most basic of tenets apparently eluded both Kirby Smith and Bragg. Their two armies appeared to many observers to wander aimlessly across the Kentucky countryside, failing to maintain adequate communications and remaining far beyond ready supporting distance of each other. In the meantime, Buell beat them to the strategic town of Louisville. The Southern generals' blunders seemed obvious to Polignac and infuriated him. On October 5 he fumed: "The inspection of the map will show the absurdity of [distancing] the two fractions of the forces so far apart with the enemy at Louisville." To Polignac, only incompetence could account for such a failure.[1]

His mood was no better the following day. Reading the confusing, often contradictory dispatches from Bragg's distant command convinced him of the general's shortcomings. He joined many of his fellow staff officers in concluding Bragg lacked the confidence and ability even to confront the Federals. That he could actually defeat Buell seemed remote at best. Polignac, like many soldiers, inevitably formulated his opinions at times from the information available to him—a notoriously unreliable mixture of camp gossip and factual reports. Despite inadequate supplies, Kirby Smith's lack of cooperation, and facing nearly two-to-one odds, Bragg had, in truth, actually protected his colleague from an attack by

Buell. Yet, writing literally within Kirby Smith's camp, Polignac illustrated the growing popular bias against Bragg. On October 6 Polignac condemned the latter's generalship: "No military operation can be conducted with success where there is no firmness of purpose on the part of the Gen[eral] comm[anding] & where the achievements *always* depend on those of the enemy. Bragg allowed Buell's whole command, not over 20,000 strong to cross the Salt river & make Louisville via Shepardsville when he himself with a superior force was concentrated at Bardstown — such a course not requiring comment."[2]

Bragg's performance during the Battle of Perryville in October reinforced Polignac's opinion, prompting him to proclaim in disgust: "He is decidedly *opposed* to concentration." Perryville, which Polignac deemed "little better than a drawn fight" despite Bragg's initial claims of success, resulted in 3,396 Confederate casualties and ultimately prompted Bragg's decision to abandon Kentucky.[3] Despite his disappointment in the failure of the Kentucky campaign, Kirby Smith acknowledged Polignac's contributions. On the twenty-first Polignac recorded: "Gen[eral] K[irby] S[mith] has written a letter to the President making a very handsome mention of my behavior on the battlefield of Richmond K[entucky] & recommending me both for my bearing & attainment for the rank of Brig[adier] Gen[eral]. Thus at least my exertion coupled with perseverance have been *brought to bear.*" Polignac remained with Kirby Smith during the retreat from Kentucky. The general's letter, furthermore, apparently carried considerable weight with Pres. Jefferson Davis. In early November Polignac left Kirby Smith's staff for Richmond, Virginia, confident that promotion was his at last.[4]

Polignac arrived in the Confederate capital a man of single-minded purpose. In quick succession he called on President Davis and Secretary of War George W. Randolph to press his case. His November 13 meeting with Randolph left Polignac bursting with confidence. The war secretary promised to take his application personally "in hand" and "have it acted upon" immediately. As he walked back to his hotel, Polignac buoyantly observed the "day fine & warm — a regular Indian Summer day." On November 16 Polignac penned: "Mr. Randolph, Secretary of War, resigned yesterday," adding flatly, "this circumstance may interfere with my plans." In light of his burning ambition, Polignac took the news remarkably well, registering only mild irritation. The reason was likely that, fresh from the wilds of Tennessee and Kentucky, he had rediscovered Richmond's rich social life.[5]

Polignac was by nature a connoisseur of fine wines, cuisine, and women. A welcoming dinner with fellow officers consisting of "wines, oysters, ham, etc., including coffee & cegars & apple sauce" proved that, at least to the wealthy, the good life was still available in wartime Richmond. The evening also contrasted starkly with another banquet five months earlier with Maj. Gen. Leonidas Polk's staff in Tennessee: "Dinner good. I say good & yet, if I had been served such a dinner in Paris at any restaurant I should have raised a bustle, abused the 'garcon,' cursed the owner of the establishment, flung my towel right into the plate, gone off in a hurry without paying, lost my temper & probably my umbrella, which would have resulted in the purchase of another & in many good resolutions for the future—all is comparative in this world."[6]

Many of Polignac's new acquaintances lived in the vicinity of the Louisiana Hospital. One of the hospital's staff, Dr. Felix Formento of New Orleans, became one of Polignac's closest friends. Consequently, Polignac was soon a familiar face in the hospital's wards and surrounding neighborhoods.[7] The Louisiana Hospital, also known as the Richmond College Hospital and Baptist College Hospital, was a component of the huge Chimborazo Hospital complex, the largest military hospital of its time in the world. Situated on commanding heights on the eastern outskirts of Richmond, Chimborazo was virtually a small town unto itself. Consisting of 150 separate wood-frame wards and boasting a bakery, brewery, soap factory, vegetable gardens, and cattle herd, it was largely self-sufficient. As the Louisiana Hospital's name suggests, each state was responsible for the care and upkeep of its own wounded and sick troops. Under the efficient eye of its chief administrator, Richmond widow Phoebe Yates Pender, Chimborazo could accommodate over eight thousand patients at a time.[8]

On December 4 Polignac described a tour of Chimborazo conducted by his friend: "Visited the Louisiana hospital under the superintendence of Dr. F[ormento]. Kept in beautiful order. Went with him through the wards—saw many wounds, amputations recently performed & one case of resection—also a man with a cancer on his jaw—a most horrible sight." Two weeks later Polignac revisited the patient, a Captain Myatt, on whom Dr. Formento had performed a resection of the elbow. He found the man's speedy recovery a dramatic testimony to the doctor's skill: "Although the patient had a piece of bone cut off in the upper part of the arm several inches long he can use his arm & bend it. This is probably the most remarkable illustration of a successful resection on record."[9]

Some of the medical procedures at the Louisiana Hospital were of a more festive nature. Smallpox had found its way into Richmond, and in an effort to control the deadly disease authorities called for mass inoculations. Richmond's elite refused to allow anything so trivial as an epidemic to spoil their social calendar. They instead made the best of it by transforming its treatment into an entertaining diversion. On December 18 Polignac recorded: "Yesterday [I] went to the Louisiana hospital to attend a vaccinating party." He found the event well attended and the women "very handsome & stylish." Polignac predicted the novel idea "will be the all engrossing topic of conversations in the social circles of Richmond for many days."[10]

Obviously finding the hospital canteen's bill of fare superior to that of many of Richmond's restaurants, Polignac dined regularly with Dr. Formento. He also made the acquaintance of a Mr. Eggleston, whose house, within walking distance of Chimborazo, served as a social center for local German expatriates. An avid amateur singer, Polignac eagerly joined Eggleston and his friends for evenings of "good German music." The Frenchman felt at home at Eggleston's house, enjoying "German chat, cards, music," and the company of the host's contented "cat sleeping by the fire, dreaming, moving & purring." Such pleasant scenes of European-flavored domesticity were enhanced by the presence of another of Eggleston's friends, an attractive young German chanteuse.[11]

Polignac became entranced with the girl. Although he thought of her constantly and quickly became her regular escort, he never mentioned her name in his diary. He instead referred to her with various code names such as "E," "Exxx," "the singer," or "the German artist." There is some evidence, however, that she was Emma Eggeling, sister of Polignac's future aide-de-camp, Lt. William Eggeling.[12] His motives for such secrecy are unclear—he often made diary entries in a personal code—but Polignac was frequently bothered by what he perceived as others prying into his private affairs. Almost immediately after his introduction to the singer, he noted his new relationship had become the focal point of Richmond's rumor mill. On November 26 he recorded: "Heard usual share of gossip about my late acquaintance with the German singer. My calls are already being trumpeted about town with the usual additions, remarks, & comments—so much for slander."[13]

Idle gossip, however, failed to deter Polignac from pursuing the relationship. He and the singer met regularly at Eggleston's house and attended the Virginia Singing Society, "made up exclusively of Germans." Polignac described a typical evening at the society as featuring an amateur theatrical production followed by "two or three choruses, next dancing, next eating supper, next adjourning, taking leave, some taking their own, some others' wives home—next, what next?" Polignac held high hopes for his own romantic future. As the singer warmed to his attentions, he mused about the evenings ahead with a rather entertaining mix of coy innuendo and martial bombast: "With a little patience I have fine prospects of some etc., etc., etc., ere long but must proceed by regular approaches until I find an opportunity to carry the position & effect a lodgement." [14]

On November 21 Polignac paid his respects to Mrs. Davis at the Executive Mansion. He found the First Lady "lively & humorous as usual." Their conversation turned on the state of Richmond's current theatrical productions. Fresh from attending a performance at the Broad Street Theater, Polignac delighted Mrs. Davis with a lively narrative of the various "amusing scenes" he had just enjoyed. She, in turn, hinted that the war had contributed somewhat to the diminished quality of recent revues. Mrs. Davis also pointedly observed that a marked lack of talent among the female performers had not adversely affected theatrical attendance. She had a ready explanation for the "rapture of the public" (which included many lonely soldiers), who thronged the mediocre productions. Noting their skimpy costumes, she rather cattily observed that the actresses "had nothing but their calves to commend them to the sympathy of the audience." As for their singing ability, she concluded, much to her guest's amusement, "a calf, you know, is known by its bleat." [15]

Polignac frequently found it difficult to make his way around Richmond. He often found it necessary to beg rides in the carriages of friends such as Dr. Formento or borrow others' horses. He at times risked his life in the small steam-powered cars that chugged along the capital's muddy streets, but for the most part he walked. In light of such inconveniences, it seems he would have welcomed the news that his horse was soon to arrive by rail. His trusty mount, however, had obviously slipped his mind in the excitement of his new surroundings. On November 30 he sputtered: "Heard that my horse will be here tomorrow. Where in the name of the Landlord of Hell shall I put him? (my horse not the Devil). I must look about [for a stable] tomorrow morning the very first thing." [16]

The news arrived in an otherwise welcome Knoxville-postmarked letter from his friend John Pegram, who had recently been promoted brigadier general for his outstanding service in Tennessee and Kentucky. Pegram offered a tongue-in-cheek explanation for the errant steed's belated arrival: "I breathe more freely—Your Bucephalus (pronounced Bucky Phalus) has been 'absent without leave' for several days and has just turned up in fine condition this afternoon with a man on his back! He (that is Bucky) was . . . seized, and is now safely lodged with the other horses of quality." [17]

Polignac applauded his old messmate's promotion, yet Pegram's ebullient tone must have piqued his ego. Pegram had achieved everything Polignac desired—a generalship and combat command. Assigned a cavalry brigade, Pegram crowed, "I have to leave for Middle Tennessee, where my bold cavaliers and much glory await me." He added with only half-feigned bravado, "I have a scheme for making a wintry dash across the Ohio river on the ice, to get fresh horses, blankets and shoes! and also to harangue the good people of Ohio, and try to bring them to a sense of their folly—General [Kirby] Smith's chief objection to my scheme is that I might be tempted to return by way of Baltimore!" Despite his own confidence, Pegram shared Polignac's reservations concerning the western commanders' abilities: "It is a matter of speculation whether the campaign in Tennessee is to be a hog-stealing expedition on our side, and Negro-stealing on that of the enemy, or whether we are to have some real hard fighting. Gen[eral Kirby] Smith received today from Gen[eral] B[ragg] a letter full of spirits, in which he says that he is 'confident of his ability to whip the enemy.' . . . It is to be hoped that when the crisis arrives, he will show greater strength in the 'vertibral column' than he did in Kentucky." [18]

Pegram's enthusiasm apparently did little to spur Polignac's efforts to reenter the fray. His sojourn in the Confederate capital began to take on the appearance of an extended paid vacation. Although he scanned the papers daily for war news and toured Richmond's military installations, he did very little to further his return to active duty. At least temporarily, Polignac abandoned the life of a soldier for that of a bon vivant. On December 4 Dr. Formento escorted his friend to one of Richmond's numerous gambling houses. Polignac thoroughly enjoyed himself and described the establishment as "kept with as much elegance as circumstances now permit. The house is a public one & a permanent inducement is held out to guests in the shape of a supper to which they can sit every night for nothing—a liberality which their gambling proclivities do more than tenfold requite." [19]

Polignac's aristocratic title continued contributing to his appeal as a sought-after celebrity. His few hours leading a regiment in a Kentucky cemetery had provided his requisite laurels as a Confederate hero as well. Reporters from such distant journals as the London *Times* requested interviews, during which the Frenchman enthusiastically urged European aid to the Confederacy. Richmond's elite found him irresistible and clamored for his presence at their many diversions. His stay in the capital subsequently revolved around the "series of dinners, dances and charades, and theatricals" that made up the social season. Privately, Polignac

chafed at his new "idle, lounging slipshod snaillike life." As he waited for
his promotion, he advanced the possibility of leading a diplomatic mission to Europe. He had maintained his contacts with Alexander Dimitri
and socialized regularly with Judah Benjamin. Throughout much of December Polignac struggled to convince the two men to allow him to
press his connections in France and England for a military alliance.[20]

Benjamin, who took the lead in the matter, advised patience. The
French consul had encouraged him to think that the deteriorating
Northern political situation might preclude the necessity of initiating
a European entanglement. Fresh from a Northern tour, the consul
reported that "a strong peace party is springing up." The emerging
"counter-revolution," as Polignac termed it, could possibly result in the
North suing for an armistice. Another scenario, according to the consul,
might prompt independently a "European intervention at an early day,"
although "not before the month of March." Registering some disappointment, Polignac glumly observed that Benjamin, "buoyant with
hopes . . . , will probably not think it necessary to send anyone abroad."[21]

Still Polignac persisted. On December 9 he engaged the French consul in a "long conversation" regarding "the intentions of Europe's states-
men with respect to the American struggle." Polignac adamantly insisted
that the Confederacy's precarious "political existence in the present state
. . . hangs on a few battles." He declared "it would be well to open the
eyes of Europe to the real dangers of the situation lest it should grow too
late for foreign nations to interfere." He advanced the possibility that
the Europeans, and especially the British, mistakenly believed "that the
north cannot subdue the south." Polignac held no such illusions. He had
witnessed firsthand the leadership of Generals Bragg, Kirby Smith, and
Beauregard. Such officers could, Polignac earnestly believed, easily defeat the British intentions of "not under any circumstances hav[ing] any
one government reestablished on this continent." Although he promised
no immediate action, the rather politically naïve Polignac recorded that
in the end, he had "won" the French diplomat "over to my side."[22]

Three days later he was still contemplating his own role in the struggle
for Southern independence. After breakfasting with Dr. Formento at
the Louisiana Hospital, he rode to the Executive Mansion. He found the
president's wife in a conversational mood and confided his beliefs "on the
different degrees of ambition & the kind of inward knowledge of their
own fate which seems to be given to great men." As First Lady, Varina
Davis had seen her share of "great men." She had also been struck by
the rarity of their talents matching their ambitions. Polignac must have
blanched slightly as Mrs. Davis cited the "many instances which have

come under her own personal observation of men who . . . were fully convinced of the great effect of their future destinies yet achieved nothing—or at least did not [realize] their end." He was, nevertheless, confident of his own future; he had come too far and risked too much to sink into obscurity.[23]

Polignac fancied himself both a connoisseur of fine horseflesh as well as a student of American ways. An auction near Governor Street one Saturday afforded him the opportunity to indulge both pastimes. In Mississippi he had been struck by the miserliness of many of his adoptive countrymen. In one instance, rather than pay a turnpike's toll near Corinth, the locals had forged an alternate (and free) "shunpike," prompting Polignac to declare "How very American!" He found the Richmond auction equally amusing as well as revealing of the American character. The bidding for an old nag, the best offering of the sale, so amused Polignac that he recorded the proceedings: "There were all sorts of prices in the crowd. 5 doll[ars] for this mare—she is a little stiff (that she was but not a little) but she looks fast when once started—'1 mile in four minutes'—voice in the crowd 'is it really so?'—owner: 'entirely!'—Gentlemen, who gives $5 for the fast mare, etc." The spirited though inconclusive bidding prompted an "elderly man" in the crowd to enter the action with an impromptu auction of his own noble steed. Tottering from the floorboards of a wagon, the old man competed with the auctioneer as he bawled out at the top of his voice "who bids for the mule—a good chunk of mule sure enough." Finding the new auction, peppered with a hefty dose of profanity, more entertaining than the original, the crowd shifted its attention. With no takers at his original price of five dollars, the old codger delighted his audience by upping his price to fifty dollars. In the renewed bidding war, Polignac chuckled "that contrary to the custom at auction sales the prices ran down instead of running up. Finally having failed to find a bidder at $5 he . . . rode off." Although such performances amused Polignac, they also brought home to him the essentially alien quality of his new country. To ease his occasional bouts of homesickness, he sought out anything that even remotely reminded him of Europe. He frequented a German restaurant on Fifth Street and even discovered a passable French restaurant. Despite being somewhat put off that the proprietor of the latter establishment was named "Jones," he made the French cafe a favored haunt.[24]

Although Polignac often found American women attractive and even charming, they at times struck him as less than ladylike. He found habits commonly affected by rural women such as smoking and dipping snuff repulsive. Their sisters in the cities, although much less addicted to tobacco, were often too forward for the Frenchman's taste. Moreover, to his exasperation, he found them predisposed to constant gossiping. In the German singer he found a fellow music lover as well as a woman free of the Americans' irritating customs. Their relationship progressed smoothly despite a minor spat. Annoyed by her swain's attentions to another woman, the singer pointedly excused herself from a party held by their mutual German musical friends. She evidently made her point, for the next day, Christmas Eve, Polignac called to beg his way back into her good graces. He had spent the morning shopping for Christmas gifts, and an early peace offering coupled with a heartfelt apology achieved the desired effect. Returning home the next morning, he cheerfully reported, "clouds blown off—sky cleared up—horizon bright. Nothing but a passing gale originating in a breath of jealousy." [25]

He was jarred awake Christmas morning by the explosions of "popcrackers" and "sky rockets." The racket began at dawn and continued "all day until dark when [it was] *not* interrupted but carried on with new energy." In the evening Polignac fought his way through the barrage to Judah Benjamin's house for dinner. Polignac and Benjamin, recently appointed secretary of state, spent the evening discussing political developments in the North and on the continent. Polignac found the recently arrived Federal casualty figures from the fighting at Fredericksburg particularly interesting. He observed that if the New York *World*'s reported total of fifteen thousand was correct, the Union had lost as many men as Wellington at Waterloo. Afterward, the last week of 1862 played itself out quietly. Polignac spent his idle hours writing and reading from the works of Bulwar-Litton and Dickens. He celebrated New Year's Eve at the German singer's house, where he "enjoyed a nice supper, music, etc., etc., etc." Upon his return home he reflected on the past year: "When I look back into [the passing year] I am in a general way pleased with the manner I have borne myself from its rise out of the mire of the Past & during its progress through Time to its downfall into eternity—Good bye 1862 forever & ever Farewell." [26]

Eighteen sixty-three "dawned in gloom, but the sun . . . soon beamed forth in great splendor upon a people radiant with smiles." Polignac celebrated the New Year by treating E to a buggy ride. In the evening he called upon Dr. Formento, whom he found "with a crowd of company." After introductions the party walked the short distance into the city for supper and further diversions. They decided to top off their evening by visiting a nearby "hell," or gambling house in soldiers' parlance. Polignac had enjoyed his previous visit to a Richmond gambling house for the same reasons as his fellow officers: Therein could be found such "lux-urious furniture, soft lights, obsequious servants and lavish store of such wines and liquors and cigars as could be had nowhere else in Dixie." They were refuges where "Senators, soldiers and the learned professions sat el-bow to elbow, round the generous table that offered the choicest viands money could procure. In the handsome rooms above they puffed fra-grant Havannas, while the latest developments of news, strategy and policy were discussed; sometimes ably, sometimes flippantly, but always freshly." Fortified by their celebrations, the men "stepped deliberately into the dining room," where, as Polignac recalled, "overtaken by peni-tence at the coolness of our behaviour we all resolved upon contributing $5 each & to fight the tiger." Satisfied with having lost only two depre-ciated Confederate dollars, Polignac merrily declared, "Bully for us," as the party adjourned to the street.[27]

The next day Polignac recorded that he had "secured a new servant, a darky by the name of Dick whom I took at $20 a month, his mother boarding him." Acquiring Dick was something of a coup for Polignac. He found it difficult both to acquire and retain servants, required acces-sories for proper Southern officers and gentlemen. He was undoubtedly a demanding employer. As a perfectionist he required strict obedience and meticulous attention to details. He also evidenced little concern for his servants as individuals. Although he interacted with them on a daily basis, he never recorded anything revealing the slightest personal inter-est in their welfare. Polignac hired servants to perform their functions and nothing more. He retained at least one white servant, "a French-man, his name Germaine." Polignac's description of Germaine was his most detailed of any of his employees: "his wages high ($20 monthly), his stature small, his references his own account of himself." Germaine, who Polignac recorded he "mustered into service of my own individual as a volunteer" on May 27, is never mentioned again. Despite the shared na-tivity Polignac apparently considered his servant's lowly caste too base to merit further attention. For the most part Polignac followed his fel-low officers' lead and either hired free blacks or leased slaves as servants. If anything, he was ambivalent to the moral question of slavery. He did, however, display at times a somewhat detached interest in the South's slave economy, for he recognized that the institution was a hindrance to gaining European recognition. Yet in Polignac's aristocratic European view, there was little practical difference in the status and uses of black slaves, Irish immigrants, or French peasants: they were all simply at the bottom of the social hierarchy and suitable only for menial tasks. Polignac joined the Confederate Army not to defend slavery but to fight for the abstract principle of states' rights and to fulfill his own sense of destiny, though mostly the latter.[28]

On January 12 Polignac's destiny seemed within his grasp. While attending a reception at the home of a mutual acquaintance, Adjutant General Samuel Cooper rather casually informed him that President Davis had approved his promotion to brigadier general. Cooper, noting that Davis thought Polignac "might be useful in Louisiana," inquired, as Polignac remembered, "whether such an appoint[ment] would prove acceptable to me." Cooper's proposal caught Polignac by surprise. He had become so immersed in Richmond's social whirl and his relationship with E that promotion had almost slipped his mind. He had at last achieved the purpose of his mission to the capital, and yet his own human frailty tempered his pleasure. Later that evening Polignac pondered his reply to the adjutant general's offer: "What could I say but yes & yet I don't feel very anxious now about being promoted. Why?? I was eager for it when I arrived in Richmond last November. Such is the course of life—it is seldom that wishes are fulfilled when they are most intense—my promotion will interfere with many other pleasant things I am now engaged in, but all must yield to one object—'one will, one end, one all pervading thought' . . . must be my motto through life."[29]

Although he often courted other women, Polignac grew infatuated with E. She was quite different from his previous lover, a French girl whom he deemed "a devilish good mistress" but "too unfaithful" to marry. Although he found E "quite pretty," he was equally fascinated by her intelligence and considerable musical talent. The attraction was mutual. E was inconsolable at the thought of Polignac's imminent departure for far-off Louisiana. On January 22, the day General Cooper handed Polignac his promotion papers, the new brigadier found the atmosphere at E's house "so gloomy as scarcely to justify . . . staying." E eventually reconciled herself to the inevitability of her lover's departure, and for the remainder of his Richmond stay the two saw each other almost daily, much to the satisfaction of local gossipmongers. Polignac's extended, unchaperoned visits to E's house struck many Richmond matrons as being beyond the bounds of decency. One, reported Polignac, "is said to give me a very bad character & to be talking a good deal about me (which means a deal of bad) at present in all the houses in which she visits." He, in turn, found Richmond society's addiction to gossip infuriating in its hypocrisy. He valued his own privacy and respected that of others.[30]

Mrs. Imogene Lyons, wife of well-known lawyer James Lyons, was a prominent Richmond hostess. Her friend Mary Boykin Chesnut once referred to the Lyonses' home, Laburnum, as the "Lyons' den" for its mistress's occasional yet spirited indulgences in "chronique scandaleuse." Despite wincing occasionally at Mrs. Lyons's tidbits of local intrigues, Polignac found her charming and enjoyed his visits to her home. On Saturday, February 7, she and Mr. Lyons invited Polignac to Laburnum for dinner. Among the guests were three other Confederate generals—William Booth Taliaferro, Sterling Price, and Charles Clark. Other dignitaries included Henry Stuart Foote, former governor of Mississippi; William Porcher Miles of South Carolina; and Col. James Chesnut, Jr., equally notable as aide-de-camp to President Davis and husband to Mary Boykin Chesnut.[31] After "a very fine dinner," the ladies excused themselves to the parlor and "speeches & sentiments began" among the men. Mr. Lyons set the tone for the evening by offering a toast to Polignac's homeland. Flattered, Polignac took the floor to praise his adoptive country, which he characterized as "the promised land of [his] youthful dreams," for which he "would be proud to die." Other speeches followed and the guests "soon after took leave."[32]

In many ways the gathering at Laburnum that frigid Saturday evening illustrates the disparity in wartime living conditions among Richmond's citizenry. The harsh winter of 1862–63 created many hardships for the city's poorer inhabitants. Many, such as War Department clerk John B. Jones, resented the comparatively privileged lifestyles of the few: "We are now, in effect, in a state of siege, and none but the opulent, often those who have defrauded the government, can obtain a sufficiency of food and raiment."[33] Polignac was aware of the profiteering and fraud so prevalent in Richmond and condemned it. In early March he described "a very sad affair" in which a doctor was "charged with having appropriated to his own use & for the benefit of his private table articles of food & delicacies contributed for the sick." Although Polignac applauded the prospect of the doctor's inevitable punishment, he took his own comparatively luxurious living standard for granted. The rarified atmosphere of Richmond's elite insulated him from the harsh realities of the common citizenry.[34] John B. Jones spoke for Richmond's rank and file: "Some idea may be formed of the scarcity of food in this city from the fact that, while my youngest daughter was in the kitchen today, a young rat came out of its hole and seemed to beg for something to eat; she held out some bread, which it ate from her hand, and seemed grateful. Several others soon appeared and were as tame as kittens. Perhaps we shall have to eat them."[35]

Such a scene contrasts sharply with the sumptuous matinees frequently given by Richmond hostesses, featuring "music & Luncheon—

oysters & wines of several descriptions—entertainment & pleasant company." On one wintry occasion Polignac spent "a very pleasant evening discussing various political topics & others over a scotch whiskey punch flavored with lemon—a luxury almost unparalleled in the annals of the Confederacy."[36] Polignac often indulged his appetites for fine cuisine and wines at the French consul's home. On one evening he marveled that "more wine was drunk than I thought there was in the Confederacy." He spent his most enjoyable hours indulging his passion for music. In early January he and his German friends, including E, were featured performers at a "matinée musicale" hosted by Varina Davis at the Executive Mansion. The gathering included a number of local celebrities. Mary Chesnut, who attended, recalled: "Miss Hammersmith sang. And Mrs. Dick Anderson—Mrs. Semmes who played—General (Prince) Polignac was there—and some Germans. Custis Lee and Mr. Davis' staff —Browne, Ives & Co. The Germans played and sang, accompanying themselves in piano and guitar." Congratulating himself that "we gave quite a concert," Polignac later walked E home, where he spent "the balance of the day."[37]

Despite Richmond's pleasant diversions, Polignac never forgot for long that he was a soldier. He read the military dispatches daily and closely followed the progress of his acquaintances actively campaigning in the field. Having served with Gen. Braxton Bragg, he was less credulous than most of Bragg's initial reports of a decisive victory at the Battle of Murfreesboro, Tennessee (December 31, 1862–January 3, 1863). As more dispatches arrived he acidly observed that "Bragg's great victory turns out to be little less than a defeat. His campaign in Tennessee can be summed up in the following—'a partial success & complete reverse.'"[38] Ironically, on the very day he accepted his promotion papers, Polignac received a letter from Beauregard requesting his services as his chief inspector general. Owing to the inefficiency of the Confederate bureaucracy and postal service, the letter had taken nearly two months to arrive from Beauregard's new headquarters in Charleston, South Carolina. The letter's delay worked to Polignac's advantage, though. His close association with Judah Benjamin and the Davis household had given him many political insights. He had learned that Beauregard's assignment to South Carolina was tantamount to banishment for his earlier defiance of the president. To have accepted his former commander's offer would have meant Polignac's own exile, estrangement from Benjamin and Davis, and a return to hated staff duties. The new brigadier general, who had already begun assembling his own staff, politely replied that he had already accepted an assignment. Although not particularly pleased with his posting to Louisiana in the remote Trans-Mississippi Department, he would at last have his own command.[39]

On February 27 Polignac's otherwise idyllic stay in Richmond was disturbed by the prospect of his imminent eviction. The news reeked of intrigue. As Polignac returned home from visiting a neighbor, his land-lord nervously accosted him at the general's door. A postal employee, the man stammered that, owing to "unexpected events," he was "compelled to leave town" never to return. He requested that Polignac vacate his room as soon as possible. Refusing to divulge any further details, the man beat a hasty retreat, leaving his baffled tenant to ponder future lodgings. Less than a week later, one of the general's acquaintances cleared up the mystery. Polignac described the scandalous particulars: "My landlord, Mr. N. was charged with having on several occasions purloined money enclosed in letters which as he held an office in the Post Dept. he had many opportunities. The two pilfered Confederate notes whose num-bers had been given by the wronged party were found in his possession. He was immediately apprehended & admitted to bail in $1000—'made skedaddle.' The balance of the family left yesterday & I am to leave to-morrow this deserted home." Despite the overcrowding plaguing Rich-mond, Polignac found new lodgings the next day. On Monday, March 2, he moved his belongings to the home of a Mr. Honneger on Ninth Street and then spent the rest of the day with E. On Tuesday, following a discreet morning tryst with an unnamed Richmond belle, he again called on E, who accompanied him to a photographer's studio for a por-trait session. In the evening he paid a series of social and political calls, a pastime that would characterize the balance of his stay in the Confeder-ate capital.[40]

On Friday, March 6, he engaged Judah Benjamin in a long discussion concerning the Confederacy's financial situation. Their conversation eventually turned away from Secretary of the Treasury Christopher G. Memminger's scheme to reduce the public debt. Prompted by a newspa-per article captioned "Long Live Abraham 1st," Polignac launched into a tirade against the Northern president. Declaring that the North had invested their executive with "dictatorial power" and "pandered to their own subjugation," he worked himself into a near frenzy of denunciation: "It was reserved to the Yankee race to invest a dull, uneducated, vulgar pettifogger with the dignity of dictator."[41]

On Monday Polignac took advantage of the fine spring weather to make a number of calls. He and Dr. Formento spent most of the day rid-ing and also visiting with the Lyons family at Laburnum. Polignac found Mrs. Lyons "charming" and as "always full of attentions for me." In the evening he visited former U.S. senator and minister to France William Cabell Rives. Polignac characterized Rives, who had been elected to the Confederate Congress in April, 1861, as "probably the first statesman of the country tho' now excluded from the councils." Polignac recorded that he "carried on quite a long conversation with the old gentleman" concerning the prospect of English military aid to the South. The two men agreed "that the greatest inducement which could be held out to England for interference would be that the South [would] eventually be crushed." Polignac and Rives believed England had withheld commitment owing to an erroneous assumption that the South could maintain the war indefinitely.[42]

They attributed the basis of England's position to such misguided Confederate propagandists as Edwin DeLeon. Polignac believed DeLeon, a member of a prominent Richmond family, was doing more harm than good. As publisher of the *Index*, a pro-Confederate journal in London, DeLeon, according to Polignac, had editorialized "that without foreign intervention the American war would not stop, as it was impossible for any of the contending parties to overwhelm the other." Although somewhat politically naïve, Polignac strongly asserted that DeLeon and his fellow agents were encouraging England's delay by mistakenly "baiting their hooks" with claims of Southern strength. Polignac held no illusions concerning England's "magnanimity" and believed that English politicians were biding their time, playing the two American nations against each other to England's advantage. "Such an untimely article is calculated to deter England from interfering as she cannot be supposed to have any desire for peace but would rather see the war carried on to such an extent as would cause both parties to sink from sheer exhaustion, whereupon she could enter the lists to snatch the spoils from both sides."[43]

The last two weeks of March marked the end of the social season. Polignac's spirits sagged as he accompanied E and his German friends to the Petersburg railroad station. He bade farewell as they set off for eventual destinations in Europe and the North. Turning unseasonably cold and stormy, the weather contributed to Polignac's gloom. After his friends' departure he spent the remainder of the day at home staring out of his window at the cheerless sunset: "The sun broke out towards the end of the day & peeped from out of the mist with a squint eye. He slouched slowly down the vault of heaven with an unhealthy complexion & had already his nightcap on, half down over his sickly face as he bade us goodnight leering at the chimney stacks & casting long shadows on the ground & cutting out strange arabesques with a golden engraver on the walls of Western exposure which were gradually mellowed to uniform darkness by the soft touch of night's pale hand."[44]

Despite the miserable weather, snow interspersed with freezing rain, Polignac's mood improved rapidly. The Germans' departure suddenly made Richmond less interesting, and the general threw himself into preparations for his own journey. Also, on March 25, he received a letter from President Davis's aide, Col. William B. Browne, requesting "some hints on the composition of the French & German organization of the staff." He plunged into the project and three days later recorded with assurance that he "Called on Mr. Benj[amin] who told me my report was read aloud today by the Pres[ident] to the Secretary of War & the Adj[utant] Gen[eral] & given much satisfaction."[45] On Tuesday, March 31, Polignac called at the Executive Mansion to take leave of Mr. and Mrs. Davis. The president, who was coincidentally entertaining a Louisiana delegation, bade the new general "farewell in kind & affectionate terms."

April 2 was a memorable day for both the president and his young general. Early that Thursday morning a crowd of "a few hundred women and boys" gathered in Richmond's Capital Square. According to one observer, "the number continued to swell until there were more than a thousand." In what became known as the "Richmond Bread Riot," the women and children, "saying they were hungry and must have food," began looting local storefronts. Gov. John Letcher, leading a company of state militia, failed to disperse the mob. Before Governor Letcher could order his troops to fire on the rioters, President Davis arrived on the scene. The president averted bloodshed by passionately pleading with the rioters to bear their "privations with fortitude." Perhaps influenced by Davis's renewed threat of a volley, the crowd eventually melted away and returned to their homes.[46] Unaware of the trouble, Polignac left the Confederate capital later that day for Louisiana with his small staff recruited from Richmond's German community—Lt. William Eggeling, formerly of the Army of Northern Virginia, and Capt. J. Ernest Cuculler. He would never again return to the city he had for months enjoyed.[47]

CHAPTER 6

"A Damn Frog-Eating Frenchman"

April 3, 1863–December 31, 1863

———◦•◦———

Polignac's new orders read: "Brig. Gen. C. J. Polignac and staff will proceed without delay to Alexandria, La., and report to Lieut. Gen. E. Kirby Smith, commanding, etc. for assignment to duty." His superiors' rather blithe assumption that Polignac could accomplish his journey "without delay" did not take into account the peculiarities of Southern transportation. Leaving Richmond on Thursday, April 2, Polignac and his quickly recruited staff, Lieutenant Eggeling and Captain Cuculler, soon found themselves stranded in Burkesville, Virginia, little more than fifty miles from the capital. Their sojourn in the small village dragged on for fifteen hours. It was an omen of delays to come—Polignac and his small party took over a month to reach their final destination. They arrived in Lynchburg the next day at seven in the evening. Failing to obtain rooms "in the hotel which is held in the highest repute," Polignac remembered the Cabell's House, the same hotel in which he had been questioned by a vigilance committee two years earlier. After Polignac reminded him of the incident, the innkeeper commemorated their earlier meeting by offering his returning guest the same room he had occupied in 1861.[1]

In Knoxville, Tennessee, the railroad conductor, "who apologized for not having done it sooner," directed Polignac and his small entourage to the "so called 'Lady's Car.'" Declaring it "one of the greatest American humbugs," Polignac did find their new accommodations "a little cleaner than the other cars." It did, however, have its peculiarly American idiosyncrasies. Polignac observed that the "Lady's Car" was "one in which gentlemen are not allowed to smoke—a restraint which 'ladies' make up for by puffing away at a rate that would throw a steamboat stack into the shade." Polignac found his feminine companions "also chew a little occasionally, but this by the bye. So much for ladyship—one of them was known to express her smoking propensities in the following manner viz, 'I wonder whether it would be considered *fast* to smoke a pipe now[?]'"[2]

It was a grueling trip. The men spent Easter on the rails to Atlanta, arriving at two in the morning. After stops in Montgomery and West Point, they finally reached Mobile, Alabama, on April 6. Exhausted, they could at least congratulate themselves for having telegraphed ahead for reservations at the "Battle House," where they checked in sometime after two in the morning. Owing to transportation delays Polignac and his staff spent a month in the strategic port city overlooking Mobile Bay. They made the best of the situation, enjoying the hospitality of the local commanders, Maj. Gen. Simon Bolivar Buckner, Brig. Gen. James Edwin Slaughter, and Adm. Franklin Buchanan. Admiral Buchanan, former commander of the C.S.S. *Virginia*, took the Frenchman under his wing. The admiral indulgently conducted the newcomer on a tour of the new C.S.S. *Tennessee*, "a gunboat (ram)" that Polignac noted was being completed "after the model of the *Richmond* but much larger."[3]

At sixty-three years old and a veteran of the old U.S. Navy, Buchanan was one of the most respected naval officers of his day. He was also proud of his new 208-foot flagship. Although seriously underpowered, the *Tennessee* was a formidable weapon. Recently launched from a Selma, Alabama, shipyard, she mounted six Brooke 7-inch rifled guns and was protected by three layers of wrought iron over stout oak and pine timbers. Polignac listened raptly as Buchanan and his crew pointed out such details as the *Tennessee*'s speed, draft, and angle of its armor plating. The powerful warship, however, was only one component of Mobile's sophisticated defenses. Confederate engineers had positioned obstructions in the already narrow mouth of Mobile Bay to restrict its entrance to less than a mile and a half. The forty guns of Fort Morgan, protected by their brick casements, challenged any vessel daring to run the gantlet of torpedoes deemed by Polignac "the best I have ever seen."[4]

He was also impressed by two of the city's island batteries, finding them "Kept in fine order." Although he thought one position "awkward," its gun embrasures "unproportionately large" and vulnerable to being "fired into from the rear," he pronounced the other "a very good battery." Polignac carefully inspected the batteries' guns, taking time to sketch their carriages and sighting instruments. The general also found the gunners better trained than the average Confederate soldiers, noting: "Discipline among the men is enforced almost like the Regular service. Schools for the instruction of noncommissioned officers & men have been established in which they are taken through an elementary handbook of artillery used in the old U.S. army. The course is obligatory for noncommissioned officers & free for privates but such alone among the latter attend it are qualified for preferrment [*sic*]."[5]

On May 5 Polignac and his staff departed Mobile for Jackson, Mississippi. They arrived the next day, Polignac wryly noting the train "ran off the tracks only once—no casualties—a most wonderful trip." Transferring to wagons, the party eventually made their way to Natchez, Mississippi, where Polignac "for the first time enjoyed the sight of the great Father of Waters." They crossed the Mississippi River on the eleventh and breakfasted in Vidalia, Louisiana. The next day the pilgrims resumed their journey by skiff on the Tensas River, their baggage following on a flatboat. The Federal Navy patrolled the Tensas, and the boatmen nervously scanned the water ahead for Union gunboats. As they approached a bend in the river near Trinity, the steersman suddenly jammed his pole into the river bottom, spinning the boat around; he had spotted the telltale bow of a gunboat lurking only yards away. Nearly panic-stricken, the boatmen beat a "precipitated retreat" three miles upriver to the relative safety of Mr. Robert Perry's plantation, where they spent the night. Congratulating themselves for their earlier vigilance, the men re-embarked the next morning. Their mood, however, soon turned to one of deep embarrassment. As they neared the dreaded site of their close call, the clear morning light revealed that their sighting was not of a gunboat but rather the ruins of an "ancient house." As the boats continued "up Little River, 21 miles from Trinity," the men erupted into waves of bickering, filling the air with recriminations and denials of blame. Most found their "over-awed steersman" the most convenient scapegoat.[6] A night spent sleeping in the cramped boat did little to improve their tempers, which grew steadily worse as the next day progressed.

The officers needed wagons for the next leg of their journey to Harrisonburg, some thirty miles away. At dawn Polignac set out on foot to negotiate with a nearby farmer. The farmer, a Mr. Breithaupt, was evidently not driven by either charity or patriotism. "An unmitigated extortioner," according to Polignac, the German charged an exorbitant "$17 to send [them] in a broken down vehicle & a broken winded horse a distance of 6 miles." As Polignac and his companions creaked and bumped along in Breithaupt's overpriced and underpowered wagon, their anger mounted. As Polignac put it, "we cherished a feeling of resentment which was soon to mature into effective & practical revenge." Rather than drop Breithaupt's rig at the agreed-upon location, Polignac determined to get his money's worth: "Pressed the old man's vehicle & horse . . . into our special service—changed our course . . . &

made directly for Harrisonburg." At Harrisonburg the officers again took to the water, boarding the steamboat *Anna*. Owing to the recent loss of Alexandria to the advancing Federals, their destination had been changed to Shreveport, Louisiana, precipitating an even more circuitous route than originally planned. In addition to traveling overland, Polignac and his staff now had to continue by way of the Tensas, Little, and Ouachita Rivers. Polignac found the *Anna*'s engineer, another German, by the name of Buchholz, a refreshing contrast to the larcenous Mr. Breithaupt.[7]

Polignac declared the engineer "a very intelligent man—one of the nicest men of his profession I ever met." It was a high compliment; Polignac considered engineering "a profession which tends to develop the powers & natural endowments of the mind more than most trades in the labouring classes of society—especially more than the plodding labour of the tillers of the soil." He also found Buchholz more refined than even the local gentry, observing, "how rough & backward are the largest planters in this section of the state." The *Anna* was no C.S.S. *Tennessee*, but Polignac was nevertheless fascinated by Buchholz's explanation of her boilers and other workings. Their conversation soon turned to slavery. The engineer complained of, as Polignac recorded, "the bad influence of the black race upon the manufacturing industry of the South," and he argued that slave labor provided unfair competition to free skilled workers. "Planters use [slaves] as mechanics which is detrimental to the white mechanics of the South—a class . . . for which little or nothing is done." Polignac had heard the complaint before and noted, "I believe it to be a growing feeling in the South."[8]

They arrived in Monroe around midnight on the seventeenth. The next morning Polignac "made acquaintance with Gen[eral] [Paul O.] Hebert, formerly governor of L[ouisiana], now a Brig[adier] without a brigade—commanding Western district North Red River." It took Polignac and his staff three days by stagecoach to travel the last one hundred miles to Shreveport. On the afternoon of May 21, Polignac reported to Gen. Edmund Kirby Smith at his home. The next day Kirby Smith informed his new brigadier that he had not yet determined his assignment. The commander explained that he had two brigades from which to choose: "The first in Gen[eral John G.] Walker's division—the second which is forming at this place—both composed of Texans."[9]

While he waited for Kirby Smith to make his decision, Polignac explored his new surroundings. True to character, he sought out the town's resident celebrities, including Brig. Gen. Henry Hopkins Sibley, who entertained him with "a long conversation on New Mexico." After taking leave of Sibley, Polignac spent the rest of the day searching for lodgings. While making inquiries at one home, Polignac experienced possibly the most memorable concert of his life. He noticed a piano in the family's parlor and they insisted, despite his frantically polite attempts to leave, in showing off their young daughter's talents. The performance, on the "played out instrument with half the keys wanting," differed somewhat from those he had attended only weeks earlier in Richmond. The determined "musical character," as Polignac called the girl, "flourished with indefatigable fingers regardless of the chords which broke forth from the worn out strings—some wanting of tone some wanting in tune & some wanting all together, the whole resulting in a perfect jangle something like the effect that might be produced by a flock of chickens played in column by two & running at double quick over the keys." At the finale of the recital, Polignac tactfully covered his "astonishment" in finding the girl was not "deaf & dumb," as he had earlier "soundly believed." The shaken music lover found the entertainment offered later that evening more to his taste. Attending a "country dance," he enjoyed the music "performed partly on the piano, partly on the guitar." He especially "had the pleasure to see some of the belles of the place go through the figures of 'swing corners, swing your partners, or the ladies' chair' with infinite grace & modesty" as they danced "'quadirilles [*sic*] & Virginia reel.'" [10]

On Saturday, May 30, Kirby Smith placed Polignac in command of one of the two Texas brigades. Every unassigned brigadier in the Trans-Mississippi must have breathed a collective sigh of relief. Kirby Smith himself considered the brigade, made up of the 22nd and the 34th Texas Cavalry along with the 17th Texas Consolidated Cavalry (dismounted), "an undisciplined mob, the officers as worthless as the men." Before the war many of the men of the 22nd and 34th had farmed the counties above Dallas in north Texas—a region not known for its strong support of the Confederate cause. Their penchant for desertion was the stuff of legends. The 17th Consolidated was a regiment in name only. The men had only recently been paroled from prison in Illinois after being captured at Fort Hindman (Arkansas Post) in January. It was a patchwork unit made up of former members of the 6th and 10th Texas Infantry as well as the 15th, 17th, 18th, 24th, and 25th Texas Cavalry (dismounted). Even their new commander, fresh from the East, had caught wind of the brigade's reputation. The wild frontiersmen of the three regiments, Polignac heard, were "said to be perfectly green, undrilled & unbroken to military duty or discipline, including the officers." To make matters worse, they were cavalry without horses. Although most had enlisted to serve in that most dashing of the military branches, the men had proven too slovenly to care for themselves, let alone their mounts. As a consequence Kirby Smith had ordered the regiments dismounted to serve as infantry. His decision destroyed whatever pride the brigade had possibly entertained. Morale plummeted. The general had even strongly considered giving up on the three regiments altogether, breaking them up and parceling the men among his more dependable brigades. Kirby Smith's motives in giving Polignac command of the brigade are unclear. It may have been an attempt to humble a haughty subordinate. Possibly he appreciated Polignac's professionalism and believed that only he could impose some semblance of discipline on the Texans. In any case, it was the brigade's last chance. Polignac's only comment on the matter was "We shall see." Before he could inspect his new brigade, however, Polignac "was laid up . . . by an inflammation of the mouth, tongue, palate and lips."[11]

While Polignac recovered, Kirby Smith's aide-de-camp, Col. William R. Trader, attempted what most considered the impossible: transforming the wild Texans into a recognizable brigade. Although a trusted officer, Trader must have drawn the short straw with this assignment. The three regiments were billeted in a "camp for instruction" a relatively safe four miles out from Shreveport on the appropriately named Texas Road. As Trader drilled his troops, Polignac exhibited a remarkable lack of interest in their progress. The general apparently considered his own participation in the instruction of his raw recruits unnecessary and below his station. While Trader worked diligently to create a brigade, Polignac found more pleasant pursuits. Three days after his initial illness, he had sufficiently recovered, if not to inspect his troops, at least to join a "riding party with ladies" followed by a "dancing party in town." Shreveport was not Richmond, but Polignac made the most of its social offerings. Although the riding party had been "intended for a romantic moonlight ride," Polignac complained "the moon failed to rise thus baffling our expectations," adding, "So much for astronomical knowledge." Refusing to allow celestial matters to interfere with their evening, the party attended a dance at which Polignac observed "the orchestra—a negro fiddler bawling out the figures . . . as he played, a scene both natural & picturesque."[12]

Polignac's most pressing concern during his first days in Shreveport involved finding more permanent housing than his cramped hotel room. On June 4 he finally "succeeded in getting a house." His coup, however, created additional problems: "I am likely to be like the man who had bought an elephant & did not know what to do with it as it is next to impossible to procure furniture & necessary articles." He found it necessary to pay another week's hotel fare before he finally "Completed the move." On the twelfth he rode out to meet Capt. John C. Moncure, his newly assigned brigade adjutant. Originally from Virginia, Moncure had moved to Louisiana, where he took up planting and practiced law. In the following months he would become Polignac's closest friend and confidant. That day they began their first of innumerable conversations "on varied topics" ranging from literature to politics. Their opinions and tastes differed only slightly, making for polite yet lively discussions. Polignac, who most admired the works of Charles Dickens, thus found Moncure's appraisal of Sir William Bulwer-Lytton as "the best living English writer" reasonable yet open to enjoyable debate.[13]

Although he lacked any other pressing military duties, Polignac did nothing to help Trader train his brigade. He instead sank into another prolonged bout of boredom and melancholy. Despite his depression, Polignac was keenly aware that his adopted country was fighting for its survival. The situation in the West was particularly acute. The fall of New Orleans in April, 1862, had denied the Confederacy its most populous city and largest port. It also effectively closed the Mississippi River. In December Maj. Gen. Nathaniel P. Banks had replaced the hated Benjamin Butler as commander of the Union's Department of the Gulf. As defined by his orders from his commander-in-chief, Maj. Gen. Henry W. Halleck, Banks's objectives were clear—he was to aid Maj. Gen. Ulysses S. Grant in the siege of Vicksburg and the opening of the Mississippi River to the United States.[14]

Formerly governor of Massachusetts, Banks, without previous military experience, had used his political connections to gain both rank and command. In the spring of 1863, leading the XIX Army Corps, he had swept aside Maj. Gen. Richard Taylor's fewer than five thousand Confederate troops to close on Alexandria. Banks's victory was spoiled, however, when his naval counterpart, Rear Adm. David Dixon Porter, commanding a small gunboat fleet on the Red River, beat him to the city, forcing its surrender. Porter's coup was indicative of a rivalry between the Federal Army and Navy that would characterize the fighting in Louisiana. Banks and Porter soon abandoned Alexandria to move on Port Hudson, a strategic fortress on the Mississippi 120 miles south of Vicksburg. Their move was a compromise: Rapids prevented Porter from advancing his gunboats farther up the Red River in pursuit of Taylor's force. More importantly, Grant and Halleck insisted on Banks's assistance in the Vicksburg Campaign. Banks faced a quandary. He lacked the transportation necessary to move his large force across hostile territory to northeast Louisiana and, if he did, the move would leave New

Orleans vulnerable to attack. By taking Port Hudson, Banks reasoned, he would strengthen his own position and could then more easily reinforce Grant.[15]

While the Federals concentrated their attentions on the two river fortresses and Trader drilled his men, Polignac received orders to travel to Alexandria. He was to preside over the court-martial of Lt. Col. Aristide Girard, charged with failure to carry out orders. He spent the week before his departure not with his men but acquainting himself with Louisiana's political and judicial systems. Polignac attended two sessions of the displaced state legislature, then in Shreveport, meeting Gov. Thomas O. Moore as well as numerous other politicians. The main topic of debate in both sessions centered on the legislative representation of occupied parishes. The discussions generated "no small degree of excitement" and illustrated "a bitter feeling between lower & upper L[ouisiana]," observed the general. It was apparent to him that if the northern, unoccupied parishes did not accommodate those of the southern, occupied regions of the state, it would "be looked upon as neglect or indifference by the loyal people of those parishes & this, owing to the very peculiar circumstances in which they are placed, may go far to estrange [them] from the cause." However apparent the gravity of the issue seemed to Polignac, it made less of an impression on the legislators. On June 20 he recorded, "The question which was under consideration yesterday is still undecided & will probably remain so as there seems to be a majority in the House & in the Senate in favor of adjourning today."[16]

He spent the remainder of the day discussing politics with Captain Moncure, whom he found to be "a Breckinridge democrat," and visiting General Sibley. The latter, still smarting from his failures in New Mexico and Arizona and facing charges for disobeying orders, was anxious to be tried by a friend. Polignac, who hated the tedium of court duty, related the uncomfortable scene: "Gen[eral] Sibley . . . told me yesterday that he would apply to be tried by the courtmartial of which I have been appointed Presid[ent]. I answered him that none of the officers composing that court were qualified to try him being all of a rank inferior to his. He rejoined that he would willingly waive his rights. I sincerely hope however that his case might not be brought up before that court."[17]

Polignac, Captain Moncure, and another officer left Shreveport for Alexandria on Saturday, June 27. Their journey by carriage was pleasant, with stops at a number of plantations along the way for meals and lodging. During a stop for breakfast in the town of Mansfield, Polignac "stumbled upon a copy of Roman History" in the local hotel. Delighted, he took the "opportunity of reading over the history of the great Caesar," his "favorite among the dead." The unexpected find prompted the ambitious officer to muse, "I wish I could for one day exchange life & soul with any other intelligent & aspiring man—the better to appreciate my own standard." Possibly slightly embarrassed by his own rather high opinion of himself, he added, "Men are apt to overrate their own merits but they should ever strive to improve their qualities." [18]

The officers arrived in Alexandria at 2:00 P.M., Wednesday, July 1. Polignac spent much of Thursday leisurely reading Dickens's *Oliver Twist* and making preliminary preparations for the court-martial. On Friday he again "read out of 'Oliver Twist' for a couple of hours, & dressed up as well as the existing circumstances & the enforcement of the blockade would permit, preparatory to driving out into the country" to attend an overnight party at a nearby plantation. The evening was an unqualified success. Polignac enjoyed himself immensely as he joined in "talk, music, dance, tableaux, charades, & dumb show, walks, flirtation, etc." The festivities continued "in uninterrupted succession until 3 of A.M. when the company adjourned to their beds." The next morning the celebrants continued their festivities with renewed energy. Polignac particularly delighted in the new and unfamiliar , to him, game of "Simon Says." He found the game "attended with high glee & expressions of mirth & roars of laughter." He also enthusiastically praised the game's anonymous inventor, declaring "nothing short of a genius" could have "framed it off in its substance & details." The game proved almost too exhilarating for one of the more delicate participants: "After half an hour in the performance, one lady, having recovered from an almost hysterical outburst of mirth declared that it was 'too exciting'—which opinion being concurred in by all present, the company adjourned into another room." [19]

On Sunday, turning his attention to more spiritual concerns, Polignac visited the town's Catholic church. He arrived "too late for the service" but made up for it by dining with the priest. Polignac found the man anything but priestly, instead rather "impulsive & even fiery & at times warlike." The priest regaled his guest about an "occasion of a yankee officer who wanted to make, in an offhand way, a transfer of property of the curate's horse—without resorting to the usual but tedious formality of sale & purchase, when the punctilious clergyman tumbled him over from his (the officer's) horse & bringing the barrel of a revolver to bear upon him thus reminded him of the law very forcibly." [20]

During his brief visit, Polignac created quite a sensation among Alexandria's gentry. As in Richmond he delighted the ladies, cutting a swath through their ranks with his unique combination of charm, wit, and title.

Given a choice among the many families extending invitations to dinners and parties, he invariably chose those reputed to have the most beautiful daughters. As in Richmond he inevitably sparked rumors of his amorous escapades. Although flattering, the local belles' attentions often confused him: "There is a notion prevail[ing] among ladies here that I am engaged in marriage with the Gen[eral's] daughter about which they are very much exercized & pretend to 'lease' me very much by frequent hints & allusion which for the most are lost upon me."[21]

On Tuesday, July 7, Polignac received word that his brigade would "probably soon . . . be ordered out in the field." He paused briefly in his preparations for another social call to ponder melodramatically: "Once more my fate is going to be tested. It must be submitted to many tests before any thing can come out of it." Moments later he joined a local planter's son in his buggy for a pleasant ride into the countryside. They arrived at the driver's family plantation at 6:30 P.M. Polignac found it a "first class" concern, "subdivided into three under three overseers" over "about 200 slaves." Impressed with the planter's self-sufficiency and prosperity, as well as noting the effects of the blockade and the loss of New Orleans, he described the planter's operations: "He used before the war to plant 3000 acres in cotton which enabled him to raise between 2 & 3000 bales. Their land is now planted in corn, as he has one million pounds of cotton on hand. Besides, he raises sugar & refines it, has a tanyard, & manufactures homespun for his slaves, makes his own leather & shoes, [and] raises sheep. . . . [T]he average revenues from his plantation is between $150,000 & $200,000 clear of expenses."[22]

Colonel Girard's long-awaited court-martial finally met, bringing an end to Polignac's more pleasant diversions. The court quickly acquitted the colonel, charged with disobeying orders in abandoning Fort De-Russy earlier in the year. Polignac arrived back in Shreveport on the fourteenth. Three days later he departed for Natchitoches to take command of the 2nd Texas Brigade.[23]

The approximately 1,255 men of the 2nd Texas Brigade—the 22nd Texas Cavalry (dismounted), 34th Texas Cavalry (dismounted), and the 17th Texas Consolidated Cavalry (dismounted)—had walked from Shreveport to Natchitoches. Camped by the Red River at Grand Ecore some three miles from town, the men were in a sullen mood. As Texans they considered service in the cavalry their birthright. Accustomed to the saddle, they had entered Confederate service with the assurance they would be mounted troops. Their designation as dismounted cavalry only served to remind them of what they considered Kirby Smith's insult in denying them horses.[24] For two months Col. William H. Trader labored diligently to transform the frustrated cavaliers into an effective infantry brigade. Although only their temporary commander, he succeeded in imposing at least a modicum of discipline on the Texans and in partially restoring their morale; as one Texan put it, he made them "toe the mark." In the process, however, he also won the men's trust and personal loyalty.[25] By contrast, their new commander had exhibited little if any concern for the brigade's progress or welfare. Despite his experiences in Kentucky, Polignac still failed to grasp the necessity of forming a personal bond with the troops under his command. Consequently, when he arrived at Grand Ecore on July 20 to assume command of the 2nd Texas Brigade, he did so as a stranger.[26]

Later that day the brigade assembled in dress parade to receive its new commander. As he inspected the troops, Polignac noticed a palpable "feeling of dissatisfaction & even a spirit of insubordination" among the men. Trader had earned the men's trust; they would follow him in battle and wanted him to stay. Polignac was a stranger, even worse a foreigner. His assignment as their commander seemed only one more betrayal by Gen. Edmund Kirby Smith.[27]

To strengthen his own position and ease the transition, Polignac played on the brigade's loyalty to Trader. After dismissing the men, he ordered their officers to form in a semicircle before him. With Trader beside him, Polignac reminded them of their duty to follow orders. His "object," as he put it, "was to put Col[onel] T[rader] in the necessity of stimulating them to obedience towards me if he was consistent with his own principles & also to show that there was no bitter feeling between us both. Col[onel] T[rader] having replied in the manner I expected, dress parade was dismissed & I withdrew."[28] A week later Polignac moved the brigade three miles to Camp Salubrity, midway between Natchitoches and Grand Ecore. All seemed well as he ordered his troops to set up a camp hospital, a bakery, and defensive works. He also "made a call on the citizens to form a mounted company . . . in order to scout on the banks of the river."[29]

On July 27 Polignac faced his first serious disciplinary crisis. A member of the 22nd Texas Cavalry had, "while in a state of drunkenness[,] drawn a knife on a citizen of Gr[and] Ecore." As punishment he was forced to suffer the indignity of being "marched between two sentinels in front of the three Regiments, with a placard on his breast bearing the inscription 'Guilty of drunkenness & unsoldierly conduct.'" After his public humiliation the offender was returned to the guardhouse to serve the remainder of his sentence. The man's punishment, although hardly unusual or even harsh during the Civil War, outraged many of his messmates. Soon after his return to the guardhouse, "a party of his reg[iment], some of them with their arms," as Polignac uneasily noted, "rushed upon the guard & rescued the prisoner." Polignac immediately called a meeting with his three regimental commanders. He found two of the men "very staunch, their regiments not having participated in the disorder." The third, Col. James E. Stevens, commander of the 22nd Texas, proved "but little disposed to help . . . to say the least of it." Owing to "the state of excitement which then prevailed" and his uneasy relationship with his subordinates, Polignac was stymied. "I thought better not to take any immediate step, especially as I did not know how far I could rely on the officers & men of the other two regiments."[30]

Fortunately, Polignac did not find it necessary to test his command's loyalty at that time. The following morning, the commanders of his three regiments reported that all was quiet in their camps. Colonel Stevens informed him "that all excitement in his regiment had subsided & that the rescued prisoner had returned of himself to the guard house." Polignac credited himself with making the subtle mixture of concessions and veiled threats that convinced Stevens of the fine line separating him from the loss of his command: "This I could do without injury to discipline, as the Col[onel] himself was interested in reestablishing order & I perceived in him some apprehension lest his reg[iment] should be disbanded by the L[ieutenant] Gen[eral] Commanding the Dep[artment]. He did this according to my advice & thus we could reconcile discipline to the exigencies of the situation." Polignac soon realized that the incident was a symptom of a deeper malaise centered in Stevens's regiment. Shortly after the disturbance Cols. Almerine M. Alexander and James R. Taylor, commanders of the 34th and 17th Regiments respectively, called their new brigadier aside. They assured him of their personal loyalty and "that their men universally condemned the attempt & indeed manifested the desire of breaking off their association with St[evens's] Reg[iment] as such scenes of disorder had become of late frequent etc." At their suggestion, during a dress parade Polignac "issued a complimentary address to the 17th Texas & Alex[ander's] Reg[iment] on account of their not having taken part in the disturbance on the day previous."[31]

During the next few days, two of Stevens's company captains made their way to Polignac's tent to disassociate themselves from their colonel. A Captain MacKnight informed the general "that his company had not participated in the disorder & with the exception of two men, he could control them. One of those two is now under arrest & awaiting trial by court martial." Polignac commented that MacKnight's information proved "that the evil is not as great in that command as had been

Colonel Almerine M. Alexander, commander of the unruly 34th Regiment, as well as Col. James R. Taylor of the 17th Regiment, was instrumental in paving the way for Polignac's acceptance by their fellow Texans. *Courtesy the Hill College Harold B. Simpson History Complex, Hillsboro, Texas.*

represented to me by Col[onel] St[evens]." Polignac later discovered, however, that the objections to his command had reached beyond his brigade's camp. The editor of the local paper, a Mr. Dupleix, provided some insights into the source of the resistance to Polignac's presence, including "rumours, remarks, gossip etc. . . , some of which fall to the lot of the Adj[utant] of St[evens's] Reg[iment], who objects to me as being *one of the Royal family* & likely to conspire against the institutions of the country." Mr. Dupleix, however, was quick to add, "'Such people . . . I never can believe to be sound.'" [32]

Polignac found further proof of at least a degree of his growing acceptance when he returned to camp. Struck by the unusually correct military deportment of the sentry guarding his tent, he paused to talk to the man. The private, "his name Pope, from one of the wheat growing counties of Texas," informed the surprised general that he belonged to Stevens's regiment. Continuing his inquiries, Polignac found that the man's company commander was one of the captains who had earlier expressed his dissatisfaction with his colonel's leadership. He found in Private Pope's attitude a cause for optimism: "Is it possible that this man's friendly disposition should be a consequence of my late conversation with that captain & that his influence should have already worked a change in the minds of some of this command?" [33]

An incident four days later partially answered his question. On the night of August 4, "40 men deserted from camp." He had little time to ponder their motives for, on August 6, he received orders from Maj. Gen. Richard Taylor, commander of the District of West Louisiana, to move his brigade to Alexandria to join Maj. Gen. John G. Walker's division. On that day, according to Polignac, "a shocking accident occurred in Stevens' Regiment during a violent storm, when lightning struck a tree under which soldiers were eating their dinner, killing two on the spot & hurting two severely." [34]

On Saturday, August 8, Polignac, accompanying the last elements of his brigade to leave Grand Ecore, boarded the steamer *Rolph*. The voyage down the Red River was uneventful, and they arrived at Alexandria "Sunday before noon." On Tuesday, after leaving his brigade in bivouac seven miles from Alexandria, he took the opportunity to call on some "Lady friends" he had met on his previous visit to the vicinity. It was evidently a memorable evening. He found the four belles "as pleasant as night, beauty, dress & a glass of Champagne could make them." He rejoined his brigade and the next morning "set forward & reached the destination of the command in the pine woods about 18 miles from Alex[andria], near a little stream called 'Clear Creek,' or Bayou Clear." While

Having served with distinction in the East, Richard Taylor was assigned to the Department of West Louisiana in 1862. Taylor quickly came into conflict with his superior, Edmund Kirby Smith, sparking a personal feud that lasted long after the war. Taylor admired Polignac's abilities and defended him against his detractors until he could prove himself in combat. *Courtesy Alabama Department of Archives and History, Montgomery.*

the brigade was engaged in "laying out the camp & 'fixing up' generally," a detachment under a Captain Caspari returned with seventeen of the deserters who had fled from Grand Ecore.[35]

Their arrival prompted the general to order the construction of a guardhouse. It was a crude affair, built "with stakes about 14 feet high, sunk 2½ feet into the ground & averaging 4 inches in diameter, running close together in a circle of 10 feet in diameter, with a small space left between two of the stakes to let the prisoners in & out. Each stake is sharpened at the top to increase the difficulty of climbing over & getting out." Polignac was bewildered by his soldiers' insistence on calling his new guardhouse "The Jug," wondering, "the point I do not see, nor can I tell the reason why." The Jug must have been a hellish place, especially with the addition of six more captured deserters to its cramped confines on the nineteenth and the onset of the rainy season.[36]

Between downpours Polignac drilled his regiments and attended to brigade business. His routine was interrupted by orders to sit on Gen. Henry Hopkins Sibley's pending court-martial. The hard-drinking Sibley, charged with disobeying orders and conduct unbecoming an officer, had unsuccessfully urged the reluctant Polignac to hear his case. Polignac had not changed his mind and, also uneasy about leaving his unruly command, wrote Gen. Braxton Bragg's chief-of-staff requesting to be relieved from the trial. His request was denied, and on August 25 he set out for Opelousas.[37]

The court-martial convened at 12:30 in the afternoon of Thursday, August 27. Polignac was highly impressed with the presiding officer of the court-martial, Maj. Gen. John G. Walker. He found Walker to be "a man of sound judgement, . . . well acquainted with the rule of evidence, . . . quiet and modest, . . . and always perfectly self-possessed." Another member of the court struck Polignac with his military bearing. He described Brig. Gen. Alfred Mouton as looking "like a lion—dark tall & handsome." The trial dragged on until early September, ending in Sibley's acquittal. For the most part Polignac found the proceedings excruciatingly dull and longed to return to his brigade. The news of a possible Federal move against Monroe further heightened his desire to leave Opelousas. The Confederate forces at Monroe, less than "1000 Cavalry & three batteries of artillery" under Brig. Gen. Paul O. Hébert, were no match for the 6,000 troops under Brig. Gen. John D. Stevenson reportedly marching on the town. Stevenson's advance was apparently part of a larger Federal offensive targeting Maj. Gen. Sterling Price in Little Rock, Arkansas, and "Fort Smith, Ark[ansas] near the Texas line." On

The commander of the Texas Division, Maj. Gen. John G. Walker supported
Polignac's attempts to maintain his authority and hold his brigade together.
Courtesy Hill Memorial Library, Louisiana State University, Baton Rouge.

August 29 Polignac fretted, "My Brigade has been ordered to hold itself in readiness to move to [General Hébert's] support & will probably have left by the time I shall be able to return to Alexandria." The Federal offensive and the Confederate response illustrated to Polignac a serious weakness in Confederate organization. Ignoring the difficulties of defending the huge territory with pitifully meager resources, he was especially critical of the Confederate commander's practice of scattering his forces piecemeal over the department. Although supposedly intended to protect the largest amount of territory with the least number of troops, he found the strategy counterproductive: "If we do not make *one army* out of the troops in Arkansas, Louisiana & Texas, we shall be overwhelmed & lose the Department."[38]

More detailed intelligence the next day convinced General Taylor that the threat to Monroe had been exaggerated. His subsequent decision to retain the 2nd Texas Brigade near Alexandria relieved Polignac of the anxiety that his command would go into battle without him. He noted, however, that the date, August 30, was "the anniversary of the Battle of Richmond, KY, in which I led my Regiment, the 5th Tennessee through the graveyard that skirted the eastern part of the town. Oh! for another day like that! for years of days like that!! & then rest and enjoy." He did not dwell on his past triumph, however, and soon found more pleasant diversions. On Friday, September 4, he attended a ball given by a Captain West, the provost marshal of nearby Washington. The ball, held in Opelousas's Variety Theater, provided the appreciative general the opportunity to observe, tongue-in-cheek, the spirited rivalry between the two towns' fairer residents: "On this occasion the beauty of Opelousas & Washington were marshalled forth in two rival camps, a most gorgeous array on both sides trying their best to out talk, out dance, out shine, out flirt, out dash, out smash, & last but not least to outwit each other & the same rivalry which was to be observed between both 'sets' was kept up between the combatants in each set, every one fighting, as the term is 'on her own hook.' As to the superiority however of either set or of individuals, both my impartiality & my sense of propriety forbid that I should express, even to myself, any opinion whatsoever—the more so as it would involve a closer observation of & a more intimate acquaintance with the privates of those two fighting bodies."[39]

Polignac arrived back at Alexandria on the thirteenth. The next day he met with Generals Walker and Taylor, and on the fifteenth he rejoined his brigade. It was an uneasy homecoming. The brigade, which had moved to a new camp on the Natchitoches Road twenty-two miles from Alexandria, was on the verge of collapse. Alarmed that the command would disintegrate completely, Richard Taylor was considering radical measures. As Polignac learned on his arrival, "The whole matter rose from Gen[eral] Taylor evincing a desire of breaking up my Brigade & distributing the regiments of which it is composed among the other Brigades of Walker's Division, on account of desertions which have taken place during [my] absence." Polignac found some support from General Walker who, as Polignac recorded, "assured me that he would take my interests in hand, adding very courteously: 'because they are consistent with those of the Division.'" The general stopped himself before mentioning the obvious—that he preferred Polignac retaining command of his rebellious misfits rather than incorporating them into the rest of his division.[40]

Polignac still failed to grasp the nature of the American citizen-soldier. He continued to maintain the attitude that soldiers must, without exception, obey all orders and endure all privations without question or complaint. His view of his brigade was thus essentially abstract, leaving no need for the personal interaction that Americans, especially Southerners, demanded. He had learned little from the lessons his experience with the 5th Tennessee had offered a year earlier; now he would find in the independent-minded 2nd Texas Brigade an even more demanding educational opportunity. Rather than taking the necessary step of acquainting himself with his men on a personal level, Polignac remained aloof. As the desertions continued, he took increasingly desperate measures to stop them, succeeding only in further alienating his men. Alarmed at reports of another planned exodus, he appealed outside of his command to General Walker, seeking cavalry support "in view of the surmised desertions."[41]

His actions quickly generated distrust among even his most trusted companies. He suspected one company of Colonel Alexander's 34th Regiment in particular of planning a mass escape. Believing "that they would not leave without taking their knapsacks & clothing," Polignac ordered their captain to have the soldiers "stack arms & pile up all knapsacks" before going out on picket duty. Having insulted one company, the general went on to humiliate the entire regiment, sparking a near mutiny: "At Dress Parade arms were stacked & a guard placed over them, which created the greatest excitement & dissatisfaction among the troops—In the Alex[ander] Reg[iment], the officers hung their swords on the stacks & said they would not take them off before the order was rescinded." Polignac was astounded by their reaction to his order. He eventually learned that his lack of subtlety had "involved both loyal & disloyal in the same suspicion." The men were fearful, moreover, that news of the affront would travel beyond their regiment, "that this measure would be mouthed about & go abroad, i.e. to Texas, & that it would be construed into a general disarming & disbanding of the troops." Unknowingly, the Frenchman had hit on the one nerve that bound his Texans together as a whole—their sense of pride and the absolute necessity of maintaining the honor of their names when they returned to their homes and families.[42]

After the dress parade the men's anger escalated rapidly. As their shaken general observed, "During part of the night, the camp was in uproar, the men hollowing & yelling, which with Texans is indicative of discontent." Their anger was fueled in part by an order issued by General Walker. A drummer named Cummings in Stevens's regiment had indiscreetly confided his intention to desert in a letter to a friend in Col. Joseph W. Speight's brigade. Walker ordered Cummings's arrest when, the intended recipient having already deserted, his commanding officer opened the letter revealing the plot. One of Cummings's friends, John Vowel, accompanied by his brother Jason A. Vowel, soon gathered a mob to free the prisoner. Polignac watched uneasily as "they went through St[evens's] Reg[iment] yelling loud, then ran past & stopped at the foot of the hill on which my tent is pitched." For several tense moments the Vowel brothers urged the crowd forward, but they had misjudged their support. Polignac was relieved to see that despite the "endeavors & entreaties of the ringleader (Jim [*sic*] V[owel]) & his earnest appeals to the seditious spirit of his followers [he could not] induce them to move one step further. They dropped off one by one & the noise which had prevailed for nearly half an hour gradually settled down into the profoundest calm." The mob's hesitation proved Polignac's salvation. Caught by surprise, he later admitted, "I was undetermined as to what I would do while the noise was loudest." His anxiety was further heightened by his inability to determine the extent to which the mutiny affected his command. Gambling that the 17th Texas Consolidated was his most trustworthy regiment, he ordered one of its companies "to repair to the guard house with loaded muskets." The 17th, however, "was late in preparing to move so that the guard house," he anxiously observed, "was left with its small guard to protect it." He also realized that he too was vulnerable to the men's rage and, "seeing that the company sent for did not arrive [I] considered for a moment whether I could not repair to the 17th R[egiment], which however I determined not to do as it might have encouraged them to go on had I been seen moving from my Head-Quar[ters]."[43]

Polignac later congratulated himself for standing his ground: "I was glad after the trouble was over, that I had come to this conclusion. I also found out that I had largely overrated the nature of the disturbance, which was confined to that little crowd above mentioned & to which the men of Steve[ns's] reg[iment] did not flock, as the ringleaders doubtless expected." The incident, however, finally forced Polignac to realize that he was in the midst of a very hostile camp. In his relief at having weathered the crisis, he also found a sort of justification for his indecision: "I might have gone out & tried to check the progress of the mob by my presence, but those experiments are hazardous as they may result in the loss of authority & prestige, especially when it is dark & men can shelter their disobedience & disrespect under the cover of night & the assurance of not being recognised, which insures impunity to their guilt." Despite his rationalizations Polignac could not escape the fact that his position as brigade commander had come perilously close to a total collapse. A night's sleep did not improve matters. The cold light of morning brought a fresh dilemma.[44]

Before roll call Monday morning, September 21, Lt. Col. John H. Caudle of the 34th Texas informed Polignac "that the officers had not taken their swords from the armstocks." The general immediately realized the officers' action was a deliberate and calculated challenge to his authority. He had lost his command of the 5th Tennessee owing to a much less overt action by that regiment's officers. He now faced the loss of an entire brigade—without ever leading it in battle. Polignac knew that he could not win in a face-to-face showdown with the regiment's officers. Unlike him, they knew their men and where they stood with them. Polignac, who had never seen fraternization with enlisted men as necessary or even beneficial, stood alone. Rather than risk an assuredly disastrous public confrontation with his subordinates, he chose strategic subterfuge.[45]

Polignac placed his trust in Colonel Caudle to help him save face and maintain order. He first ordered the colonel "not to let any [of his fellow officers] know that he had as yet reported to [him] this breach of discipline." If the officers did not take the opportunity to back down quietly, Polignac ordered Caudle to leave them behind and march the regiment to the parade ground without them. That his general placed such a responsibility on Caudle says much for the colonel's character and sense of duty. His fellow regimental officers would certainly have seen his obedience of their foreign general's order as a betrayal of his own kind. Fortunately for Caudle, his loyalty was not put to the ultimate test. Confident that the junior colonel would do his best to calm his colleagues in Alexander's regiment, Polignac felt the pulse of the 17th Texas. His visit to their camp revealed "the same dissatisfaction prevailed, altho' not manifested by any seditious measures or dispositions." He concluded, "having talked to the men in the different companies, I left them well satisfied about the scope of the order & reconciled to it." However slowly, and with Caudle's indispensable advice and support, the new brigadier was learning how to lead his Texans. Having laid the groundwork by finally talking to his men on a personal level, he addressed them as they stood in formation. He spoke to the 34th Texas first, gratified that Caudle had convinced its officers to cooperate at least temporarily by retrieving their swords and turning out with their men. Then, in a tone that he calculated was "alternately emphatic & colloquial, almost jocular at times," he expressed his "astonishment at the dissatisfaction caused by the late orders." He went on to explain to the troops (with a remarkably straight face) that the orders were for "their own protection, as they had to refund the Government the value of their arms if lost, that they were surrounded by jay-hawkers, who would gladly seize any opportunity of arming themselves at their expense." He concluded "that if their pride had been offended, at what they considered as a slur on them, my feelings were hurt by their belief that I thought them disloyal, etc." Miraculously, such a transparently disingenuous argument delivered in what they considered a hilarious accent calmed the men's tempers. Unaware that he had also inadvertently become a form of entertainment to the now smiling and supposedly childlike Texans, Polignac triumphantly dismissed the regiment.[46]

Polignac went on to give a similar address to Stevens's regiment, after which he appealed to General Walker for support. Walker was more than cooperative and, as Polignac noted, issued "a general order, directing arms to be stacked & guarded in the whole Division, & embodying some of my remarks to the troops—thus the point was carried & at the same time the spirit of insubordination & dissatisfaction was quelled." Walker presented Polignac with another opportunity to redeem himself before his men by returning Private Cummings. Having spent so little time among his troops, Polignac was surprised to find the object of such excitement to be "a mere boy & evidently frightened almost to death." He wisely seized the chance to win a reputation as a merciful disciplinarian. Knowing the man would later relate the proceedings to his comrades, Polignac intentionally allowed Cummings's guard to witness the interrogation. The general began by declaring Cummings's guilt in as "vivid colours as [his] thoughts would suggest." Seeing that he had made his point, the youth already visualizing the inevitable firing squad, Polignac changed tack: "I therefore told him that I would on account of his age have mercy upon him—that the letter he had written & which contained the only evidence of his guilt was in my possession & that I would tear it up & burn it, which I did then before him. I saw tears gathering on his eyelids as I held out my hand to him & made him promise that he would never desert. Thereupon I released him."[47]

The desertions, however, continued throughout Walker's command. To boost the men's sagging morale, Walker ordered a full review of his entire division on September 22. "One of his motives," according to Polignac, "indeed the chief one . . . , was the men being very apt to over-rate numbers, from a mere glance at troops formed in line, they would draw a great source of comfort & much confidence from that sight & the idea of their strength which it would convey." Walker's psychological experiment succeeded. Although realistically estimated at "about 4,500 present, probably a little over," Polignac learned that some of his brigade "put down the strength of the Division at 10,000 men." Even their most optimistic estimates were dwarfed by the over 30,000 Federals massing to the southeast. Kirby Smith and Taylor quickly guessed that the Union commander, Maj. Gen. William B. Franklin, intended to invade Texas. They did not, however, know his projected route, a vital piece of information. Having only limited numbers of troops to defend his vast department, Kirby Smith desperately needed more information in order to use his sparse resources most efficiently.[48]

On September 25 Taylor, determined to obtain more intelligence, ordered General Walker to march his division to Morganza. Polignac's brigade led the column as it marched southeastward in the suffocating, humid heat along Bayou Boeuf, passing alternately through pine woods and the small towns of Lecompte and Cheneyville. On September 28 they arrived in Evergreen. "The road," Polignac recorded, "was exceedingly dusty & very severe on the feet of the soldiers, badly shod for the most—the hot dust driven through the seams of their shoes by their tramping would raise blisters on their skin." Although his troops were "more accustomed to the practice of the horse than to long walks," Polignac was pleased that they "compared very favorably with the marching of the other brigades of the same division." On September 28 Walker ordered Polignac to station his brigade in the little village of Evergreen "to guard his rear from a possible movement of the enemy from Simmesport." He then took "the balance of the division on towards Morgan's Ferry on the Atchafalaya [River]."[49]

Polignac made a thorough survey of his new theater of operations. Situated on the left bank of Bayou Rouge, Evergreen lay about forty miles from Walker's destination at Morgan's Ferry. Three roads connected the town with Simmesport to the northeast. Ranging in length from twelve to twenty-five miles, they were the most likely routes for a Federal flanking attack. Determined to "put Evergreen beyond the possibility of surprise," Polignac dispatched scouts to Simmesport and other nearby hamlets and farms. He was relieved to find Simmesport already garrisoned not by Federals but by one hundred isolated Rebels. During the subsequent days he established an efficient network of scouts and couriers linking Evergreen with Simmesport and strategically placed picket posts.[50]

With Polignac securing his rear, Taylor sent Brig. Gens. Alfred Mouton and Thomas Green against the small Federal garrison at Morgan's Ferry. On September 29 they struck "in a driving rainstorm." According to Taylor, "Green, with his horse and a part of Mouton's brigade of Louisiana infantry, crossed the Atchafalaya at Morgan's Ferry, and attacked and routed the enemy on the Fordoche, capturing four hundred and fifty prisoners and two guns. Green lost a hundred in killed and wounded; the enemy, who fought under cover, less than half that number." Interrogations of the captured Federals and Franklin's later moves convinced Taylor of what he already expected. Rather than subject his army to the barren wastes of southwestern Louisiana, the Union general intended on approaching Texas by way of the Red River Valley. Although a less direct line of march, the northwestern route did offer the advantages of better forage as well as the river itself. Federal strategy in Louisiana was adapting to the state's unique systems of rivers, lakes, and bayous. By following the Red River, Franklin knew he could rely on the U.S. Navy's river fleet to provide transportation and artillery cover. Franklin moved cautiously, allowing the Confederates time to develop their response. Gen. Thomas Green aggressively harassed the invaders, staging effective hit-and-run cavalry attacks on outlying Federal posts. Such successes, however small, helped strengthen Taylor's confidence that he could resist Franklin's advance.[51]

In mid-October Kirby Smith ordered a reorganization of Taylor's forces. In the evening of Wednesday, October 14, General Walker informed Polignac that he was transferring his brigade to Brig. Gen. Alfred Mouton's 2nd Infantry Division. Polignac also learned that his own command would "be increased by the addition of the brigade formerly commanded by Col[onel] [Joseph W.] Speight." The next morning Polignac marched his brigade to nearby Moundville some two miles from Washington near Bayou Boeuf. There General Taylor ordered them to pitch their tents in the pinewoods outside of town. Shortly afterward, a tight-

Angered at the loss of the command of his brigade to Polignac, Col. Joseph W. Speight launched a vendetta to undermine the Frenchman's authority. Although he almost succeeded in sparking a full-scale mutiny among his Texans, he found no support from his own more conscientious subordinates. *Courtesy the Hill College Harold B. Simpson History Complex, Hillsboro, Texas.*

jawed Colonel Speight reported to surrender command of his own brigade, composed of the 15th Texas Infantry and the 31st Texas Cavalry (dismounted) regiments.[52]

Taylor soon realized that he had done Polignac no favor. The harddrinking Speight and his fellow officers deeply resented Polignac's authority and even encouraged open opposition to his command. His former "brigade," composed of Texans from the farmlands around Waco and Millican, had recently arrived from Arkansas, where casualties and desertions had reduced them to a mere "seven hundred muskets." Their morale was abysmally low. As Taylor himself admitted, "The men . . . were much discontented." Their dissatisfaction soon turned to open mockery. "Probably most of these Texas soldiers," a commentator later noted, "had never seen a Frenchman before. . . . He was certainly, both in appearance and manners, unlike any of the Rangers, whom it had been their happy fate to follow in other battles." Moreover, none of the Texans could seem to come anywhere near a correct pronunciation of their new general's name. Their alternative was typically Texan as they "with derisive laughter dubbed him 'Polecat!'"[53]

Felix Pierre Poché, an officer in another brigade, noticed that "Prince Poleignac on account of his foreign and illustrious birth, excited a great deal of interest among the troops." Poché's own impression is revealing: "He is a light complected man, with blue eyes, sandy hair, rosy cheeks, and almost red whiskers, his size is rather under medium height, and is rather slim. He seems very plain from his appearance, wears a small loose grey cloth coat, blue pants and plain boots, [and] a two-cornered hat, 'a la Napoleon.'"[54] The new influx of Texans rekindled the others' resistance to Polignac's authority. Taylor soon learned that they had sworn "that a damn frog-eating Frenchman with a name they could not pronounce, and whose orders they could not understand would never command them." Faced with a potential mutiny within Polignac's brigade, Taylor took personal action. In his memoirs he recalled, "I went to their camp, assembled the officers, and pointed out the consequences of disobedience, for which I should hold them accountable; but promised that if they remained dissatisfied with their new commander *after an action*, I would remove him."[55]

For Camille de Polignac it was not the mysterious and unseen forces of the Fates determining his destiny in Louisiana but the even-handed intervention of Richard Taylor. He was indeed fortunate, nevertheless, to have Taylor as his advocate. The son of Pres. Zachary Taylor, who had encouraged his children to study French, Taylor's background, education, and outlook closely paralleled those of Polignac. Taylor had traveled in Europe before graduating from Yale and also shared with Polignac a touch of romanticism combined with the ingrained paternalism of both the Southern and European aristocracies.⁵⁶ The perceptive commander also recognized his subordinate's military skills. Equally important, he was untainted by, as a contemporary noted, "the aversion to render justice to a foreigner, generally attributed to the Southerners, who are jealous of any one else sharing their own glory." From Col. Joseph W. Speight's point of view, Polignac had not only robbed him of his glory but his brigade as well. It was Speight, Polignac soon learned, who had instigated the current "petty spirit of opposition." Although Speight and, as Polignac recorded, "some officers of late . . . cast a slur on [his] southern feelings," he also found that having "no standing at home," they also carried limited influence among their men.⁵⁷

Taylor, who also had little regard for Speight, kept a close eye on the situation. He observed with a touch of humor: "Order was restored, but it was up-hill work for General Polignac for some time, notwithstanding his patience and good temper. The incongruity of the relation struck me, and I thought of sending my monte-dealing Texas colonel to Paris, to command a brigade of the Imperial Guard."⁵⁸ Polignac's "patience and good temper" served him well. Although snubbed by their former commander, he soon gained the confidence and friendship of a number of his new officers. Such men as Lt. Col. James E. Harrison exemplified the sort of conscientious subordinates who had chafed under Speight's command. A South Carolina native, Harrison had moved to Mississippi and had entered state politics. Harrison laid most of the blame for his brigade's poor morale and discipline on its officers. Following Speight's example, many of his colleagues had ignored their troops' welfare in favor of more pleasurable pastimes including drinking and gambling. In Polignac, Harrison and a core of like-minded officers saw their opportunity to redeem their brigade and transform it into an effective military force.⁵⁹ Their combined efforts were soon rewarded. On October 27 Polignac, pleased yet still incredulous, recorded: "I went to see the troops of my brigade which were on picket & as I rode up to the 17th Tex[as] the men raised a loud cheer & hurraed me heartily—upon my enquiring for the cause of their cheers they answered that they were glad to see me."⁶⁰

November and December settled into a dreary routine, the rainy weather accentuating the desolate countryside of southern Louisiana. The once-prosperous region had suffered immeasurably from the better part of a year of constant warfare. As one melancholy Rebel described it: "This section of country might have been termed the 'paradise' of

A lieutenant colonel when Polignac arrived in Louisiana, James E. Harrison saw in Polignac an officer who could instill discipline and restore pride in his unruly Texans. Harrison later achieved the rank of brigadier general. *Courtesy the Hill College Harold B. Simpson History Complex, Hillsboro, Texas.*

Louisiana before the war; but alas, what a change has befallen it now! The houses are all deserted; occasionally you meet with a few old, faithful negroes, left by their owners to take care of their place until their return. Here you can behold mansion after mansion, including costly sugar-houses, now going to decay."[61] In early December, while in "command of the outposts in the immediate vicinity of Morganza," Polignac contemplated the fate of that unfortunate town: "Morganza, formerly a little village which had sprung up there, on account of its being a convenient landing, is now entirely burnt down; smouldering ruins only tell of its former existence & bear testimony to the vandalism of the enemy."[62]

Although Banks ordered his troops into winter quarters in lower Louisiana, Federal riverboats continued to ply the state's waterways. In mid-November Polignac marched his brigade to the confluence of the Red, Atchafalaya, and Mississippi Rivers with orders to harass the enemy's river fleet. The ironclad gunboats that shepherded the Federals' more vulnerable transports particularly fascinated Polignac. He spent hours concealed in the underbrush along the riverbank observing the squat U.S.S. *Osage*, *Choctaw*, and others through his telescope. Despite his efforts he reported with disappointment that by the end of November, "Our expedition has so far been utterly unsuccessful as we have not sunk one single transport at Red River landing & only stopped one which I am told went down [the river] the next day." For the remainder of the year, Polignac led his men along the Atchafalaya and Red Rivers toward Alexandria.[63]

In December a number of factors contributed to a renewed wave of discontent among the Confederate troops. Rations, the perennial concern of all soldiers, were limited in both quantity and variety. Many soldiers found their meals consisted solely of sweet potatoes, the only food their commissary officers could find in abundance. Such boring fare sparked unexpected innovation. While attending to his routine correspondence, Polignac took time to describe a new invention: "The lamp by which I am writing deserves a special mention. It is a sweet-potato cut in half, dug out & filled with lard in which a cotton wick is soaked projecting a little above the edge of this vessel of a new description. It is upon the whole a most successful contrivance & as it does not require snuffing it claims a marked superiority over the tallow candle."[64]

Abysmal weather contributed to the troops' misery. Mid-December was marked by days-long downpours of "heavy rains" during which the "wind whistled in a frightening manner" through the "sad & monotonous pine woods." On December 23 Polignac recorded "the rain falling in torrents & the wind blowing almost a hurricane." Another officer reported many of his men were injured as pines "fell by the hundreds," themselves victims of the high winds.[65] Cold, hungry, and bone tired, with many suffering from "heavy colds," Polignac's soldiers splashed along a road "like a canal full of water" as they trudged toward Alexandria. When they stopped along their route, they invariably found the "ground covered with water," making for "wet equipment & bedding" and "miserably cold night[s]" made worse by the difficulty of maintaining campfires.[66] Shortly before Christmas, Polignac and his staff found shelter for the night at Mansura with two surgeons from General Mouton's division. They pooled their resources to concoct "a bowl of delicious eggnog, which with the proper ingredients soon brought out the musical abilities and loquacious qualities of the company." Polignac enjoyed himself immensely and, as one of the party remembered, "was soon sufficiently mellow to be entertaining, and enlivened the house by singing every few minutes a verse of a song which had reference to one 'Madame Gregoire' whoever she may have been."[67]

Polignac's brigade spent what one miserable soldier remembered as a "sad Christmas Day . . . marching as usual, in the mud and cold with empty stomachs and the same irksome life of a soldier." In the evening they camped on the Richardson Plantation some seventeen miles from the "pretty little village" of Monroe in northern Louisiana. The command was somewhat diminished on December 20 with the detachment of elements of Ashley W. Spaight's 11th Texas Infantry Battalion to southern Louisiana. Despite their loss in numbers, his remaining Texans nevertheless outdid themselves in maintaining their unsavory reputation among neighboring Confederate units. On December 29 an officer in a Louisiana regiment recorded: "Today we had beautiful sunshine, and wonderful weather. I was busy almost all day moving a load of salt at Trenton. Poleignac's Brigade had the Ferry, and consequently I had a great deal of trouble getting it across. Those Texans are exceedingly boorish and insolent." Only hours later, but with infinitely more loathing, the same officer reported on what passed for recreation among some of Polignac's men: "I learned tonight that one of those Texas clodhoppers had killed a little boy in Monroe. He shot him with his rifle while the latter was quietly riding his horse. The little boy is the son of Mr. Baker, one of the prominent citizens of these parts."[68]

Despite such incidents, the majority of Polignac's Texans were anxious to test their mettle against the Yankee invaders. Their opportunity finally arrived on December 29. Ordered to disrupt Federal naval activity aimed toward Harrisonburg, Polignac marched his troops into concealed positions along the Red and Black Rivers. During the last days of

1863, his gunners and marksmen played havoc with the Federal sailors, inflicting heavy casualties with comparatively little loss to themselves. Their success may possibly have been due in part to a marked change in the outlook of their commander. On December 24, after a lengthy discourse in his diary concerning the roles of ambition and fate in his life, Polignac concluded emphatically that he "should deal with the *Present* more than with the *Future*."[69]

CHAPTER 7

"I Will Show You Whether
I Am 'Polecat' or 'Polignac!'"

January 1, 1864–April 6, 1864

—·•·—

F riday, January 1, 1864, "a cold bright day. Thermometer 5° in the morning: one of the hardest frosts on record in this section of the country." Polignac penned his first diary entry of the new year in the comparative luxury of what he wryly referred to as his "private apartments." Although admittedly "neither more nor less than a negro cabin, perfectly ventilated," his quarters were infinitely superior to those of his suffering men.[1] A soldier in a nearby regiment recorded, "The oldest residents of these parts declare they never felt such cold in this region." The last day of 1863 had begun with rain that, as the temperature plummeted, turned to snow. To add to the men's misery, having been soaked by weeks of heavy downpours, the piney woods could offer but little dry firewood. The ragged soldiers, many without shoes or tents and often suffering from pneumonia, shivered against the wind with "practically no fire" to warm themselves. In the morning they awoke to find the "ground completely frozen" beneath them. The plight of his men was no longer lost upon their general. Having overcome the Texans' initial resistance to his authority, Polignac had at last grasped the necessity of attending to their needs. He therefore took steps to procure new shoes for some of his troops as well as to find a more suitable campsite south of Monroe. Although his men appreciated Polignac's newfound concern for their welfare, they nevertheless continued to complain.[2]

On January 10, determined to restore at least partially his men's morale, Polignac addressed his assembled regiments. He focused on their two most pressing concerns—the miserable weather and the "inferior quality" of their beef ration. Although hardly a rousing call to arms—he essentially reminded them that both complaints were the result of "unavoidable circumstances" and "chargeable to none of their commanders"—his oration was well received. In the evening the regimental band of the 15th Texas expressed their comrades' appreciation by serenading their formerly despised commander. Polignac correctly interpreted the concert as a further indication of his acceptance by his troops. He also seized the opportunity to ingratiate himself anew, at least with the musicians. Now much less aloof and much more aware of the need to "talk up" the Texans in order to retain their support, he resorted to unabashed flattery and thanked the bandsmen in a carefully prepared speech. The men answered his brief oration with appreciative applause after which the general retired to his cabin to celebrate his new popularity with "a cup of very bad tea."[3]

On January 11 rumors of a Federal move from Trinity up the Ouachita River to threaten Monroe reached Confederate headquarters. To counter the anticipated expedition, Maj. Gen. Richard Taylor ordered Polignac to set up defensive positions along the riverbank near his camp. Polignac quickly sent out pickets to establish outposts and vedettes along the river. He also ordered Capt. Thomas A. Faries of the Louisiana Pelican Battery to place his artillery in a position commanding a sharp bend in the river. As an added precaution, an advance party of cavalry waited downstream to provide early warning of an enemy approach.[4] The attack, however, never materialized, and on January 16 Polignac received the "unwelcome piece of news" that Taylor had ordered his brigade to Harrisonburg. On Monday, January 18, Polignac's brigade marched south along the Ouachita River accompanied by two sections of Faries's artillery, consisting of a pair of 3-inch Parrott rifles and two 12-pounder howitzers. One section of 6-pounder smoothbores remained behind in Monroe to support Mouton's brigade.[5]

On the twentieth they arrived at what one soldier described as "the ugly and insignificant little village of Columbia." Aided by the small steam ferry *Ruby*, Polignac crossed two regiments and the artillery to the right bank before nightfall. The difficulty of the operation prompted Polignac to take measures to avoid what he viewed as a potential threat to his operation. During the march from Monroe, the Confederates had found ample forage and provisions on the left of the Ouachita. Their new route lay on the relatively barren right bank of the river. As Polignac noted, "should the enemy's gunboats run up, we should be cut off from our usual channel of supplies & compelled to haul our stores from Alex[andria], a distance of about 50 miles." Unwilling to risk what he calculated as an eight-day delay such a round trip would entail, Polignac "gave orders to collect a supply of meat & corn" around Columbia. On the twenty-second the brigade resumed its march, the supply laden *Ruby* descending the Ouachita paralleling their route. Although slowed by the hilly terrain along the march, the Confederates arrived at their destination on

Sunday, January 24. At Harrisonburg Polignac happily found the boat *Conley* docked along the bank "with 2500 bushels of corn," adding that it was enough to "supply the wants of men & stock for a week."[6]

Taylor had assigned Polignac's brigade to Harrisonburg to provide protection for a detachment of engineers rebuilding Fort Beauregard. Demolished by the Federals the previous September after its evacuation, the fort sat on a hill commanding the Ouachita. After establishing his main camp near Harrisonburg, Polignac posted regiments covering the three land approaches to town to guard against attack. Despite a "long spell of dry & beautiful weather," the Texans disliked their new posting. The bleak surroundings of Harrisonburg accentuated the monotony of camp life. In a letter to his son, Lt. Col. James E. Harrison of the 15th Texas Infantry described the environs of the town as "a poor miserable hilly pine woods country on our side [of the river], and swamps on the other." Their tedium was briefly relieved when, on the twenty-fifth, workmen uncovered some buried wreckage that had been smoldering since the fort's destruction. As Polignac described the scene, "[when the timbers,] being brought in contact with the air, the fire was suddenly revived & blazed out instantaneously, raising a high flame which could be seen all night waving & flaming from the top of the south eastern bastion of the fort."[7]

Barely a week later the war returned to the vicinity of Harrisonburg. At daybreak on February 3, Polignac reported, "a party of 100 mounted yankees, mostly negroes, crossed the Tensas [River] at Percy's Ferry." The raiders caught the Rebel pickets at nearby Mandersonville's Ferry, "some six miles above" Harrisonburg, by complete surprise. Polignac registered disappointment in his troops' performance, noting that they "were thrown in utter confusion & left their ground precipitally allowing two of their scouts & five men who were gathering cattle, to fall into the hands of the enemy." Determined to return the insult, Polignac requested permission from Taylor to attack Vidalia, the closest Union outpost. Taylor viewed such a move as potentially advantageous for a number of reasons. Located on the Mississippi River opposite Natchez, Vidalia had become a focal point for Unionist activity in the region north of the Red River from Alexandria to Lake Concordia to Harrisonburg. Bands of deserters and jayhawkers, desperadoes who were often evading conscription, ravaged the area at will, often attacking unwary loyal soldiers and citizens.[8]

On the evening of February 3, the same day as the Union raid on Polignac's men at Mandersonville's Ferry, "jayhawkers and deserters" attacked two of Taylor's officers near Alexandria. Noting that one of the officers "was very severely wounded," Taylor quickly declared, "such outrages must be punished with a strong hand." On February 4 Taylor's assistant adjutant-general, Maj. Eustace Surget, dispatched orders to Polignac "to scour this portion of the country thoroughly, and every man found with arms in his hands, against whom reasonable suspicion exists of a determination to resist the laws will be shot by you on the spot. Such men are not to be arrested. You will further arrest and send to this post [Alexandria] every man capable of bearing arms, of whatever age, who cannot give substantial proof of his loyalty to the government."[9]

During the first week of February, Taylor learned that the Natchez garrison had been reduced by two regiments, transferred to Maj. Gen. William T. Sherman's army at Vicksburg. Noting that "only two regiments of white troops and some negro organizations" remained in Natchez, Taylor considered that Polignac's proposed Vidalia raid held a reasonable chance of success. In addition to "the moral effect of such a demonstration," Taylor stressed his additional objectives of securing "all the able-bodied negro men and mules, horses and transportation" in the area. He again stressed, "If jayhawkers are taken in arms they will be summarily executed; if not, they will be sent in irons to these headquarters."[10]

At midnight on February 6, Polignac led "two reg[iments] & the relics of a third one, in all about 550 men," across the Ouachita River. They left behind "another Reg[iment]," reduced to only "about 250 men strong," to guard their escape route at Mandersonville's Ferry. On the afternoon of February 7, transporting their rations and supplies on pack mules—the roads being too muddy for wagons—the attach force took positions in a stand of trees some two miles from Vidalia. Scanning his objective across the open field separating his concealed troops from town, Polignac realized he had lost the element of surprise. Alerted by three Confederate deserters, the Federal commander in Vidalia had ordered its streets blockaded with bales of cotton, plainly visible to the Confederate troops two miles away. Adopting the third person narrative of his hero Julius Caesar, Polignac described his reaction: "The commanding General having heard of these things & that the enemy had blockaded the streets of Vidalia with cotton bales, put field batteries in position & removed their stores, abandoned the idea of making an assault upon the town, as it seemed inconsiderate to sacrifice eventually a large number of men in the capture of a place the momentary possession of which would be without advantages." However, he could not, "deeming [it] inconsistent with the honour of his troops & his own . . . , retreat." Polignac decided to buy time for his foraging parties ranging through the local plantations by staging a rousing diversionary attack on Vidalia. Two roads

led from the Confederate positions into the village, "the ground between
. . . intersected with ditches & small ponds & mostly open with the exception of an intervening strip of timber." [11]

Polignac decided on a two-pronged attack: his meager cavalry was ordered to take the left road while his infantry advanced along the town's right approach. The cavalry, reinforced by a small number of infantry, closed on the left of the village and "in order to deceive the enemy by the appearance of a large force . . . , brisk firing & moving to & fro deluded the enemy so entirely into the deceived belief as to cause him to concentrate his fire on this point." [12] Polignac had long fumed in private over his despised Texan nom de guerre. As the Federals focused on his cavalry, he galloped to the head of his infantry on the right, where the general "raised himself in his stirrups and brandishing his sword aloft he led his men in person, shouting at the top of his voice, 'Follow me! Follow me! You call me 'Polecat,' I will show you whether I am 'Polecat' or 'Polignac!'" With "an answering shout" his Texans followed. [13] Lt. Col. H. A. McCaleb, commanding between three and five hundred men of the 2nd Mississippi Heavy Artillery (Colored), reported that the enemy "came in splendid style, carrying their arms at a support, presenting a most formidable front." The Texans must have indeed presented a "splendid style" —the Yankee officer estimated their numbers "from 1,200 to 1,500 men in all." "One splendid volley, well aimed," according to McCaleb, caused the attackers "to falter and lie down." He did not mention in his report that the Texans had also come under fire from four Federal gunboats that arrived on the nearby river. [14]

After regrouping in the woods, the Confederates made one last assault on the town. They were no match for the combined fire from the Federal gunboats and barricaded infantry. Despite the withering fire, one Texan, Alfred T. Howell, adjutant of the 22nd Texas, found humor in a desperate situation. In typical Texan fashion, he wrote to his brother after the engagement that his horse, panicked by the heavy fire, "ran away with me in the direction of the Federal lines. I turned him, however, before he got very far, and as I came back, our men shouted that my horse was a Yankee." With night falling Polignac, satisfied "that enough had been accomplished to vindicate the honor of the troops & to justify the object of the undertaking," called off the assault. The action had cost his brigade six killed, ten wounded, and eight missing. Both Polignac and Taylor considered the losses a reasonable trade-off for the nearly four hundred sorely needed cattle, horses, and mules brought in by the expedition. [15] More importantly, Polignac had at last won the respect of his troops. Taylor's prediction had proven correct, even if it had indeed been "up-hill work." But during the preceding weeks, Polignac already had won the hearts of many of his men with his newfound concern for their welfare. He had impressed others with his surprising mastery of swearing, a cherished art form among the Texans. Still, some troops had continued to hold their noses as he approached, unaware that their commander had already discovered "the play upon his name." A contemporary noted that Polignac had "maintained a discreet [sic] silence, and never revealed his knowledge or his indignation" until his call to attack at Vidalia. It was his "revenge," and after the raid no Texan "had a word of ridicule more for the gallant little Frenchman."[16] Yet their subsequent return to Harrisonburg plunged the Texans' mercurial general into renewed melancholy. Garrison duty always bored Polignac, often resulting in frequent headaches and depression. On February 23 he dejectedly penned a single diary entry: "Forgot I was alive."[17]

The engineers continued their construction at Harrisonburg and Trinity, where they planned to mount three heavy guns. By 4:30 in the afternoon of March 1, they had mounted only one 32-pounder when lookouts sounded the alarm. Pickets stationed at Beard's Point on the Black River passed on the unwelcome news that six Federal gunboats were closing rapidly on their positions.[18] The ironclad U.S.S. *Osage*, leading the more lightly armored "tinclads" *Fort Hindman, Cricket, Ouachita, Lexington,* and *Conestoga,* had left its anchorage on the Red River earlier that morning. Under Lt. Cmdr. F. M. Ramsey, the small river fleet came under carbine and rifle fire some fifteen miles below Trinity. Fifty Rebel cavalrymen under Capt. W. H. Gillespie, concealed behind a levee, proved the source of the minor annoyance. The horsemen quickly scattered under a rather more lethal answering barrage of shrapnel, grape, and canister. Undaunted, Gillespie's determined troopers continued to harass the Federal crews from the river's west bank "all the way up to Trinity."[19] There, Polignac's most formidable weapons—the three heavy guns—were useless: two were without carriages and his only mounted piece lacked ammunition. To avoid their possible capture, Polignac ordered the two gun tubes dumped into the river while the engineers buried the third gun. With luck, he counted on recovering all three after the Federals' departure.[20]

No one had warned artillerist Lt. Oscar Gaudet of the gunboats' approach. When the squat, 180-foot *Osage* suddenly rounded the bend less than three hundred yards away, he and his men were standing totally exposed on the open riverbank. Oscar Gaudet was not a man who frightened easily, however. With remarkable coolness he ordered his gunners to swing around and train their two ridiculously light-caliber 12-

pounder field howitzers on the approaching monster. Lacking proper armor-piercing solid shot (it would have made no difference anyway), Gaudet opened with unfused shell. Predictably, his improvised projectiles slammed into the *Osage*'s six inches of armor plate and glanced "upward . . . without effecting any injury or retarding her progress."[21]

As if to avenge the minor scratches to its paint, the ironclad's single forward-mounted turret slowly rotated in their direction. Scant yards away, Gaudet and his gunners found themselves staring down the eleven-inch muzzles of two massive Dahlgren smoothbores. At such range they most probably heard the gunnery officer's order to fire echo within the *Osage*'s turret. They just as probably heard little else. The deafening roar of the ironclad's twin heavy guns at point-blank range, followed by a terrific concussion, smoke, and flame, caught the Rebel gunners full in the face. Miraculously, the *Osage*'s two 121-pound projectiles passed harmlessly just over their heads to smash into the outskirts of Trinity. Such close range worked to the Rebels' advantage—although nerve and ear shattering, it at least saved their lives. Only some fifty to one hundred yards away, the Federal gunners could not depress their Dahlgrens low enough to bring the Confederates into their sights. But as the opposing gunners banged away ineffectively at one another, one of the tinclads steamed up the mouth of the Little River on Gaudet's right. His crews exposed on the flat spit of land bordered by the two rivers, Gaudet decided it was time to leave. With the tinclad's grapeshot whistling dangerously around them, the Confederates limbered up and made for the rear. Despite the fury of the unequal duel they had not lost a man.[22]

The gunboats paused briefly to hurl a few more shells into Trinity before continuing upriver. Determined to give them a warm reception at their by now obvious destination, Polignac ordered his infantry and Gaudet's two howitzers to Harrisonburg. As night fell Speight's, Hawpe's, and Alexander's regiments, followed by Gaudet, set out to make the twelve miles to Harrisonburg before dawn. In a decision he would come to regret, Polignac entrusted Trinity's defense to his ranking cavalry officer, Capt. James B. Randle. The route to Harrisonburg followed what one soldier described as "the worst road I ever saw, some of the boys left their old shoes sticking in the mud." Apart from difficult marching and lost shoes, the previous day's heavy rains created a more serious problem. The road, which Polignac also described as "almost impassable," was intersected just below Harrisonburg by Bushley Bayou, "a navigable stream," where he feared "the enemy could easily head me off." Tempers flared as officers hurried to ferry their men and equipment over the swollen waters.[23]

The ever-contentious Col. Joseph W. Speight, commanding the rear guard, and Lieutenant Gaudet, fresh from his duel with the *Osage*, nearly came to blows. Usual procedure called for crossing artillery first so it may be "placed in position on the opposite bank to cover the crossing of troops and trains." To Gaudet's exasperation Speight ordered him to stay behind until the very last of his infantry had ferried over the bayou. In the end it made little difference—Speight had already ordered the lieutenant to abandon his heavy caissons in the mud six miles behind, and without ammunition Gaudet's guns were useless. Speight's actions cost Polignac half of his artillery. Capt. Thomas A. Faries, however, commanding the Louisiana Pelican Battery, was determined to put his remaining two guns to deadly use. He selected his ground with care. At dawn on Wednesday, March 2, he positioned his 3-inch Parrott rifles "on a large circular Indian mound in an old field about midway between Harrisonburg and Bayou Bushley." From his position "200 yards from the right bank of the river," Faries planned to ambush the gunboats before they reached the town.[24]

Polignac next ordered two infantry regiments to take positions along the riverbank below town. Soon after, at 10:00 A.M., the *Osage*, leading the four tinclads, hove into view. As the gunboats came into range, the Confederate infantry offered a volley from their exposed positions along the bank. Almost instantaneously, Faries joined the din with his two guns. There was a brief silence from the gunboats, "but then," according to a private on the river's edge, "I tell you they opened on us heavy." As the *Osage* neared Faries's Indian mound, it slipped from view behind the towering riverbank and, as he later reported, "her funnel alone indicated her movements." It made no difference; his own 3-inch rifles would have had as little effect as Gaudet's howitzers. The tinclads, on the other hand, were much more vulnerable. As the *Osage*, guns blazing, steamed invincibly upriver, Faries turned his attention to its thinner-skinned companions.[25]

Faries knew that the tinclads' armor was impenetrable to musketry but vulnerable to well-placed artillery fire. Within a matter of minutes, his gunners fired sixty-three times at the vessels, Faries reporting, "Nearly all of the shot and shell from the two 3-inch rifles took effect in the pilot-houses and upper works of the four tin-clads, all of which lay together in a mass." Polignac, directing his infantry by the river and close enough to the gunboats to read their identification numbers, reported "gun-boat No. 13 was badly crippled by the fire [of Faries's] artillery." Indeed severely damaged, *No. 13*, or the U.S.S. *Fort Hindman*,

Although sketched in 1862 near New Orleans, Allen C. Redwood's drawing of
Confederates ambushing Federal gunboats accurately depicts the type of warfare
Polignac's troops waged along the bayous and rivers of northern Louisiana.
From Johnson and Buel, eds., Battles and Leaders of the Civil War, *2:28.*

drifted in the current to below the mouth of Bayou Bushley. The other
gunboats ran the Confederate gantlet and continued upstream.[26]

During the approximately two-hour fight, Harrisonburg and its defenders had, according to Polignac, endured a hail of "not less than 1,000
rounds, out of 24 & 32 pounders & 12-pounder Parrott guns & guns of
smaller caliber, a great deal of grape, cannister, & spherical case, & some

8 & 11 inch shells." Although casualties were surprisingly light, both of Polignac's aides, Capt. S. Cuculler and Lt. William Eggeling, had their horses shot from under them. Captain Faries lost his mount as well while he "was in the act of reporting to General Polignac for orders near the bank of the river above the mound." As the last gunboat steamed out of sight above Harrisonburg, Polignac misjudged their intentions and prematurely ordered his men back to their camps about a mile from town. It was a costly mistake. With Harrisonburg undefended the fleet doubled back and landed a three-man raiding party to burn the village. Polignac, alerted by the resultant smoke, rushed his troops back into town only to fall into the fleet's ambush. Suddenly, from the point of view of Pvt. Billy Flinn, "we were in the hotest fire of all, because they could see us from the River, and had a fare sweep on us." "The Town," recounted Flinn, "was riddled all to pieces and 3 houses burned we saved the rest of it when the gunboats came up from Trinity they gave no time to the Families to get out of town and those 3 houses that was burned lost every thing that they had."[27]

The gunboats, with the *Fort Hindman* in tow, continued downstream and anchored for the night one mile above Trinity. The next morning, March 3, they renewed their attack on the small village. They met little resistance. Polignac placed the blame for the Federals' virtually uncontested assault squarely on the shoulders of the officer he had left to protect Trinity: "Capt[ain] John G. Randle, by some unaccountable mistake, took his cavalry up Little River, so that the duty of guarding the town devolved on Captain Gillespie alone." Although Capt. W. H. Gillespie "behaved throughout with coolness, energy, & judgment," he and his few cavalrymen were no match for a fleet of gunboats. Complicating matters, his superior, Captain Randle, continued to demonstrate a remarkable dedication to incompetence. Although in the immediate vicinity, Randle made no attempt to prevent one of the gunboats from ascending the Little River and destroying a critical pontoon bridge. Forever earning Polignac's contempt, he also neglected to report that the *Fort Hindman* had "swung to at the mouth of the Little River & run aground." Polignac later bitterly complained that if Randle had immediately informed him of the gunboat's plight, the helpless vessel "would . . . have fallen into our hands." By the time he learned of the unfolding fiasco at Trinity and forded his infantry past the debris of the wrecked pontoon bridge, the gunboats were nearing the Mississippi River.[28]

To Polignac's intense embarrassment, the warships had significantly increased their ordnance inventories. Randle's sudden departure had afforded the Federals time for a leisurely survey of the works at Trinity and

Fort Beauregard. A rapid drop in the river's water level exposed both of the submerged guns, and search crews, on the evening of March 2, had located the other buried in the fort's earthworks. Within hours had salvaged all three of the hidden cannon. The loss of the valuable ordnance sparked a brief skirmish of recriminations among the local Confederate commanders. Polignac, who rarely found fault with his own judgment, blamed not only Randle but also a Captain Devoe, chief of engineers at Trinity and directly responsible for the pieces. At the first sign of danger, Devoe had proven his mastery of the fine art of discretion; by the end of the day he had already reached Alexandria. To Brig. Gen. St. John R. Liddell, commanding the seven-hundred-man cavalry brigade operating on the Ouachita, it was Polignac alone who bore the responsibility for the loss of the cannons and the destruction of property in Trinity. Liddell was a contentious man by nature—he was an outspoken critic of Taylor's overall strategy and, because he was the senior brigadier in the area, resented Polignac's autonomy. (Six years later Liddell would die aboard a riverboat during an altercation with a neighboring planter and his two sons.) Although Liddell acknowledged that his cavalry scouts had frequently provided Polignac with faulty information, he emphatically asserted that on the day of Ramsey's attack the cavalry's intelligence was superb. Polignac, according to Liddell, rashly ignored both the scouts' and Liddell's personal warnings until it was too late to rescue the guns or defend the town. "Thus," Liddell claimed, "Polignac utterly failed in the special object he had been sent to do, that is, the protection of the works and guns."[29]

Union rear admiral David Porter, commanding the Mississippi Squadron, was understandably pleased with Lieutenant Commander Ramsey's performance during the Ouachita expedition. After the gunboats' return to the Mississippi on March 5, the admiral praised their officers and crews: "The rebels, about 2,000 strong, under General Polignac, were driven from point to point, some extensive works captured, and three heavy 32-pounders brought away. The works were destroyed. The enemy suffered severely from our guns, and the vessels brought away all the cotton they could find. They also destroyed a pontoon bridge." Porter considered Ramsey's losses minimal: "We lost two killed and fourteen wounded and the *Fort Hindman* was badly cut up with shot and shell, being struck 27 times, but nothing to impair her efficiency."[30]

Polignac's superior, Gen. Richard Taylor, fully appreciated the trying conditions under which his subordinate was forced to operate. Defending an extensive area with only some two thousand men, inferior equipment, and difficult terrain, he deemed Polignac's performance exceptional. Moreover, despite the failures of Randle, Devoe, and Speight, Taylor commended Polignac for his success in driving off the gunboats at a cost of only three killed and thirteen wounded. Only the bitter Liddell seems to have disagreed: "This shows how easy it was for a designing commander to put the best construction upon that for which he himself is open to censure for not opposing, if not approving. Taylor knew that he had to bear some portion of blame in this matter, hence he took this course to ignore everything but the bravery of his own troops." Taylor later assessed the actions at Trinity and Harrisonburg as the turning point in Polignac's career: "The gunboats were driven off, and Polignac, by his coolness under fire, gained the confidence of his men, as he soon gained their affections by his care and attention. They got along famously, and he made capital soldiers out of them."[31]

However, the Ouachita River expedition was merely a prelude to a larger all-out offensive being outlined by Federal generals and politicians. Both Secretary of State William A. Seward and General-in-Chief Henry W. Halleck pressed for a renewed attempt to invade Texas. The operation seemed necessary for a number of reasons, all of which had been repeatedly debated in the North's upper circles for some time. Of primary importance, occupation of the state would cut off the vital avenue for supplies and war matériel entering the South through Mexico. That country's occupation by French forces since June of the previous year also elicited another concern. Northern authorities agreed that a strong Union presence in Texas would discourage the French from more actively aiding the Confederacy. Furthermore, Texas itself was an attractive prize as a source of cotton, foodstuffs, and livestock.[32]

Confederate generals Richard Taylor and Edmund Kirby Smith held no doubts as to the Federals' intended route. Early in the year Kirby Smith, as overall commander of the Trans-Mississippi Department, advised President Davis, "The only true line of operations by which the enemy can penetrate the department is the valley of the Red River, rich in supplies; with steam-boat navigation for six months of the year, it offers facilities for the co-operation of the army and navy, and enables them to shift their base as they advance into the interior."[33] As early as January Taylor had guessed the Federals would move against him in the early spring. By March 7 his spies' reports of an "Increased activity and concentration at Berwick's Bay, and a visit of [Gen. William Tecumseh] Sherman to New Orleans to confer with [Maj. Gen. Nathaniel P.] Banks" confirmed that the offensive was imminent.[34] Taylor quickly moved to assemble his widely scattered forces to meet the anticipated onslaught.

On March 7 he dispatched orders to Polignac to abandon the no longer essential Fort Beauregard and move his brigade to Alexandria. Taylor planned to merge Polignac's brigade with that of Brig. Gen. Alfred Mouton and march their combined forces down Bayou Boeuf to reinforce Maj. Gen. John G. Walker's Texas Division near Fort DeRussy.[35] Despite Taylor's scornful protests, Kirby Smith considered the unfinished bastion the keystone of the lower Red River Valley's defenses. Taylor, as did Walker, deemed DeRussy untenable and a waste of valuable resources. The latter were proven correct on March 14 when, as Polignac observed: "Fort DeRussy fell almost without a struggle."[36]

Although Polignac initially blamed the fort's loss on Walker's "hasty retreat," subsequent intelligence confirmed the Texan's sound judgment. With less than four thousand troops he could hardly have stopped Brig. Gen. Andrew J. Smith's ten thousand veterans drawn from Sherman's army at Vicksburg. After occupying DeRussy, Smith, reinforced by nineteen ironclads and gunboats of Adm. David D. Porter's squadron, continued up the Red River. On the morning of the fifteenth, Taylor bowed to the inevitable and evacuated Alexandria. That afternoon the first of Porter's fleet arrived at the town's docks. Smith's troops filed into town the following day.[37]

Although formidable, Smith's and Porter's combined forces were only one component of the massive operation to be known as the Red River Campaign. Their overall commander, Massachusetts politician-turned-general Nathaniel P. Banks, planned a three-pronged invasion. His own seventeen-thousand-man XIX Corps began to file into Alexandria on March 19. Later that month Banks planned to link up in Shreveport with an additional ten thousand troops under Maj. Gen. Frederick Steele marching from Little Rock, Arkansas.[38]

Taylor had no choice but to fall back and marshal as many troops as possible in the countryside. Polignac described the exodus: "On the 15 March Alexandria was evacuated. My Brigade had reached the place the day previous. The whole infantry force of the District was concentrated that evening on Bayou Boeuf. The next morning we took up their line of retreat across the Pine woods towards Carroll Jones, where upon arriving after a few days' march, we halted."[39] Taylor had established "a depot of forage" near the home of Carroll Jones, a well-to-do free black, some thirty miles above Alexandria. The arrival of Walker's Texas Division, Polignac's Texas Brigade, and Mouton's Louisiana Brigade, under Col. Henry Gray, on the seventeenth and eighteenth prompted Taylor to reorganize his command. He consequently merged Polignac's Texans with Gray's Louisianans to form the 2nd Infantry Division. He then placed the new division under command of the Louisiana Brigade's former commander, Brig. Gen. Alfred Mouton.[40]

Taylor assumed that, sharing two common languages, Mouton and Polignac would become friends and work well together. His assumption proved only partially correct. Although only three years Polignac's senior and more comfortable with French than English, the Acadian general was a much different man than his new subordinate. Too diplomatic to state his true opinions openly, the ascetic Mouton's private correspondence revealed a personal distaste for the French nobleman's character. Still, although Mouton frowned on what he considered Polignac's "excessive drinking and carousing," he nevertheless respected his intelligence and military abilities.[41]

The combined strength of Mouton's new 2nd Division and Walker's Texas Division afforded Taylor barely seven thousand infantry. His cavalry was almost nonexistent, crippling his ability to screen his movements and monitor the Union advance. The March 19 arrival of Col. William G. Vincent's Louisiana cavalry regiment promised at least some capability in tracking Banks's progress. Taylor quickly dispatched Vincent the fifteen miles to Bayou Rapides to monitor Banks's army in Alexandria, twenty miles to the south. Although sorely needed, Vincent's Louisianans were, as Taylor observed, "jaded by constant service and long marches." Miserable weather and renewed skirmishing took a further toll on their effectiveness. According to Taylor, "The 21st proved to be a cold, rainy day, with gusts of wind." That night, exhausted by frequent skirmishing with enemy cavalry patrols in a soaking rain intermixed with hail, Vincent's troopers dropped their guard. Their camp on Henderson's Hill seemed safe enough. The constant rain had turned the scrubby woods at the base of the hill into a nearly impenetrable swamp. Consequently, Vincent posted few pickets out in the dripping woods, allowing the majority of his men to cluster around their small fires. Their lack of vigilance allowed Brig. Gen. Joseph A. Mower, leading six infantry regiments and one brigade of cavalry, to quietly surround the camp. Guided by local jayhawkers, the Yankees, who had braved mud at times "belly deep" to their horses, quickly overcame the few Rebel pickets. They then rushed through Vincent's camp, capturing some 250 prisoners, most of his horses, and Capt. William Edgar's four-gun artillery battery. Although Vincent escaped—"in his slippers!" according to Polignac—his command virtually ceased to exist. Taylor later rationalized the loss of Vincent's cavalrymen, stating, "In truth, my horse was too ill disciplined for close work," but he was again without his eyes and ears.[42]

Down in Alexandria his opponent was assembling the largest force ever amassed in the Trans-Mississippi. Banks's Department of the Gulf had contributed two divisions each of the XIII and the XIX Corps as well as Brig. Gen. Albert L. Lee's cavalry division. Gen. A. J. Smith's two divisions of the XVI Corps, one division of the XVII Corps, and Brig. Gen. A. W. Ellet's Marine Brigade made up the detachment sent from Sherman's Army of the Tennessee at Vicksburg. These thirty thousand troops and their 90 guns would be supported by Admiral Porter's approximately sixty vessels that included transports, gunboats, and ironclads, offering a combined total of 210 naval guns.[43]

Faced with such unequal odds, Gen. Edmund Kirby Smith, from his headquarters in Shreveport, ordered Taylor to fall back toward that town. Polignac's Texas Brigade thus retreated northward to Beasly's depot on the twenty-second and camped near the Cane River on the twenty-fourth. Banks's pursuit was somewhat slowed by unpredictable river levels, so critical to his fleet's passage, and a rush to confiscate as much Rebel cotton as possible. To deny the enemy this valuable commodity, Taylor reluctantly ordered the burning of thousands of bales along his retreat route. Their desolate wake of "smoldering ruins of gin houses and piles of half-burned cotton" prompted one of their Federal pursuers to write: "From the day we started on the Red River expedition, we were like the Israelites of old, accompanied by a cloud by day, and a pillar of fire by night."[44]

Banks's relentless advance reached Natchitoches on the last day of March. On April 3 his floating headquarters, the *Black Hawk*, anchored at the tiny settlement of Grand Ecore, four miles upriver. Taylor, who had abandoned Natchitoches on March 30, hurried to concentrate his own forces near Pleasant Hill, a small village thirty-six miles to the north. On April 1 Mouton's and Walker's infantry and artillery arrived, later joined at last by Brig. Gen. Thomas Green's and Col. Xavier B. DeBray's cavalry. The next day Taylor ordered Polignac to form a line of battle on the Natchitoches Road below the town. Taylor continued to deploy his troops northward, and on the third Polignac encamped his brigade ten miles south of Mansfield. On April 4 the brigade marched up the Shreveport Road through Mansfield, where they rested until the seventh. The sound of distant cavalry skirmishing soon alerted them to the Federals' approach.

The firing announced the turning point of the Red River Campaign. Banks's staff had advised the general of two roads leading north to Shreveport. The longer hugged the riverbank, thus offering his troops the protection of marching under the guns of Porter's fleet. Banks, anxious to reach Shreveport as quickly as possible, nevertheless decided on the more direct and westerly overland route. Although the road passed through Mansfield and Pleasant Hill, occupied by Taylor's main force, Banks evidenced little concern. Taylor's prolonged retreat had lulled him into the belief that the Confederates were unwilling to make a stand under any circumstances. On April 6, therefore, the Federal Army abandoned the protection of the river to march through the "howling wilderness" of northwestern Louisiana.[45]

CHAPTER 8

"Follow Your Polignac!"

April 6, 1864–April 10, 1864

———•-•———

Maj. Gen. Richard Taylor was anxious for a fight. His "long re-treat of two hundred miles from the banks of the Atchafalaya to Mansfield" had strained his patience to the breaking point. In his frustration he blamed Lt. Gen. Edmund Kirby Smith for denying him sufficient troops to face Maj. Gen. Nathaniel Banks and his Union invaders now ravaging Taylor's adopted state.[1] For his part Kirby Smith feared initiating an error that could cost the Confederacy the en-tire Trans-Mississippi Department and ultimately the war. The very ex-istence of his meager command significantly affected the overall equation of the greater conflict. So long as he kept his armies intact, Kirby Smith forced the Federals to maintain Banks's and Maj. Gen. Frederick Steele's proportionately much larger forces in the Trans-Mississippi to contain the Rebels. Should he be drawn into a disastrous defeat, Kirby Smith knew that not only would he lose his department, but thousands of Union sol-diers would be freed for duty in the East.[2] On April 6, determined to come to some understanding with his difficult subordinate, the depart-mental commander rode to Taylor's headquarters at Mansfield. As their own contradictory accounts attest, they accomplished little during their meeting. Kirby Smith did promise to send Brig. Gen. Thomas J. Chur-chill's 4,400 men to Keatchie, midway between Mansfield and Shreve-port, but little else. Denied authority to initiate an engagement, Taylor waited for Banks.[3]

For Polignac's foot-sore Texans Thursday, April 7, was a welcome day of rest. It was just as well. As they lounged in their camps north of Mansfield, a neighboring soldier scratched in his diary: "This day has been cloudy and rainy, occasional showers of rainfall all the day." That afternoon they could hear distant firing as Brig. Gen. Tom Green's "wild horsemen" skirmished with Banks's advance guard, Brig. Gen. Albert L. Lee's cavalry, some three miles above Pleasant Hill at Wilson's Farm.

Forced to withdraw before superior numbers, Green growled prophetically to a fellow officer: "We haven't had much show yet, but we will give them hell tomorrow."[4] The short fight at Wilson's Farm convinced Taylor, who had joined Green during its latter stages, that the next day would indeed by eventful. "Leaving Green," Taylor recounted, "I returned to Mansfield, stopping on the road to select my ground for the morrow." Arriving at his headquarters, Taylor lost no time in alerting his staff and brigade commanders of the coming engagement.[5]

That evening the ladies of Mansfield offered a soiree in honor of their gray-clad protectors. Although Polignac did not mention the affair, attended by Taylor and his generals, he could hardly have resisted an opportunity to socialize with the local belles. The generals gallantly assured their worried hostesses that no hated Yankee would ever set foot in their little town.[6] The following day, April 8, was to be, according to a proclamation by Pres. Jefferson Davis, a day of "national fasting, humiliation, and prayer." Well before dawn "the pattering rain," observed a tired Confederate, "ceased, and the silver stars [began] to show themselves." An officer recalled, "at 2 o'clock the order was received to send the troops forward on the road to Pleasant Hill, and the wagons to follow in the rear with the exception of the ammunition wagons and the ambulances." At 6:30 A.M., to the rousing strains of "Dixie," Polignac's Texans led the Confederate column as it marched over garlands spread on Mansfield's main street by the town's ladies. Anxious to confront the invaders at last, their spirits quickened as the soldiers passed Taylor, Walker, Mouton, and Green as the generals held a war council beside the road.[7]

At the Moss Plantation some three miles from Mansfield, Taylor directed his 5,300 infantry into their positions. Partially concealed in the edge of a pine forest, Mouton's division took the left of the road leading to Pleasant Hill as Walker's Texas Division formed its line of battle on the right. They looked out upon what Taylor described as "an open field eight hundred yards in width by twelve hundred in length, through the center of which the road to Pleasant Hill passed. On the opposite side of the field was a fence separating it from the pine forest, which, open on the higher ground and filled with underwood on the lower, spread over the country."[8] Polignac's Texas Brigade anchored the Confederate left. Mouton's other brigade, Gray's Louisianans, stood to their right next to Col. Horace Randal's brigade of Walker's division. Brig. Gen. James P. Major of Tom Green's command dismounted his cavalry to protect what Polignac deemed his "much exposed" left flank. Twelve artillery batteries positioned "from place to place at the most advantageous points" and

3,000 cavalry brought Taylor's strength, not yet reinforced by Churchill's command, to about 8,800 effectives.[9]

Brushing off the warnings of his leading cavalry commander, Brig. Gen. Albert L. Lee, Banks continued his advance to Sabine Crossroads. His virtually uncontested march across Louisiana had lulled the Union commander into the belief that Taylor would not make a stand before reaching Shreveport. He therefore saw little danger in abandoning the protection of Porter's guns for the single narrow road leading to Mansfield. The road, as Lee tried to warn his commander, although offering their most direct route, posed their most significant threat.[10] Though the Federal column boasted some eighteen thousand troops, their deployment was dictated by the narrow confines of their path. In places barely wide enough for a single wagon, the road passed through a hilly, almost impenetrable pine forest. Lee was particularly concerned over the placement of the supply trains; his own stretched some two or three miles to the rear blocking both retreat and reinforcements. Lee's anxiety was further aggravated by his own relatively green troopers' performance in the face of stiffening Confederate resistance at Wilson's Farm. To placate his cavalry commander, Banks ordered Maj. Gen. William B. Franklin to send Lee infantry reinforcements. On the morning of April 8, reinforced by two infantry brigades from the 4th Infantry Division, XIII Corps, Lee's forces numbered some 4,800 men. By late morning the Federals had driven Confederate skirmishers before them through the pine thickets until they reached a low wooded ridge known as Honeycutt Hill.[11]

Gazing toward the new Federal positions, a soldier in Walker's division on the Confederate right described the intervening landscape: "The battle ground marked out is several farms connected under one fence, —some of the land ploughed—some fallow, and some woodland; with many crossfences, and a lane running through the whole. The whole fencing and woodland comprises perhaps four thousand acres."[12] An officer in Gray's Louisiana Brigade, to Polignac's immediate right, described the scene before Mouton's division: "Our position was on a rather high hill at the edge of a forest behind a fence, with a large field before us, ending in a forest on a very high hill facing us. In that position we awaited the enemy whose cavalry made its appearance about midday on our left, at the moment when our brigade was marching by the left flank to spread more to the left."[13]

Richard Taylor was confident of his men and his positions. At 9:40 A.M. he dispatched a message to Shreveport. Implying that a confrontation with Banks had become unavoidable, he almost casually concluded, "I consider this as a favorable point to engage him at as any other." Around noon, noting that his fellow Louisianans were "inflamed by many outrages on their homes, as well as by camp rumors that it was intended to abandon their State without a fight," Taylor reined-up before Mouton's division. Turning to the Louisiana Brigade, he shouted out, "as they were fighting in defense of their own soil [he] wished the Louisiana troops to draw the first blood." His prophetic speech was cut short when a number of Confederate cavalry burst from the opposite tree line. Close on their heels some one hundred Yankee troopers galloped derisively "shouting sooe! sooe! as though they were driving hogs." As they closed to within twenty feet of Mouton's concealed troops, a wild shot struck Taylor's saddle. A single Confederate volley, however, discouraged any further advance.[14]

Across the field on Honeycutt Hill, Albert Lee, who was joined by Banks at about one o'clock, was still unsure of Taylor's intentions. Recent events indicated a stiffening Confederate resistance, yet Taylor's well-chosen positions effectively concealed his divisions from the Federals' view. Lee again ordered his cavalry ahead to reconnoiter the Confederate positions. Close by Polignac's Texas Brigade, Felix Pierre Poché, an officer in Gray's Louisiana Brigade, observed: "The Yankee Cavalry numbering five hundred, silently emerged from the woods, and coming very bravely toward our lines, were at first mistaken for our own men, and our generals did not recognize them until they were about 200 feet from our line. And Gen[eral] Mouton then ordered the 18th La to open fire on them, which orders were promptly obeyed, and with the second discharge the enemy's Cavalry broke, fleeing in great disorder leaving some ten wounded and as many prisoners whose horses had been killed."[15]

As the Rebel cavalry wheeled to return the favor to their recent pursuers, Mouton's lines erupted in "three cheers for Louisiana." Their excitement was contagious, fueling Taylor's enthusiasm as he rode past their front offering his congratulations. The Federal cavalry probes and reports of infantry massing in the woods opposite Gray's and Polignac's brigades promised an attack on his left. He consequently ordered Randal's brigade of Walker's division across the road to reinforce Mouton's right. To mask their maneuver he deployed additional skirmishers into the field and advanced Col. Xavier B. DeBray's cavalry across the central road.[16]

About midafternoon Poché observed, "the enemy's infantry and artillery arrived and arranged themselves in battle formation, facing us at the edge of the woods." Polignac and Gray quickly sent forward several companies of skirmishers to harass the newcomers and perhaps goad them into a rash charge. To add weight to their challenge, at about two o'clock Taylor ordered up a Texas battery, "which," Poché observed, "took a position on the high ground on the left of the road just in front of Polignac's Brigade and opened fire on the Federal line." Their fire was effective for, according to Poché, "the Federals, who had posted their artillery on Honeycut [*sic*] Hill, ordered forward a battery of nine rifled guns which took position on the hill on the right of the road, and a fierce artillery duel ensued, in which three of the five Confederate guns were put out of action, but the other two stood firm and returned shot for shot." [17]

The growing afternoon heat coupled with Yankee disinclination to cooperate with his plans began to try Taylor's patience. He was, as he later recalled, confident "of success in the impending engagement" owing to his "accurate knowledge of the Federal movements, as well as the character of their commander, General Banks, whose measure had been taken in the Virginia campaigns of 1862 and since." Banks's obvious reluctance to attack across his carefully prepared killing ground at last convinced Taylor to seize the initiative.[18] At approximately 3:30 P.M. Taylor rode across his lines to confer with Walker. Twenty minutes later he had made up his mind. Barely controlling his excitement, Taylor made for Mouton's lines, now the center of renewed skirmishing. Polignac was the first to hear his decision. As he galloped abreast of the Texas Brigade, Taylor paused long enough to shout to its commander: "Little Frenchman, I am going to fight Banks here, if he has a million men!" The bitter Confederate retreat would end at Mansfield. Taylor then hurried on to Mouton, ordering him to begin the attack immediately. Taylor appeared almost serene as he observed the unfolding drama from his vantage near the central road. With one leg resting casually across his saddle, he casually enjoyed a cigar as Walker's and Mouton's ragged divisions emerged from the woods. Upon their shoulders he had pinned his career and the fate of the Trans-Mississippi. It was a little past four in the afternoon.[19]

Mouton's customary reserve evaporated at the prospect of at last turning on the hated Yankees. Fiercely drawing his sword, he paused just long enough to roar to Polignac: "Let us charge them right in the face and throw them into the valley!" As an officer recalled, "Immediately after that we were ordered to leap over the fence, and with resounding yells we began running and stormed the enemy." Taylor reported their charge as "magnificent." "Yelling like crazed demons," the Texans and Louisianans followed Polignac and Mouton into what Taylor described as "a murderous fire of artillery and musketry." Confederate soldier H. C. Medford shuddered as "The elements begin to fry with the passing of balls." [20]

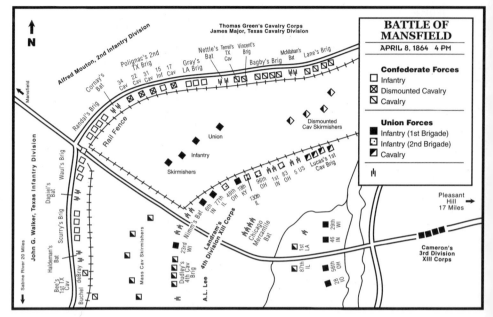

Map by Jeff Kinard and Quentin Cline

Another Confederate remembered: "At a distance of one hundred fifty feet the enemy opened fire and we were severely battered by musket fire and a really terrific cannonade. The balls and grape shot crashing about us whistled terribly and ploughed into the ground and beat our soldiers down even as a storm tears down the trees of a forest." As Polignac's brigade closed on the Union positions, the intensity of firing and its resulting casualties mounted. "Shots plow gaps through them," observed an awed Federal on the ridge ahead, "shells burst in their midst and form caverns in the mass of living men."[21]

Taylor had indeed chosen a superb killing ground. Unfortunately, his new decision to carry the attack to the enemy now required his own men to cross the exposed field. Over hundreds of yards, jogging at the double-quick, the Rebels "charged down a hill, over a fence, through a ravine, then up a hill, right in the teeth of the guns." In addition to their heavy casualties, Polignac's men "were nearly breathless when they struggled up the ravine." Before ordering his division into the final attack, "Mouton commanded them to throw themselves prostrate a moment to recover breath." As the prone Rebels exchanged shots with the Yankees concealed in the woods, a courier from Gen. Edmund Kirby Smith found Taylor. Taylor, however, had fully anticipated both Kirby Smith's or-

Shortly after the Battle of Mansfield, Sam Houston, Jr., of McMahon's Texas
Battery sketched Polignac's Brigade charging the Federal lines.
Courtesy Mansfield State Historic Site.

ders to avoid battle as well as the messenger's tardiness. Scanning his superior's now irrelevant instructions, Taylor crowed: "Too late sir! the
battle is won."[22] Determined to fulfill Taylor's prophecy, Mouton and
Polignac renewed their charge. "Barracaded [*sic*] behind piles of rails,"
the Federals greeted them with point-blank double canister and volleys
of musketry. "The cost," a Confederate remembered, "was terrible." The
Midwestern troops behind the barricade were no pasty-faced Northern
clerks, but "American farmers who did not shoot and run away, but stood
up manfully, realizing that they held the key to the situation and that victory or defeat depended on their being able to hold their position."[23]

"The Crescent Regiment struck them first and at close range received
a volley from the [130th] Illinois Regiment that killed fifty-five men including a field officer of the regiment, and wounded 150." To the Crescent Regiment's left, Polignac led his Texas Brigade, "scarcely stronger
than a good regiment," into the teeth of nine field guns supported by the
161st New York Zouaves and the 77th Illinois Regiment. Glancing back
as his Texans staggered in the muzzle blasts of the cannons, he bellowed

over the din, "Come on boys, come on, these things do make a hell of a noise but don't hurt much[!]" Fierce "Texas yells" soon drowned out the Yankees' cheers, which had erupted after the first volleys.[24] A local resident later remembered that, as the Texans crashed into the Union lines, "It looked like the immovable had been struck by the irresistible and that something had to happen." Scanning the smoke-shrouded battle through his binoculars, Taylor looked on as Polignac's little brigade and the Louisianans "reached the fence, paused for a moment to draw breath, then rushed into the wood on the enemy." Savage hand-to-hand fighting raged as Polignac's Texans grappled for possession of the Federal artillery on Honeycutt Hill. Within minutes dozens of dead and wounded lay sprawled around the guns.[25]

Although "literally shot to pieces," the Rebels pressed their attack. Reveling in the heat of battle, their Acadian general rode into the thickest of the fighting. "Mouton," recalled one Louisianan, "was always in the front." Another soldier marveled, "He was all the time in a glee of laughter, cheering his men and officers, telling them that our arms would be victorious today." Close behind their general the Confederate flag-bearers and regimental officers paid a high price for leading the assault. In all, seven soldiers fell killed or wounded as "man after man grabbed the fallen colors and tried to bear them forward, only to fall as fast as they took them." Impressed by their bravery, Taylor recorded, "As these officers went down, others among them . . . seized the colors and led on the men."[26] "In this moment of furious fighting and utter confusion," remembered Confederate J. E. Hewitt, "General Mouton and staff rushed forward and placed himself at the head of the leaderless, but still fighting Crescent. One of his staff had brought forward the blood-stained regimental flag when it was again blasted with a volley from the stubbornly resisting Federals and again fell to the ground, this time stained with the life-blood of Gen[eral] Alfred Mouton . . . , five balls had pierced his manly breast."[27] The initial assault also claimed a potentially crippling number of field officers, including Lt. Col. Sebron M. Noble, killed while leading the 17th Texas Consolidated. "Despite these and other heavy losses," wrote Taylor in his report, "the division never halted for a moment nor even fell into confusion, but under the gallant Polignac pressed stubbornly on."[28] Taylor credited Polignac's cool professionalism as he assumed command after Mouton was killed "and pressed the shattered division steadily forward." The circumstances of Mouton's death added to the Confederates' fury. A Rebel remembered that as soon as "The guns were taken after a desperate struggle . . . , the Federals broke and fled. Mouton turned, lifting his hand to stay the firing of the Confederates upon [a] group of prisoners: as he did so, five of the Federals stooped down, picked up their guns, aimed them at the generous Confederate and, in a moment . . . , Mouton dropped from his saddle dead, without a word or a sigh. The Confederates who witnessed this cowardly deed gave a yell of indignation, and before their officers could check them, the thirty-five Federals lay dead around Mouton."[29]

After placing Col. James R. Taylor of the 17th Texas in command of his own brigade, Polignac renewed the attack. Texans and Louisianans alike coldly leveled their bayonets to extract their revenge. "With tears of grief and rage in their eyes," his troops took up a new battle cry, shouting "Mouton!" as they surged forward. Chaos ensued as Federal regiments such as the 130th Illinois and 48th Ohio finally disintegrated. Remnants of many companies, their cartridge boxes empty, simply surrendered en masse. Others continued to fight a running battle as they stumbled back through the pine thickets toward the main Union force. As the survivors fled into the shelter of the forest, the Texans seized three of their abandoned guns. Within minutes they had turned the pieces around and were merrily reissuing Federal ordnance to its former owners in ten- and twelve-pound parcels.[30]

If, however unlikely, Taylor had harbored reservations concerning his decision to attack, Confederate successes quickly dispelled all doubts. Confident in Polignac, now reinforced by Lt. Col. John H. Caudle's 34th Texas and protected on the left by Green's cavalry, Taylor ordered in Walker's division. Soon Brig. Gens. Thomas N. Waul's and William R. Scurry's brigades joined Randal's regiments already fighting in the far woods on Polignac's right. Even the failure to flank the Union left by Colonels Buchel's and DeBray's cavalry under Brig. Gen. Hamilton P. Bee counted for little. As Bee's cavalry foundered in the dense woods and swamps, Scurry ordered his brigade to fix bayonets and, according to Taylor, "advanced, and swept everything before him." As the entire Federal line collapsed and made for the rear, the exultant Rebels followed. Confederate H. C. Medford remembered: "In this pursuit no tongue, or pen can express the excitement—the joy of our men and officers. The undergrowth is all run over, without any knowledge of its being an obstacle."[31]

By five o'clock, in an attempt to counter Polignac's seemingly irresistible momentum, some Federal gunners resorted to extraordinary measures. One soldier reported: "Each piece was loaded with a case of grape and cannister, spherical case shell, and a sack of bullets containing about three hundred." Federal artillery claimed a gruesome toll as the Confederates crashed through the dense pines against their new posi-

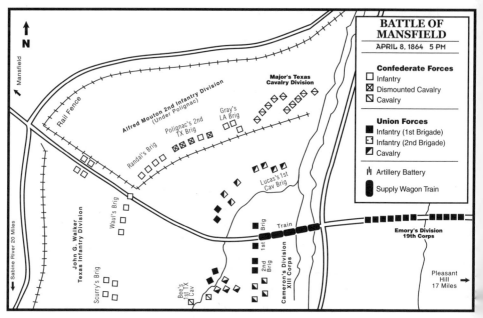

Map by Jeff Kinard and Quentin Cline

tion. A Louisiana soldier recalled: "We passed this thick wood in a continuous and terrific shower of cannon balls accompanied by grape shot, and arriving at the fence of the next field we discovered the enemy's second line and received a concentrated shelling which killed a great number of men."[32]

Polignac, braving the hail of artillery and musket fire at the head of his division, urged his men onward. Despite their general's personal efforts to steady their lines, Banks's men again lost their nerve. John Russell Young, a Northern reporter accompanying the expedition, recorded the ensuing panic: "suddenly there was a rush, a shout, the crashing of trees, the breaking down of rails, the rush and scamper of men." As Young found himself "swallowed up, as it were, in a hissing, seething, bubbling whirlpool of agitated men," Surgeon John Homans noted an almost comical scene. Himself battered and jostled about by the fear-stricken soldiers, Homans observed a long string of their comrades desperately aligning themselves behind the doubtful shelter of a lone sapling.[33]

Polignac dryly recorded that his "Division[,] charging the enemy vigorously[,] routed him completely, capturing all the artillery he had in his front." As Louisianan J. E. Hewitt put it: "The Federals, seeing their line broken by the Louisiana brigade on their right, their line doubled up and demoralized by [Gen. Tom] Green's attack on their left, their artillery driven back by Polignac in the center, and their own front threatened, did not wait upon the order of their going, but went at once. . . . Thus the whole Federal line was driven pell-mell from their original positions, and, panic-stricken . . . joined the stampede."[34] Flinging aside such by now maddening encumbrances as rifles, knapsacks, canteens, and coats, the fugitives continued their headlong flight. A Confederate later recorded, "The Yankees were routed and all their army fled hotly pursued by our men who killed them at every step." One Texan gave his own impression of the carnage: "Horses and men, by hundreds, roll down together; the road is red with their blood." Stumbling over their own wounded, the Union mob finally reached the road only to find it hopelessly clogged with their supply train. Upon hearing the cheers of Polignac's approaching Rebels, the Yankee teamsters had cut their mules' traces and joined the retreat. Unable to negotiate the tangle of wagons and ambulances, the Federal artillerymen abandoned their precious guns unspiked in their haste to escape.[35]

Although humiliating, the loss of Lee's supply train proved something of a blessing in disguise to the beleaguered Federals. Where Union artillery, musketry, and bravery had failed to halt the Confederates' advance, the sight of the bulging wagons stopped the hungry Southern soldiers in their tracks. What Banks had considered the barest essentials for campaigning to the gaunt and tattered Rebels seemed the most wondrous of luxuries. Taylor's men temporarily abandoned their pursuit to gorge on such unimaginable delicacies as canned meats and fruits and to cast off their rags for new, albeit blue, uniforms. Others' belief in a benevolent God was confirmed by the discovery of keg after keg of potent army-issue whiskey. As the Rebels swarmed over their unexpected bonanza, many Federals made good their escape. The delay also gave Brig. Gen. William H. Emory time to lead Union reinforcements free of the clogged road.[36] Emory, a West Point graduate and professional soldier, ignored the warnings of the panicked survivors and pushed his division through the panicked mob. Shortly before dusk he expertly deployed his troops along Chapman Hill, a steep ridge fronted by a shallow creek and an orchard known by locals as Pleasant Grove. His single division was all that now stood between Banks's helpless column and Polignac's approaching Rebels. Declaring that they must stop the Confederates "at all hazards," he ordered his men to fix bayonets.[37]

In one of the many ironies of the war, Richard Taylor was no longer intent on the immediate destruction of Banks's force. He was, however, in desperate need of water for his men, and the creek in front of Emory's

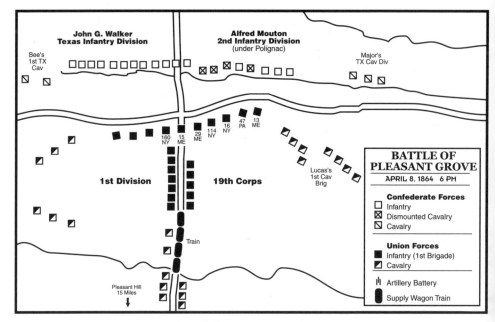

Map by Jeff Kinard and Quentin Cline

line was the only readily available source.[38] At 6:16 P.M., moments after Emory had positioned his men, the first Rebels crashed out of the orchard. Polignac, now commanding Mouton's division, again led the Confederate left. Although "Fatigued and disordered by their long advance through the dense wood," the Rebels came "rushing and yelling as if they had everything their own way." One of Emory's soldiers attributed the Texans' and Louisianans' aggression to their brief dalliance among Lee's wagons: "On they came, flushed with victory and spoils, to which the liquors had not a little bit contributed."[39]

A fierce rendition of "Hail Columbia" by the XIX Corps' band added to the somewhat unreal quality of the ensuing twilight battle. As Polignac's men reached the creek, Brig. Gen. James W. McMillan, commanding Emory's 2nd Brigade on the ridge above, ordered his men to fire. Blazing out in the gloom, their volleys staggered the Confederate line. An officer remembered: "The very air seemed dark and hot with balls, and on every side was heard their dull, crushing sound, as they struck that swaying mass, tearing through flesh, bone, and sinew." Again and again Polignac's determined troops hurled themselves against the stubborn Federals on Chapman Hill. Although the fighting lasted no more than twenty minutes, a Yankee veteran later vowed its intensity rivaled that of Champion's Hill and Shiloh. By the time darkness finally put an end to the bloodletting, the Confederates held the "all-important" stream. They had paid a fearsome price, though, as among their heaps of dead lay "the gallant" and respected Col. James R. Taylor. Only two hours earlier he had, upon Mouton's death and Polignac's assumption of divisional command, relinquished the leadership of the 17th Texas Consolidated to lead the Texas Brigade.[40] Huddled some four hundred yards behind their earlier position, Emory's men could hear the Rebels celebrating their victory down by the creek. At 10:30 P.M., to "the sounds of jollity and mirth" echoing through the pines, General Taylor dispatched another report back to Kirby Smith. He was convinced he had achieved a total and decisive success that day. He later claimed that "Twenty-five hundred prisoners, twenty pieces of artillery, several stands of colors, many thousands of small arms, and two hundred and fifty wagons were the fruits of victory in the battle of Mansfield."[41]

The action, called the Battle of Sabine Crossroads in the North, had indeed been costly for the invaders. Out of Banks's total force of some 12,000 effectives, losses included 113 killed, 581 wounded, and 1,541 missing: a total of 2,235 men. In addition, Federal quartermaster and ordnance officers found their inventories reduced by hundreds of small arms, twenty artillery pieces, nearly one thousand draft animals, and between 156 and 250 wagons.[42] After his initial flush of victory, Taylor reflected on his own considerable losses: "Sitting by my camp fire . . . I was saddened by recollection of the many dead, and the pleasure of victory was turned to grief as I counted the fearful cost at which it had been won. Of the Louisianans fallen, most were acquaintances, many had been neighbors and friends; and they were gone. Above all, the death of gallant Mouton affected me. . . . I thought of his wife and children, and of his father."[43]

Two-thirds of the Confederate losses—about 1,000 men out of a total of 8,800 troops on the field—were from the 2nd Infantry Division. After Mouton's death in the first minutes of the attack, Polignac had personally led its Louisianans and Texans into the thickest fighting. His own Texas Brigade, which had entered the battle "scarcely stronger than a good regiment," had suffered staggering losses. A letter home by Pvt. A. L. Neems of Polignac's 34th Texas Regiment to his wife and parents reveals the human cost among the close-knit north Texans: "I have sad news to write you . . . of the death of our friend and brother James N. Carr. He was shot dead on the battlefield last Friday. He was shot in the breast. Wm. Butler was killed. George Buster was killed. Wm. Thornton was slightly wounded in the thigh, Wm. Short mortally wounded, Wilber Hill, slightly wounded, Thomas Taylor, slightly wounded all, of Co E Alexanders regiment."[44] Persistent if not talented, Banks still held on to his scheme to take Shreveport. Taylor had stopped him at Mansfield but, by rejoining Porter and Brig. Gen. Thomas Kilby Smith's detachment of the XVII Corps at the Red River, the Federal commander believed he could salvage his expedition. Under cover of darkness Banks quietly evacuated Pleasant Grove for Pleasant Hill, some fourteen miles to his rear.[45]

Declaring, "The safety of our country depends upon it," Taylor spent a sleepless night of April 8–9 preparing Banks's destruction. At dawn he accompanied Tom Green in his pursuit of the Federal rear guard. Trudging a few miles behind came Brig. Gen. Thomas Churchill's newly arrived division followed by Walker's with Polignac's bringing up the rear. The road and surrounding countryside bore ample evidence of the destruction inherent in war.[46] Few farmhouses had escaped pillaging and burning during the Yankee advance. Their former occupants, mainly women and children, now looked on, hollow-eyed, as their own army passed by. The road itself was filled with the detritus of earlier panic—weapons, equipment, clothing, burning wagons, and the dead. A Texan riding in the rear with Polignac's and Walker's troops described the march to Pleasant Hill: "through the battlefield [Mansfield], where the dead are lying as they were killed. The infirmary corps are not yet done taking up the wounded. The slain horses and men are to be seen every where, over an area of at least nine square miles. Hundreds of negroes and straggling soldiers are plundering the battle field—robbing the pockets of the dead. Here a dead negro in the road, in Yankee Uniform, over whom a hundred waggons [sic] have rolled. He is mangled until he has scarcely any resemblance of the human shape. Meet time and again with quantities of prisoners going up who have been taken this morning. We have taken in these fights, a great number of the Zouave troops, so peculiar in their dress."[47]

Their face-to-face confrontations with some fugitives from Banks's army sparked mixed reactions among the relatively provincial Texans. Many evidenced disgust that they had been fighting ex-slaves in the form of Col. William H. Dickey's 1,500-man Corps d'Afrique. Nearly all of Walker's and Polignac's troops reacted with wonder, which quickly gave way to hilarity, at the sight of the exotically garbed New York Zouaves. The New Yorkers' blue vests, bright red fezzes, and scarlet bloomers—which to the western Confederates looked suspiciously like ladies' undergarments—contrasted sharply with their own array of gray and butternut rags scattered with bits of captured blue uniforms. One Texan remembered his friends' mock derision as they "threw down their guns and de-clared that if they were to fight any more women they would go home."⁴⁸

A resort before the war, Pleasant Hill sat on a picturesque, square-mile plateau along the Mansfield and Fort Jessup Roads. With a popula-tion of about two hundred, the village included a Methodist church, post office, hotel, three storehouses, a school for girls, and the Pearce Payne Methodist College for boys. Arriving at the town's outskirts around nine o'clock, Taylor was somewhat surprised to find the Federals forming a line of battle.⁴⁹ Taylor suspected that the infantry before him was merely masking Banks's main movement—his retreat to the river. The South-ern commander could not, in any case, test the Federals' true intentions without his infantry. When Churchill finally arrived around noon, he found the general waiting on a pine log, absently whittling a stick. De-spite Bee's reconnaissance reports indicating the Federals were prepar-ing formidable positions, Taylor was determined to attack. As Taylor put it later, he "did not wish to lose the advantage of the *morale* gained by success on the previous day." By keeping Banks off-balance he believed "the Federal forces would be widely separated, and might be destroyed in detail." Yet Taylor had not counted on human frailty. Polignac's and Walker's men had fought a pitched battle the previous day, and Chur-chill's soldiers had marched forty-five miles in thirty-six hours. Reluc-tantly, Taylor allowed his troops, now totaling some 13,500 men, two hours' rest before opening the engagement to be known as the Battle of Pleasant Hill.⁵⁰ Taylor carefully studied the Federal lines extending "across the open plateau, from College Hill on their left to a wooded height on the right of the road to Mansfield." Below the main battle lines and batteries on the plateau he spotted their forward skirmishers de-ployed along a dry gully "bordered by a thick growth of young pines, with fallen timber interspersed." Separating the Confederate positions from their enemy was a deadly "open field, several hundred yards wide near the road, but diminishing in width toward the west." "The Federal commander," Taylor wrote, "had concentrated some eighteen thousand, including A. J. Smith's force, not engaged on the previous day."⁵¹

At 3:00 P.M., disregarding his opponent's superior position and num-bers (he had actually overestimated their strength by five thousand men), Taylor set his attack in motion. Pinning his strategy on Churchill's rela-tively fresh troops, Taylor ordered two divisions southward in a flanking maneuver. Within an hour and a half Churchill's brigades, led by Brig. Gens. James C. Tappan and Mosby M. Parsons, stood in line of battle across the Sabine Road.⁵² Taylor's plan was the essence of conventional military thinking. It called for Churchill's troops to launch a decisive

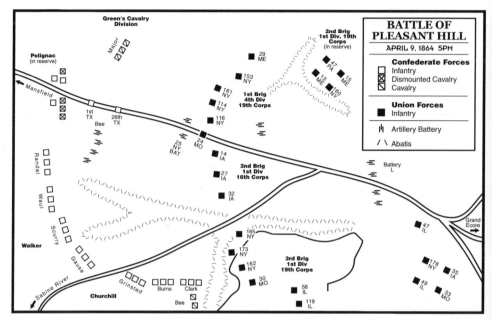

Map by Jeff Kinard and Quentin Cline

attack on the Union southern flank, rolling it in upon itself. As the enemy line collapsed, Walker was then to throw his division against Banks's center while Bee's cavalry disrupted Federal attempts to regroup. Polignac's survivors, who had borne the worst of the Friday fighting, were allowed to rest as reserves on the Confederate far left.[53]

The tranquility of the beautiful spring afternoon was shattered at 4:30 P.M. Moving his twelve guns to within seven hundred yards of the Union center, Maj. Joseph Brent ordered his gunners to pull their lanyards. Soon after, with "a most hideous yell," recalled a Yankee officer, "such as Texans and Border ruffians alone can give," the entire Confederate line surged forward. As they closed with the bayonet and saber, the Federal line erupted in a terrific volley. A Northern newspaperman reported: "The death-signal was sounded. Words can not describe the awful effect of this discharge. Seven thousand rifles and several batteries of artillery, each gun loaded to the muzzle with grape and cannister, were fired simultaneously, and the whole centre of the rebel line was crushed down as a field of ripe wheat through which a tornado had passed . . . hurried to eternity or frightfully mangled by this one discharge."[54] After over an hour of such desperate and costly fighting, Taylor feared the worst. Although Churchill was making headway on his far right, Confederate assaults on the Union center had made little progress. As Walker's brigade commanders struggled to maintain their momentum, Taylor ordered up Polignac's division.[55]

Polignac again formed his line between Green's dismounted cavalry under Brig. Gen. James Major and Walker's left brigade under Col. Horace Randal. It was the Frenchman's defining moment. Standing erect in his stirrups, Polignac brandished his sword toward the Federal positions and roared: "My boys, follow your Polignac!" The 2nd Division surged forward, the Louisianans mingling their new battle cry, "Mouton!" with the Texans' Rebel yell.[56] Ahead, Col. William T. Shaw steadied his 2nd Brigade of Brig. Gen. A. J. Smith's 3rd Division of the XVI Corps. Rooted behind a splintered fence, Shaw's tough Iowans and Missourians had broken every previous assault Taylor had thrown against the position. In volley after volley they had littered the field before them with the grim testimony to their determination. Now Polignac's troops swept past the bloodied heaps of gray and butternut to wreak their own vengeance. Engulfed in a suffocating pall of smoke so dense "that the sun was entirely obscured," the Rebel and Yankee lines merged in savage hand-to-hand fighting.[57]

As Shaw's brigade grudgingly gave way before Polignac's, Walker's, and Green's combined onslaught, the Federal left collapsed. Sweeping aside all opposition "as if it were chaff," Churchill's men captured a Federal battery and dozens of prisoners. As Polignac later correctly observed, however, Tappan and Parsons "followed the enemy with more courage than discretion up to the edge of [Pleasant Hill]." Just as it seemed the battle was won, a tremendous volley ripped through the Southern ranks. Moments later a second blue line burst from the woods, halting the Confederate advance and pushing it back upon itself. The Federal counterattack crushed Taylor's critical flanking movement and with it his hopes of a second victory. Pressed steadily by veteran regiments of A. J. Smith's division, Churchill's men fought stubbornly but at last fell back into the pines. Never without an opinion, Polignac later that night assessed their failure: "As they moved too quickly, they could not be properly supported by Walker's division & lost the artillery they had captured and some of their own."[58]

Not yet aware of the potential disaster unfolding on his right, Taylor continued to press the Union center. But unforeseen factors—largely of Taylor's making—now began to dictate the battle. As he had done the day before, the Confederate commander began his attack late in the day —Polignac recorded that his own division was not called up until shortly after 5:00 P.M. Moreover, his men were reaching the end of their considerable endurance. Their two-hour respite could hardly have erased the effects of days of continuous marching, fighting, and lack of sleep. Roiling amidst the lengthening twilight shadows, the intense fighting in the center grew increasingly chaotic. As the light failed, Taylor called off his assault.[59]

Notwithstanding his troops' profound exhaustion and the fading light, Polignac faulted a fellow general for the Confederate failure to break Banks's line. That evening after the fighting he wrote: "A great deal of confusion prevailed during the whole fight . . . owing to the want of judgment of Maj [sic] Gen [Thomas] Green, who was intoxicated & caused our troops to fire at one another." Although Green's condition may have slightly contributed to Taylor's ultimate decision to call off the assault, it was by no means a critical factor. Writing in his own diary not far away, Felix Pierre Poché offered a more balanced overview of the battle's last moments: "Due to the thickness of the forest and the approaching night a part of our troops[,] particularly Mouton's [Gray's] and Polignac's Brigade[s] at one end of the line and Scurry's Brigade and Churchill's Division to the right, did not recognize one another and exchanged shots for quite a while but fortunately without much damage." The problem of firing upon one's own was not confined to Southern troops. Poché took some consolation in observing that the "Yankees fought boldly among themselves" as well.[60]

There was little of the dramatic to close the Battle of Pleasant Hill. There were no decisive rushes followed by pulse-quickening pursuits of a panicked foe. There was only exhaustion. For a while, shadows exchanged ineffectual flashes in the dark. Soon they too abandoned the woods to the dead and wounded, who moaned and cried in pain and isolation. No one felt the disappointment of the day's outcome more deeply than Richard Taylor. A scant four hours earlier he had been certain that his small army would repeat its success at Mansfield. Now, standing amidst the wreckage of that army, he tended to its survivors. Most of his men had long since emptied their canteens and were suffering the effects of dehydration. He therefore ordered the bulk of his force back to the stream for which they had paid so dearly the previous evening. To cover their withdrawal and medical parties administering to the wounded, he posted Bee's cavalry brigade on the battlefield. Finally, as he later recorded, "worn out by fatigue and loss of sleep, I threw myself on the ground, within two hundred yards of the battlefield, and sought rest."[61]

Around 10:00 that night a very agitated Edmund Kirby Smith roused Taylor from a deep sleep. The lieutenant general had been in the saddle since 2:00 that morning when he had received Taylor's Mansfield report.

Passing Taylor's columns heading for the stream convinced him that, as he later attested, "Our repulse at Pleasant Hill was so complete and our command so disorganized that had Banks followed up his success vigorously he would have met but feeble opposition to his advance on Shreveport." Kirby Smith immediately assumed overall command of Taylor's forces and, as a precaution, ordered Polignac to remain on the battlefield in support of Bee. His fears, however, were eventually laid to rest as stragglers from the front brought in reports that Banks had resumed his retreat. The Union general thus, as Kirby Smith came to realize, "convert[ed] a victory which he might have claimed into a defeat."[62]

Although incomplete in that Taylor failed to annihilate Banks's force, Mansfield and Pleasant Hill rank among the decisive Southern victories of the Trans-Mississippi. Taylor, in somewhat less than six hours of intense fighting, succeeded in reversing the Union's plans to subdue western Louisiana and invade Texas. In that sense the combination of Federal blunders and Confederate audacity contributed as much in prolonging the Confederacy as any number of the more heralded eastern battles. Both sides suffered heavy casualties during the two days' fighting. Federal records added the 152 killed, 859 wounded, and 495 captured at Pleasant Hill to the losses of the previous day. Taylor estimated his total losses for both engagements at 2,200.[63]

Simple statistics often gloss over the reality of war. A shaken Felix Pierre Poché's account of the morning of Sunday, April 10, is more revealing:

I took a walk over the field of the Battle of Pleasant Hill and we saw great numbers of dead, dying and wounded. The field presented a very dismal and sorry spectacle with its dead[,] the greater number of whom were mutilated, some without heads, the faces of other[s] completely mangled, others again had their legs crushed, their feet torn away, one in particular[,] a Confederate[,] had had his right side torn away by a bullet, his ribs crushed and turned inside out, leaving his entrails exposed to view and one could see the flies crawling all over them. A wounded Yankee had his teeth driven in, his jaw crushed by a bullet which had lodged in his neck. With his face swollen as large as a pumpkin, unable to speak, he was truly a terrible sight. Many of the wounded had fallen in lonely and secluded spots, had not as yet been found or given any help, and were suffering a veritable martyrdom. It appeared that there had been a regular butchery of horses as the field was covered with the corpses of those poor animals, innocent victims of the civil war, who were brought here in spite of themselves only to be left here for their bones to whiten.[64]

As commander of the only reasonably intact force left on the field, Polignac had little time to ponder the tragedies of war. He had again proven his value to himself and the Confederacy, and soon he would reap the rewards of his efforts. In the meantime the French general would hold together the nucleus of the Confederate Army in northern Louisiana.

CHAPTER 9

"Twelve Hundred Muskets"

April 10, 1864–June 8, 1864

———•✦•———

ew of its principals found total satisfaction in the decidedly peculiar aftermath of the Battle of Pleasant Hill. Both Banks and
Taylor had committed grievous errors yet neither fully exploited
the other's blunders. The Federal retreat to Grand Ecore on the
Cane River, however, effectively nullified the success at Pleasant Hill.
Maj. Gen. Nathaniel P. Banks thus converted the two days' costly fighting from a Union tactical success to a Confederate strategic victory. It
also cost him the confidence of his subordinate generals as well as his
troops. While Brig. Gen. A. J. Smith briefly entertained the notion of
deposing his commander in favor of Maj. Gen. William B. Franklin his
men mocked their politician-general as "Napoleon P. Banks."[1] For his
part, Maj. Gen. Richard Taylor's victory and subsequent rewards—the
adulation of his troops and the Southern press as well as promotion to
lieutenant general, recommended by Lt. Gen. Edmund Kirby Smith—
rang maddeningly hollow. Taylor's success failed to sway Kirby Smith
from his conviction that his greatest threat came from Arkansas. In a
decision that would spark a lifetime of mutual acrimony, Kirby Smith
therefore ordered Taylor north to Shreveport. There he would hold
his troops in readiness to counter Maj. Gen. Frederick Steele's long-
expected attack. Taylor was convinced that his superior had robbed him
of the opportunity to finish the work begun at Mansfield. He nevertheless consoled himself by dispatching Brig. Gen. Thomas Green's cavalry
after Banks to monitor his movements and harass his rear guard. The
popular Green's death while engaging Federal gunboats at Blair's Landing on April 12 added the tinge of grief to Taylor's frustration. It was in
the blackest of moods that he arrived in Shreveport with Walker's, Churchill's, and Parson's divisions—the bulk of his command.[2]

Only Polignac's division, "reduced to some twelve hundred muskets"
according to Taylor, remained behind to harass Banks. On April 13 its

somewhat incredulous commander jotted in his diary: "I have been promoted to the rank of Maj[or] General, to fill the vacancy occasioned
by poor G[eneral] Mouton's death, who was not commissioned a Ma-
j[or] Gen[eral] though he command[ed] a Division. Yesterday Gen[eral]
Green was killed—he was since a short time a Maj[or] General. Thus
owing to these two untimely deaths, I have had a most extraordinary
preferment, as on the 8th I was the 6th or 7th Brig[adier] Gen[eral] in
this army, of which I am now the 3d Major General."[3] Polignac had little
time to ponder the fortunes of war. His new division, consisting of Mouton's legacy of Louisiana troops and his own Texans, was now barely
larger than a full-strength regiment. Both brigades had suffered heavily
in the recent fighting. Of his original Texas Brigade, the 17th Texas Consolidated Cavalry (dismounted) had lost 23 killed and 45 wounded; the
34th Texas Cavalry (dismounted), 7 killed, 58 wounded; The 22nd Texas
Cavalry (dismounted), 4 killed, 30 wounded; the 31st Texas Cavalry (dismounted), 3 killed, 25 wounded, and 1 missing; and the 15th Texas Infantry, 2 killed and 14 wounded. In all, the already under-strength brigade had suffered a total of 213 casualties.[4]

On Sunday, April 10, Polignac marched his battered division back to
its camps above Mansfield for rest and reorganization. As they passed
through the village that would lend the April 9 battle its Southern name,
one Texan noted, "the whole town . . . is a hospital." Confederate medical personnel had converted every available space, both public and private, into makeshift wards and operating rooms. A Louisianan grimly
observed: "What a pitiful sight were those hospitals crowded with the
wounded, the dying and the dead, friends and enemies side by side, some
calling for help, others groaning in pain that I left with a heavy heart."
The same soldier also further remarked, "on the other hand the sight
of the ladies who rushed on all sides bringing food and comfort to the
suffering of their country was a spectacle upon which the patriotic eye
feasted."[5] Mansfield had presented the Confederacy with two more aristocratic martyrs to the Southern cause. Many soldiers stopped to pay
homage to the bodies of Brig. Gen. Alfred Mouton and Col. Leopold
Armant as they lay in state. Felix Pierre Poché remembered, "The two
creole leaders were laid beside each other and were buried side by side."[6]

On the twelfth, quartermasters issued some of the spoils from the
abandoned Federal supply train to Polignac's grateful troops. Shining
new belts, cartridge boxes, canteens, and other accoutrements added a
touch of uniformity to the otherwise ragged infantrymen. Satisfied that
his troops were rested, fed, and reequipped, Polignac ordered a general
review of the division.[7] The Frenchman had proven himself to his Tex-

ans. In an effort to win over Mouton's Louisianans, he now astutely praised their beloved former general. Modestly crediting the Creole's leadership with the victory at Mansfield, he lauded Mouton's "energy which insured the success of the onslaught." He invited his men to join his own grief in mourning the loss of the hero who "fell while facing the foe and urging our troops to victory." Polignac's speech displayed his new mastery in the art of effectively commanding Southern soldiers, a combination of selfless personal leadership and unabashed flattery: "Thanks to your valor and untiring energy, the host that had invaded the country and was moving up spreading devastation . . . has been repulsed and is now in full retreat. . . . On the 8th of April, you made . . . a charge worthy of an army of veterans . . . which shows that numerical strength must give way to a well settled determination of a just cause."[8]

Casualties and other factors necessitated extensive reorganization of Polignac's command. Col. Joseph W. Speight, who had led the initial resistance to Polignac's assignment to the Texas Brigade, officially resigned on April 15. Few regretted his departure. Recently promoted Col. James Harrison of the 15th Texas temporarily assumed command of the Texas Brigade. He was replaced, however, much to both Harrison's and his men's disappointment, by newly appointed Brig. Gen. W. H. King of Walker's division. Although a competent officer, King was unable to assume command as a result of wounds suffered at Mansfield, and the position later devolved upon Col. Robert D. Stone of the 22nd Texas.[9]

Taylor still entertained hopes of cutting off Banks's now entrenched 25,000 troops at Grand Ecore. The Red River itself seemed to cooperate with his designs, dropping to an unusually low level and temporarily stranding Porter's fleet upriver. Harassed by a mere three thousand Rebel cavalrymen, both Banks and Porter pondered the specter of the total defeat of their separated commands. If the river conditions continued to deteriorate, the admiral stood the risk of having to destroy his own fleet—to abandon it to the Rebels was unthinkable. In that case Banks would be denied the by now obvious advantages of the ships' guns and transportation capabilities. For his part Porter needed Banks's land forces to protect his sailors as they struggled to free their repeatedly grounded vessels. For a while, however, Banks seemed paralyzed with indecision, convinced that he faced numbers equal or superior to his own.[10]

The arrival of Polignac's division at Grand Ecore on April 16 raised the combined Confederate strength in the area to approximately 4,500 to 5,000 effectives. With characteristic efficiency Polignac assumed command of the combined force and prepared for future action. As the general recorded, he "sent an officer to Blair's [L]anding with some men to establish a line of couriers from that place with a view to communicating with [Brig.] G[en.] [St. John R.] Liddell. Ordered scouts to be sent to Red River . . . moved the regiments on pickets on the lower Natchitoches road forward to the fork of the Alexandria Rd. which I ordered to be strictly watched—pushed our outposts into town—at dusk occupied the town with a company. Sent a scout to St. Maurice on the Red River below Natchitoches." Although facing odds of five-to-one, Polignac could congratulate himself that he had effectively hemmed in the mighty Red River expedition.[11]

Polignac still faced the all too familiar problem of Confederate commanders in the Trans-Mississippi Theater: he simply did not have enough men to counter his far more numerous Federal forces effectively. At Grand Ecore, however, Polignac realized that he held a psychological advantage over Banks and his dispirited army. He credited his ability to hold them in check to the "effect of defeat & the extent of the demoralization it may spread into an army."[12] Taylor, whose services in Arkansas Kirby Smith had curtly deemed unnecessary, arrived at Grand Ecore on the twenty-first. Accompanying Taylor was the accomplished cavalryman Maj. Gen. John A. Wharton, who had been assigned to replace "the lamented Green." The generals soon realized that they faced an impossible task. Having dispatched a cavalry detachment of "about 2200 strong . . . to operate in the Cane River valley & on [the] Red River against the gun-boats," Polignac had of necessity reduced his force by half. The remainder of his troops were holding various outposts between Natchitoches and Grand Ecore, where he maintained "a very small force . . . to keep up appearances." Mere appearances could not hold even Banks indefinitely. On the twentieth the Federals moved toward Natchitoches and, upon securing the town, opened an escape route south toward Alexandria. By the end of the next day, they had abandoned Grand Ecore, leaving little more than their empty trenches and a few smoking ruins.[13]

The Federals continued their destruction as they marched south to Cloutierville, thirty-two miles away. After preparing two days' rations, the Confederates followed on the twenty-second. Close on Banks's heels, Polignac was dismayed that the Federals were "burning the plantations as they went, the private dwellings, the cotton, the corn, etc." He felt, however, that such depredations "plainly indicated that they had given up their former faith in their ability to subdue the South . . . and were taking a wanton revenge . . . upon the non-combattants [sic]." In typically melodramatic fashion, Polignac interpreted the Federals' actions as indicative of "the frantic madness of despair."[14] In truth, Banks was barely managing to maintain the distinction between a controlled retreat and outright rout. Marching along the east bank of the Cane River, his column was, in effect, trapped between it and the Red River. By crossing his troops at Monett's Ferry, four miles south of Cloutierville, Banks hoped eventually to gain the safety of Alexandria. In the meantime Wharton's cavalry pressed relentlessly on his rear, claiming numerous casualties and prisoners. Reports of more Rebel troops converging around the crucial river crossing added a noticeable sense of urgency to the Federal flight.[15]

Richard Taylor had ordered Brig. Gen. Hamilton P. Bee ahead with 1,600 cavalry and four batteries to hold the ferry. As Taylor observed, the brigadier had a formidable force and, "after several days to examine and prepare his ground, might well be expected to hold it with tenacity." Polignac's infantry and newly arrived Brig. Gen. William Steele's seven-hundred-man Texas cavalry brigade would then close and assault Banks's rear. Taylor was convinced he held the advantage: "If Bee stood firm at Monetts' we were in position to make Banks unhappy on the morrow, separated as he was from the fleet, on which he relied to aid his demoralized forces."[16] "But Bee," as Taylor later grumbled, "gave way on the afternoon of the 23d, permitting his strong position to be forced at the small cost to the enemy of less than four hundred men, and suffering no loss himself." Although Bee's fifty casualties may have taken issue with Taylor's assessment, Bee had blundered badly. Guided by a cooperative slave, a number of Federal regiments waded across the river two miles above the ferry. Their subsequent flanking attack on Bee's left in conjunction with a cavalry feint to his right prompted him to order a retreat. In his report, Taylor lamented that had Bee held out "a few hours longer, even the small force under my command must have compelled the surrender of Banks's Army." After thoroughly upbraiding his hapless yet admittedly inexperienced subordinate, a furious Taylor ordered him to Alexandria.[17]

Arriving too late to participate in the action, Polignac's division camped at the ferry on April 25. While his men enjoyed some much-needed rest, Polignac received word that one of Porter's gunboats had run aground nearby on the Red River. Losing no time, at two the next morning he ordered Col. James Harrison, the trusted commander of the 15th Texas, to march his regiment upriver to attack the hapless vessel. After marching all night—a distance of some eighteen miles—Harrison discovered that Polignac's information had been "totally incorrect." Instead of finding a single helpless gunboat, he picked out in the gathering light of dawn "three Iron clads, two Transports fitted up with guns, and one Transport with Sharpshooters." Not one to be put off by trivial details, Harrison ushered his men "noiselessly through the thick woods and under growth to within one hundred yards of the Bank." Finding the Federals "wooding on the oposite Bank and plundering a Resedince," Harrison cautioned his men to hold their fire until his signal—the report of his "six shooter." At 9:00 A.M., Harrison reported:

> I selected a Big portly Captain sitting in a Big arm chair. When my pistol fired he tumbled out of his seat like a Turtle off a log, and through the hatch he went. My whole line opened at once. Such consternation I never saw. It was fully ten minutes before Th[e]y could arrange themselves to fight, but when they did by going above and below us and in front, the shells and missles came like a hail storm. The whole Earth shook. Timber and Bushes were litterly torn to pieces. I made my men fire and fall flat on the ground and Load and shoot deliberately. We did them great damage, in killed and wounded, during the Engagement. The Best Boat, a Large Ironclad Monster in turning to give us a Brode side grounded so fast she could not get off, and we would not let her have help. She blew up, Shaking the Earth, and scattering her large timbers in some instances for two hundred yards on the Bank. She Burned, another in going off got aground and was fired and Burned, the woodend ones were litterly riddled by our Balls.[18]

Losing only one killed, five wounded, and two missing, Harrison, whose fighting abilities far outweighed his spelling skills, had forced Porter to destroy his most formidable ironclad. The U.S.S. *Eastport* had become hopelessly snagged as the Red River's water level steadily dropped. Unable to free the vessel and under Harrison's spirited attack, the admiral decided at least to deny its use to the Rebels. He therefore ordered the *Eastport*'s Lt. Cmdr. S. Ledyard Phelps to destroy his ship. The massive explosion of three thousand pounds of gunpowder placed below decks very nearly claimed both Porter and Phelps as they made their escapes in small boats. Still under a hail of musketry, Porter steamed on with his remaining three tinclads and two transports for Alexandria.[19]

But Polignac had developed a taste for Union river craft. He ordered Lt. Col. John H. Caudle of the 34th Texas to set up another ambush near the mouth of the Cane River. At about six in the evening, fifteen miles below the site of Harrison's attack, the crew of Porter's flagship, the *Cricket*, spotted activity on the right bank. Moments later the tinclad opened fire with her bow guns. The four guns of Capt. Florian O. Cornay's St. Mary's Cannoneers immediately replied with a devastatingly accurate fire. As Cornay's gunners rapidly registered hits on Porter's hapless fleet, Caudle's two hundred marksmen picked off any exposed crewmen.[20] The interiors of Porter's boats were crammed with the crews of previously lost vessels and contrabands—slaves the Federals had seized in raids on riverside plantations. Although the tinclads' thin plating could deflect musketry, it was useless against artillery, and the unprotected transports were vulnerable to both types of fire. As Polignac's troops intensified their firing, bedlam broke out below decks in the Federal fleet. On board the *Cricket*, Porter himself barely escaped injury or death from "the pelting shower of shot and shell" that Polignac's men hurled at the vessel. The admiral later remembered "every shot going through and through us, clearing all our decks in a moment." It was, he claimed, "the heaviest fire I ever witnessed."[21]

The ordeal of the *Cricket* was a mere prelude to the hell that soon erupted within the transport *Champion No. 3*. Just as the *Cricket* steamed out of the Confederates' range, a twelve-pound shot slammed through the transport's boiler. Trapped within the claustrophobic lower decks, a hundred contrabands were scalded to death as a boiling cloud of steam exploded from the shattered engine room. Although a few of the casualties were sailors, the vast majority were innocent victims of war—men, women, and children. Richard Taylor later blamed the Federals for the pointless deaths: "the loss of life on the transport was fearful. One hundred dead and eighty-seven severely scalded, most of whom subsequently died, were brought on shore. These unfortunate creatures were negroes. . . . The object of the Federals was to remove negroes from their owners; but for the lives of these poor people they cared nothing, or, assuredly, they would not have forced them, on an unprotected river steamer, to pass riflemen and artillery."[22] Cornay's and Caudle's men next turned their attention to the *Champion No. 5* and the *Juliet*. The two transports were lashed together, but Confederate artillery fire quickly crippled the *Juliet*, which began to drift out of control. Despite considerable confusion, the *Champion No. 5* managed to tow the helpless *Juliet* safely back upstream. With the *Juliet*, *Champion No. 5*, and *Fort Hindman*, now under Phelps, above the battery and the *Cricket* below, Porter waited until the next day to try and continue his escape.[23]

The next morning the *Fort Hindman*, with the *Juliet* in tow and followed by the *Champion No. 5*, again tried to run the gantlet. Cornay and his gunners were waiting. They quickly reduced the *Juliet*'s superstructure to splinters and much of her machinery to scrap iron. Another well-aimed shell carried away much of the *Fort Hindman*'s steering mechanism. Although unsteerable, both vessels miraculously drifted downstream to safety. The *Champion No. 5* was not as lucky. Remarkably rapid and accurate Confederate fire quickly disabled the transport, forcing her crew to beach her on the opposite bank. Caudle's men subsequently captured a number of Union sailors, including the *Champion*'s pilot, as they attempted to escape.[24] At Monett's Ferry Polignac personally interrogated the pilot. The man was talkative, offering details of the Federal ships' capabilities as well as Porter's dispositions. The information also satisfied Polignac that his tiny force had wreaked significant damage on the Mississippi Squadron. His men had destroyed two valuable transports and the mighty *Eastport* had been reduced to debris, which littered the banks and bottom of the Red River.[25] Polignac's own losses had been remarkably light in comparison. The second engagement claimed only two additional Confederate casualties—a wounded rifleman and gallant but unlucky Captain Cornay, who was killed at his guns. Ironically, the greatest tribute to the captain's contribution in the action was unintentionally penned by Porter himself. Cornay's four-gun field battery had performed so efficiently that the admiral officially reported that he had faced at least eighteen heavy guns.[26]

The last of the battered Union fleet limped into sight of Banks's entrenched army at Alexandria on April 28. To Porter's dismay he could go no farther. The river over the rapids above town had dropped over six feet since his fleet had passed a month earlier. The water rushing over the rocky bottom of the falls now measured a scant three feet, four inches; Porter needed a minimum of seven feet of water to float the heaviest of his ten gunboats and dozens of transports safely past the barrier. Fearing that the demoralized Banks might withdraw—abandoning his two-million-dollar fleet to the enemy—the admiral fumed at the absurdity of his situation.[27]

Fifteen miles away the architect of much of Porter's dilemma was on the march. Having faced and humbled some of the most technologically advanced warships to that point in history, Polignac and his tiny division now hurried south. As Taylor's only infantry, they were a key factor in his new plan to trap the Federals in Alexandria. Taylor's scheme called for his new cavalry commander, Maj. Gen. John A. Wharton, to divide his troopers into three detachments. Polignac's division would then stand ready to support Wharton as needed. The odds were nevertheless preposterous—Taylor now faced Banks's recently reinforced army of over thirty thousand with less than five thousand.[28] Yet Taylor was determined to play the role of David. He divided Wharton's horse into three detachments, as he later wrote, "each a thousand strong, and accompanied by artillery. The first, under [Brig. Gen. William] Steele, held the river and Rapides roads, above and west of Alexandria; the second, under [Brig. Gen. Arthur P.] Bagby, the Boeuf road to the south of that place; while

[Brig. Gen. James P.] Major, with the third, was sent to Davide's Ferry, on the river, twenty-five miles below. Polignac's infantry, twelve hundred muskets, was posted on the [Bayou] Boeuf within supporting distance of the two last."[29]

Despite his mounting disdain for Kirby Smith, Taylor still clung to the hope his superior would return Walker's division. He was confident that the Texans' additional manpower would enable him to finish the job begun at Mansfield. In the meantime he employed a number of devices designed to keep the Federals both immobile and miserable. Such ruses as frequent drumrolls, bugle calls, and the constant clatter of wagons driven back and forth just out of sight convinced many Yankees that they faced hordes of Rebels. Polignac and the cavalry commanders were charged with removing or destroying any livestock or other useful supplies within reach of the enemy.[30] His division spent the first week of May in a constant series of marches and skirmishes in the vicinity of Alexandria. Overall, the Confederate strategy was remarkably successful. Polignac's artillery continued to harass Union river traffic while his infantry repeatedly held their own against numerically superior ground forces. While work crews salvaged a number of cannons from the wrecked gunboats upstream, Major's cavalry continued to make gunpoint acquisitions of Federal property downriver. The troopers captured or sank several Union transports below Alexandria, gathering tons of supplies, scores of prisoners, and effectively blocking the river. On May 9, Polignac's troops surprised a Union force near the river, "capturing some of the enemy's tents, horses, & even their breakfasts."[31]

However, on May 13 a burly, thirty-eight-year-old former Wisconsin lumberman accomplished the impossible for the Federals. Lt. Col. Joseph Bailey, acting chief engineer of the XIX Corps, finished his dam. Overcoming Porter's initial derision and a near-disaster on the eighth, Bailey's work details completed a series of obstructions across the 758-foot-wide rapids. The improvised dam succeeded in raising the river level sufficiently to allow Porter's fleet to escape through a 150-foot chute in its center. The following day Banks's army evacuated Alexandria. Behind them the town erupted in flames as A. J. Smith's men, known as his "gorillas," gleefully applied the torch.[32] The outraged Confederates followed. On May 14 Polignac's division marched six miles from their camp at Marksville to Bayou de Glaize. The next afternoon they prepared to delay the Federal retreat at Mansura, overlooking the beautiful Avoyelles Prairie. Col. James E. Harrison, commanding the 15th Texas, described the meadow as "about seven miles long (Through which the Road ran) by one [and] a half miles wide, at the Lower end of which in a small ravine, and among some scattered timber the little Viliage of Mansura is nestled."[33]

Taylor formed his line of battle before dawn on May 16. Bagby and Major assembled their troopers on the Confederate right while Polignac's division and some cavalry formed the left. Thirty-two artillery pieces added weight to their position. Soon line upon line of blue-coated infantry emerged from the trees on the far side of the grassland. "All was quit and still as death," Colonel Harrison recorded, "excep the passing to and fro of officers giving orders. On the dark lines press[ed] until within 1000 yds, open prairy, when all at once as if the heavens had been rent asunder thirty two pieces of our artilary opened them, Throwing them into confution. They retired But soon advanced with their entire force 30,000 Strong. With Their artilary in front. Our little divission stood before them like a stone wall for two hours. The scene was grand and sublime beyond description. Language becomes poor when I attemt a description."[34] Nearly all present agreed that the engagement at Mansura presented a most impressive martial spectacle. Although actually numbering only some ten thousand troops at the beginning of the action, the Federal Army would still have appeared grand to the outnumbered Confederates. The wide Avoyelles Prairie allowed both armies, regimental flags snapping, to deploy in parade ground precision. And yet it was happily a relatively bloodless battle. The Confederate artillery, nearly doubled in strength from guns captured in earlier actions, opened fire at 6:00 A.M. Union gunners returned their fire and for almost four hours they maintained a largely ineffectual long-range artillery duel.[35]

At about ten o'clock Polignac observed Union reinforcements arriving on his front. The fresh troops from the XVI Corps brought Federal strength up to some eighteen thousand men. Both Taylor and Polignac realized the futility of making a determined stand against such overwhelming odds. As the opposing batteries banged away at one another, Polignac ordered his men to fall back. Joining Taylor's withdrawal toward the village of Evergreen, Polignac was pleased with his men's performance: "Our retreat began in good order all along the line. The enemy as soon as we had retired into the woods, marched off by the left & took the road to Simmsport [sic] at a 'doublequick'!"[36] That evening Polignac rested his troops four miles from Mansura along Bayou Rouge. An additional ten-mile march on the seventeenth brought the division to within nine miles of Norwood's Plantation. Ahead, Banks continued on to Simmesport, by then a war-devastated village on the Atchafalaya

River. There, Union engineers, again under Lieutenant Colonel Bailey, struggled to complete an improvised pontoon bridge—Banks's escape route—across the river. On the eighteenth, determined to buy time for the work crews, A. J. Smith ordered Brig. Gen. Joseph A. Mower back to stall Taylor's approaching forces.[37]

Leading three infantry brigades and one of cavalry, Mower retraced the Federals' course over Yellow Bayou. As his cavalry skirmishers fell back before Mower's advance, Taylor called up Polignac's infantry and Wharton's cavalry. Polignac marched his division the nine miles from their camps and arrived at Norwood's Plantation early in the afternoon. Wharton's dismounted cavalry took their positions on the Confederate right while Polignac's units again formed the left.[38] Two brigades of cavalry and some eight to ten artillery pieces were already engaged with Mower's well-positioned troops when Polignac arrived. Brig. Gen. James P. Major's cavalry opened the assault from the Confederate left, sweeping aside the Federal cavalry on his front. Polignac's division, to Major's right, then surged forward in a wild charge. Mower's infantry and artillery waited for the Rebels to emerge from the willows and scrub brush before opening a staggering fire of musketry and lethal double-shot canister. Reeling from the shock, the survivors broke for the rear as Union infantry rushed forward with the bayonet. Having dealt with Polignac's troops, Mower next turned his batteries on Major's troopers with similar results. Polignac, however, soon reformed his regiments, bringing up the 18th Louisiana from reserve. As the Louisianans arrived to the cheers of the Texans, the Rebel artillery renewed its "deadly fire [on the Federals] and immediately put them to flight."[39]

Polignac next formed his lines in a large field broken by numerous ditches and gullies. Former acting commander of the Texas Brigade, Col. James E. Harrison, now leading the 15th Texas, described the next murderous assault:

> We had the advantage of a large ditch with others to fall Back on. We remained here, for half an hour, our artillery, just in front shelling. . . . When Genl Wharton ordered our line forward, we formed in another ditch two hundred yds in front of our first position, still a good one. . . . We advanced to the Edge of the field, the fence having been burned away. He[re] we were halted, in ten paces of a wall of thick undergrowth. . . . [Skirmishers] had not advanced more than sixty steps before they were in ten feet of the 16th Army Corps, rising up in four lines and demanding their surrender. Some of them escaped and got Back, when the four

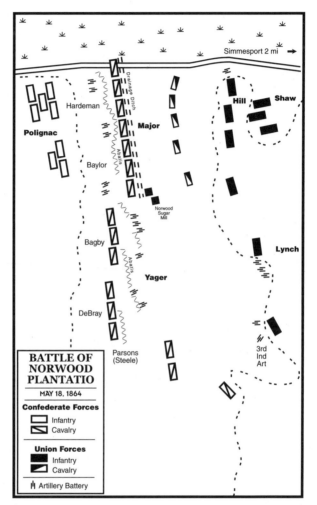

Map by Jeff Kinard and Quentin Cline

lines were precipitated upon us, and the fight became desperate. I . . . was engaging four lines to my front at a distance of 25 and 30 paces, Thy constantly demanding my surrender. I replied with Enfield Rifles, holding them steady. [We] cut down their flag Bearers twice, [but] Thy were promptly raised, and the demand repeated surrender you damned Rebels or we'l kill you all. . . . I fell Back, to the ditch alluded to and opened fire on [the Union] advance forcing them Back to the Bushes, and then met our reserve with the artilary when thy were driven Back entirely and we held the field.[40]

A seesaw battle of Confederate attacks and Union counterattacks, the fighting at Norwood's Plantation raged four hours under a blazing sun. Owing to Wharton's seniority, Polignac chafed in his role as subordinate field commander. Typically, he found fault with the cavalryman's leadership. Wharton's haphazard troop deployment, as Polignac alleged in his diary, could very well have led to a Confederate disaster: "My division was sent for & the enemy having stopped advancing, Gen[eral] Wh[arton] moved to attack him. But . . . he massed his troops on the right, while the strength of the enemy was opposing our left, which was the wing to be strengthened as it covered our line of retreat."[41]

For many soldiers the battle consisted of small but fierce encounters in the dense thickets and gullies along the bayou. Smoldering wadding from the intense rifle and artillery fire added to the chaos as it ignited the dry underbrush. The flames' heat and choking clouds of smoke soon made it impossible for even the most determined warriors to continue fighting. One sergeant from the 32nd Iowa remembered that following "volley after volley at close and deadly range, . . . the 'wily Prince of France,' Polignac, certainly felt that he had spent life enough." At last Taylor gave up his costly attacks. The Confederates withdrew under the covering fire of the St. Mary's Cannoneers and Polignac's infantry.[42] An officer in Polignac's Louisiana Brigade recalled the last moments of the battle: "Meanwhile nightfall was approaching and our troops having been in action for more than 3 hours and harrassed [*sic*] by fatigue were quietly withdrawn from the field. The enemy's artillery was then placed in position and exchanged a few shots with ours, but this last duel lasted but a few minutes, and peace at last reigned over the bloody field of carnage. . . . Our poor soldiers dead with fatigue and blinded with dust were marched to the camp on Bayou Black water [L'eau Noir] four or five miles from the battlefield."[43]

The Battle of Norwood's Plantation, called Yellow Bayou in the North, involved only some 5,000 Confederates against Mower's 4,500-man detachment. Yet Taylor's insistence in pushing the offensive against Mower's well-positioned troops cost him dearly—608 casualties to Mower's 350. The Texas Brigade alone suffered 208 of the Confederate total loss. Acting brigade commander Col. Robert Stone, slain while reporting to General Wharton, was among the thirteen officers killed or wounded during the action. Col. James E. Harrison, who had noted Stone's lack of leadership during the fight, afterward resumed command of the Texas Brigade. The wounded were carried to a nearby plantation where field hospitals had been set up in the slave cabins. One officer commented on their lot: "Those unfortunates suffer greatly in the heat, and are truly bothered by the flies and other insects."[44]

And Banks completed his escape; Mower's stand at Norwood's Plantation allowed Bailey the time he needed to complete his bridge. By dusk on May 20, the entire Red River Expedition had crossed the Atchafalaya over the bridge and by ferry. The Federals were at last safe, but they had failed in their objective. Richard Taylor assessed the Red River Campaign's final battle: "We held the field, on which the enemy left his dead, but our loss was heavy. . . . Polignac, in charge of division, was conspicuous in this action. The following day, May 19, 1864, the enemy crossed the Atchafalaya and was beyond our reach. Here, at the place where it had opened more than two months before, the campaign closed."[45] Although arguably less eloquent than their commander, Taylor's troops offered their own opinions of Banks's expedition. Their new marching song celebrated their success and mocked the invaders' predilection for confiscating valuable Louisiana cotton:

> But Taylor and Smith with ragged ranks,
>> For Bales For Bales;
> But Taylor and Smith with ragged ranks,
>> For Bales, Says I;
> But Taylor and Smith with ragged ranks,
>> Burned up the cotton and whipped Old Banks,
>> And we'll all drink stone blind,
> Johnny fill up the bowl.[46]

Richard Taylor would have found bitter irony in the song's lyrics. If anything, he passionately believed he had ejected Banks in spite of Kirby Smith's opposition. In his memoirs Taylor damned his superior's "sheer stupidity and pig-headed obstinacy" for not supporting his efforts to destroy Banks and in allowing his escape. Kirby Smith's focus on Arkansas, in Taylor's view, directly contributed to the Confederacy's downfall. "From first to last," charged Taylor, "General Kirby Smith seemed determined to throw a protecting shield around the Federal army and fleet."[47] For all his railings against his commander, Taylor had only praise for his subordinate generals and their soldiers: "the divisions of Walker and Polignac had held every position intrusted to them, carried every position in their front, and displayed a consistency and valor worthy of the Guards at Inkermann or Lee's veterans in the Wilderness!" Although inflicting no decisive defeats upon the invaders, Taylor's men indeed deserved the highest praise. During the sixty-seven day Red River Campaign, they repeatedly faced and defeated superior numbers of superbly equipped opponents. The Confederates' total losses in Louisiana of approximately 4,275 men were proportionally much larger than the Federals' 5,412. Taylor's firm and typically Rebel belief in aggressive assaults accounted for much of the disparity in casualties. At Mansfield, Pleasant Hill, and Norwood's Plantation, Polignac's division made repeated bayonet charges against strongly held Federal positions. His losses were predictable.[48]

Federal matériel that the Confederates destroyed or captured added to the sting of Banks's defeat. In addition to thousands of small arms, their ammunition, and various types of accoutrements, the expedition lost some 3,700 government-owned cavalry and draft animals and 822 wagons. Union reports did not include the significant losses of civilian-contracted animals and transportation. Including naval guns from Porter's fleet, the Federals also lost fifty-seven artillery pieces, many put to good use by their captors. As a further humiliation, Taylor's forces, with Polignac playing a significant role, claimed nine Union rivercraft. The army lost the *Woodford*, a hospital vessel, as well as the transports *Emma*, *City Belle*, and *John Warner*. Porter's losses included the two transports *Champion No. 3* and *Champion No. 5* as well as the tinclads *Signal* and *Covington* and the ironclad *Eastport*.[49] His dismal performance during the campaign also cost Banks his command. Looking "dejected and worn, and . . . hooted at by his men . . . ," the politician-turned-failed-general returned to New Orleans and surrendered his department to Maj. Gen. Edward R. S. Canby. Ironically, Kirby Smith temporarily assigned Banks's nemesis a similar if not as universally applauded fate. On June 10, no longer able to ignore Taylor's incessant criticism and insubordination, Kirby Smith relieved him of duty and ordered his arrest. Taylor had, however, been lionized by the Confederate press and Congress for his successes during the campaign. Later that summer he returned to duty east of the Mississippi as a newly promoted lieutenant general.[50]

Polignac emerged from the campaign as an undisputed Confederate hero. He had proven to his men not only his concern for their welfare but his bravery as well. In charge after charge he had led from the front exhibiting little concern for his personal safety. Under his guidance they shed their reputation as misfits to become the backbone of the Confederate Army in Louisiana. On June 1, while in camp by Alligator Lake near Yellow Bayou, the officers of the Texas Brigade presented Polignac with a field horse. In a carefully prepared speech, Col. James E. Harrison, commanding the brigade, spoke for his fellow officers. The horse was, he declared to the general, "a slight testimonial of our confidence in you as an officer, and our esteem for you as a gentleman." Polignac accepted the mount, graciously dubbing him "Texas," with heartfelt gratitude and an impromptu speech matching Harrison's oration in eloquence. His days of being jeered as a polecat must have seemed remote indeed.[51]

Life along the bayous eventually drifted into a routine of marches interspersed with boredom and drill. May's drought gave way in June to almost daily downpours, thickening the air with humidity and swarms of mosquitoes. The Louisiana Brigade was camped "on Lake William, the water of which is of a green color, filled with small animal life, and which is not fit to use for washing." The "physical disorder" of "Camp Eggling," as the Louisianans called it, with its "horrible smell," mud, mosquitoes, and heat, quickly fostered an ugly mood among its inhabitants. One of Gen. Henry Gray's officers railed at his surroundings and army life in general: "We are still in the same abominable camp on Lake William, and moreover the surgeons responsible for making inquiries about the condition of the camp reported to Gen[eral] Polignac, that the troops, having dug wells, had water in abundance, without having to use that from the Lake, and we will now be kept in this atrocious camp until the fine day arrives when we cross the Atchafalaya."[52]

The monotony was briefly interrupted on June 8, when three Union gunboats shelled Simmesport. A two-gun battery attempted to fend off the raiders, but during the fierce artillery exchange one of the Rebel cannons exploded. The battery commander called for support from the nearby Crescent Regiment. The Crescent's commander, Capt. W. C. C. Claiborne, Jr., however, refused to risk his men in what he considered a pointless venture. A sympathetic fellow Louisianan explained: "The only way to save the pieces was for the regiment to charge across the field, but Capt[ain] Claiborne knowing that it would cost him many men decided not to risk any more lives, knowing that the cannon was not worth fifty or sixty men, who would inevitably be killed. The Yankees had one or two men disembark who tied a rope around the cannon, pulled it aboard the boat, and left rejoicing in their good fortune."[53] The loss of the gun, a valuable Parrott rifle, sparked something of a rift between Polignac and his Louisianans. Responding to the battery commander's complaint that "although he called for help, the soldiers of the Crescent Reg[iment] refused to advance to his assistance," Polignac ordered Claiborne's arrest. The officers of Claiborne's brigade sided with their fellow Louisianan in the matter, one writing: "Public opinion favors Claiborne, and Gen[eral Henry] Gray in particular does not like the severity of Gen[eral] Polignac's punishment of Claiborne." To Polignac the affair was a minor disciplinary problem not even worthy of mention in his diary. Again bored with the routine of camp life and marching, the general had found other diversions. During the rest of the summer, he would devote his spare moments to his "Transatlantic Letters to an Englishman," his self-described "long contemplated pamphlet upon the doctrine of Non Intervention." [54]

CHAPTER 10

"Lafayette of the South"

Oh gone is the soul from his wondrous dark eye,
And gone is her life's dearest glory.
The tales of fond lovers unheeded pass by,
Her heart hears a single sad story;
How her gallant young hero fell asleep and will never
Awake from his dream by the banks of the Red River.

The melancholy lyrics of "On the Banks of the Red River" expressed the dark mood of Polignac's men during the summer of 1864. The surviving victors of the Red River Campaign now found themselves in endless, seemingly pointless movements across north-central Louisiana. While Lt. Gen. Edmund Kirby Smith fretted over his next move in Shreveport and Lt. Gen. Richard Taylor fumed, Polignac's troops marched. On June 9 they marched from Mansura to Marksville, arriving on June 11. On July 4 they left Marksville for Pineville, reaching that village above Alexandria two days later before recrossing the Red River on the seventh and continuing to McNutts Hill. By the seventeenth they were tented at "Camp Boggs" on Beaver Creek.[1]

On July 22 Gen. Braxton Bragg, acting independently from Columbus, Georgia, as Pres. Jefferson Davis's chief military advisor, issued Kirby Smith new orders. Bragg, who had not yet heard of Taylor's dismissal, urged "that the President orders a prompt movement of Lieutenant-General Taylor and the infantry of his corps to cross the Mississippi. Such other infantry as can be spared by General Smith will be followed as soon as possible. General Taylor on reaching this side of the Mississippi will assume command of the department." Under increasing Union pressure, Confederate commanders east of the Mississippi were desperate for reinforcements. Taylor and his veterans seemed the most obvious source of manpower. Having driven Banks from the Red River

Valley, Bragg now wanted Taylor, with Walker's and Polignac's divisions, to counter Union advances toward Atlanta or Mobile.[2]

In response to the new directive, Polignac's division again took to the road. Retracing many of their earlier routes, they recrossed the Red River to Pineville, marched to the vicinity of Trinity on the Black River, and returned to Harrisonburg on the seventh. At Harrisonburg Polignac's Texans reunited with Gray's Louisianans and Walker's Texas Division. While Taylor attempted to find means to cross the Mississippi, Polignac's troops dug trenches and grumbled.[3] Morale plummeted as Polignac's men contemplated crossing the river. Their sacrifices in Louisiana had seemed perfectly justified: they had defended their homes and families against the foreign invaders. But to cross the Mississippi would take them into territory to them as alien as the moon. The men would no longer be fighting for a tangible goal, but the abstract concept of the Confederacy. Many found no logic in fighting for a government in faraway Richmond—a government that had shown little interest in their own welfare. Moreover, the vast expanse of the river would create an almost insurmountable barrier between the soldiers and their loved ones. One Texan expressed the sentiments many of his comrades were feeling: "As for my part I take crossing in mine although it is a bitter pill. . . . I cant believe the present suffering of the soldiers will last long. This Hell roaring war cant exist long . . . it is rather cool for a man to leave his home exposed to the enemy an[d] go to protect one that is all reddy over run though I cant tell what is best neither do I give a darn blew button." Few, at least in their writings, seemed to notice the irony that their general's home and family lay half a continent and an ocean away.[4]

In August, desertions began in earnest among Polignac's Texans. Richard Taylor recognized a number of reasons for their exodus, including the "non-payment of the troops for a period of twelve months," the absence of a "very large proportion of the field officers," and "recent changes which had taken place in the commanders on the division and brigade levels." On August 17 one of Henry Gray's officers noted: "I understand that the troops generally do not like the idea of crossing and the Texans in particular are violently opposed and it is feared that these cads will give us trouble." Two days later the Texans confirmed the officer's fears: "We learn today that because of our contemplated move, the infamous Texans have deserted in great numbers yesterday and last night. Two hundred out of Walker's Division returned of the four hundred that had deserted and one hundred thirty-five deserters of the Texas [Polignac's] Brigade in our Division."[5] The dense, humid heat of the late Louisiana summer added to the soldiers' misery. Polignac attributed his own renewed bouts of malaria to the almost tropical conditions: "Another attack of fever came suddenly upon me about 8 P.M. The Louisiana climate is beginning to tell on me. This is my second summer in this state which is said to be the most trying. The weather has been hotter than last year. For the past few days it has been quite sultry, with a warm breeze blowing by gusts 'simmoun or sirocco' like."[6]

By the end of August, both Kirby Smith and Taylor recognized the futility of trying to force Texans across the Mississippi. Even if they could evade the numerous Federal gunboats patrolling the river—a doubtful proposition—they would have too few troops to make any difference in the East. News of the impending fall of both Atlanta and Mobile provided the final argument to retain the troops west of the river. Polignac's and Walker's divisions, now commanded by a harsh disciplinarian, Maj. Gen. John H. Forney, could be, Kirby Smith decided, better used in Arkansas. He therefore ordered them north as reinforcements for the state's new district commander, Maj. Gen. John B. Magruder.[7] Again on the move, Polignac's division reached the Boeuf River on August 31. They camped two days by the river while their pontooneers constructed a ninety-yard-long, ten-boat bridge. Passing through Columbia on the Ouachita River, they next moved to Monroe, camping north of the town on September 5. Fever, despite the availability of quinine, continued to plague both the soldiers and their general, and water was scarce along their route. On September 4 Polignac noted the misery of his troops as they trudged along the sandy road: "The weather for a week past exceedingly warm, unusually so for this season causing many men to faint under the scorching rays of the sun, while on march." Himself weakened by the heat, Polignac suffered another recurrence of malaria on the sixth.[8]

Throughout the desertions continued. Polignac was often relatively lenient with repentant soldiers but, according to common practice, court-martials meted out harsh penalties to ringleaders and habitual offenders. On Friday, September 9, Polignac recorded the fate of one such unfortunate from the 34th Texas Cavalry with a professional detachment: "This morning at 6½, a man belonging to this division was shot for desertion. His brigade was drawn arms for the execution on three sides of a square. The culprit was placed on the fourth side, the 12 men appointed for the execution in front of him; the field and Staff [officers] of the Brigade in the center of the square. A suitable number of guards were placed along the sides, to prevent crowding. The most perfect order prevailed."[9]

On the evening of Sunday, September 11, Polignac received orders directing his and Forney's divisions to Monticello, Arkansas. They set out at dawn on the thirteenth. Marching along Bayou Bartholomew, Polignac's troops passed through Bastrop and camped above Knox's Ferry, crossing the bayou "on a foot bridge hastily put up by the Engineer Corps" on the fifteenth. The weather cooled somewhat as the division marched by Berlin, Arkansas, on the sixteenth and then on to Hamburg and on again to Flat Creek, where they pitched their tents on the seventeenth. The next day they camped about three miles south of Monticello, Surgeon David Wallace of the 15th Texas Infantry finding their new environs "as poor as poverty to begin with, foraged upon by a large body of troops, quartered here for a month, the prospect for something to sustain man and beast do not look promising. We are getting very poor rations for ourselves, our animals worse. We are getting ten ears of corn per day for our horses. This, as well as the meal we eat, has to be transported sixty miles. From present indications, if a campaign is attempted here, our saddle horses will starve before spring." Indeed, Magruder planned to move soon. On the evening of the eighteenth, the district commander sent for Polignac, Wharton, and Parsons to confer "on the practability of a campaign." "Nothing of importance" was decided upon according to Polignac, who turned his attention to setting his division in order. For the next week little disturbed the routine of camp life save another bout of malaria and the delivery of a letter from E, postmarked and dated London, June 3, 1864.[10]

Dubbed "Prince John" for his predilection for tailored uniforms and lavish display, Magruder quickly lived up to his reputation. On Monday, October 26, he ordered a grand review of his newly acquired legions. To the stirring strains of "Dixie" and "Hail to the Chief," carriage loads of local belles thrilled to the sight of Prince John, resplendent in ostrich-plumed hat, galloping "like a comet" past his massed troops. They may have been somewhat less impressed by a parade four days earlier described by Felix Pierre Poché: "By Gen[eral] Polignac's order our Brigade passed in review led by Gen[eral] Gray. Feeling indisposed I obtained permission from the Gen[eral] not to participate in the review. But I learned that our Regiments were not very distinguished by their dress as three men were not completely clothed and were without their shirts. They were placed under arrest."[11]

For all his martial splendor, Magruder failed to impress Polignac with his generalship. A meeting with his brother "noble" the day after the celebrated review prompted Polignac to observe: "Was called to a Council of War at Gen[eral] Magruder's H[ead] Q[uarters] this morning at 9 o'clock, which lasted untill [*sic*] nearly 4 P.M. & convinced me, if conviction was needed, of the uselessness of Councils of War."[12] In truth, Magruder was a bit bewildered as to his next move. His first inclination was to use his infantry to screen Maj. Gen. Sterling Price's weary and "totally demoralized" raiding expedition then returning from Missouri. Federal activity, however, in the vicinities of Little Rock and Fort Smith, Arkansas, next seemed to invite a countering maneuver toward the northwest. On Friday, September 30, Magruder called for Polignac. The district commander, as he recorded, now "anticipate[d] a raid of [Maj. Gen. Frederick] Steele on a larger scale into Texas." As a countermeasure Magruder ordered Polignac to move his division to Camden by way of Warren, Arkansas.[13] The miserable six-day march to Camden took the division through the dense woods and swamps of southern Arkansas. "Wet and weary" from earlier torrential rains, the men splashed along mud trails made "slippery & very boggy in some places" by a steady rain. The waterlogged troops arrived at Camden on the October 6 only to be put to work the next day scraping out trenches around the town. Polignac next moved the division on the eighth to "Camp Bragg" near Washington, where he hoped to set up a more permanent camp.[14]

The 2nd Division, however, amid the mud and squalor of Camp Bragg, was on the brink of collapse. Endless marches; shortages of food, clothing, tents, and blankets; and the resulting fevers and other maladies had taken their toll. Sickness, desertions, and casualties had reduced the division's strength to only 1,132 privates with predictable effects on their morale. On October 9, his command in near open revolt, their general vented his rage and frustration in his diary: "'Odi profanus vulgus et arceo!!' Oh that Horace had been with an army [of] volunteers & had known their constant complaints, recriminations, petitions, suggestions, desertions, & had heard their yelling. How it suggests to the mind the [aborigine (?)]!!! To say that in this wide world the vast majority of human creatures live purely a material life without an ennobling thought, solely bent upon the gratification of instincts, differing very little from those of animals!! O! monstrous, monstrous!!!" One could hardly say that his mood had improved by the next day, his only diary entry being, "O (retrospectively)."[15]

Although disgusted with his troops' brutish behavior, Polignac could not long ignore the simple truth that the men had endured the unendurable. With winter approaching, few could survive without the food and supplies hoarded by Kirby Smith's bureaucrats at Shreveport. Despite his own recurrences of fever and depression, Polignac concluded that only direct action could pry such bare necessities from the quartermaster and commissary officers. On the twelfth he informed some of his troops, the

Creoles of the 18th Louisiana, in French that he would personally inter-
cede on their behalf.[16] Having suffered another bout of fever and chills
en route, Polignac arrived in Shreveport at 8:00 A.M. on Sunday the sixteenth. For the next few days he "rummaged in the different D[epart-
ments]," as he put it, "looking to the relief of my poor naked soldiers."
He was particularly galled by the sleek rear-echelon officers in the capital of "Kirby Smithdom." During his "search of favors & indulgencies,"
he noted, "that a *right* has to be purchased like a favor"—an observation
Richard Taylor would most certainly have seconded.[17]

Yet Polignac's charm and considerable negotiating skills stood him
in good stead in Shreveport. "A long interview" and dinners with Kirby
Smith helped procure much of what he sought. Louisiana's newly elected
governor, Henry W. Allen, "promised," as Polignac recounted, "to supply my troops with a quantity of clothing sufficient to make up for any
deficiency which might still exist after drawing from the clothing bureau."[18] On Saturday, October 22, he attended "a congratulatory dinner"
in his honor. He was escorted to the home of a Mr. J. A. Sigur, "a refugee
from lower Louisiana," where he was met on the front steps by Governor Allen. After a short speech Allen, "in state and with a great display of
ceremony," descended the steps and presented Polignac with a sword.
Polignac thanked the gentlemen with a prepared speech before being
escorted into the house. His hosts then treated him to a dinner "which
might have been called almost sumptous in good times & which, under
the circumstances exceeded every body's expectations." Then, "After
dinner," the guest of honor recorded, "toasts as usual: The President
of the Confederate States, Gen[eral] Beauregard, Gen[eral] Lee & myself were successively toasted." Life among the gentry of the Trans-
Mississippi indeed had certain advantages.[19]

Polignac remained in Shreveport until October 27 attending to unfinished business and making social calls. His journey back to Camden
was uneventful, although he was amused by one of his hosts along the
way: "Stopped at . . . Mr. Allen's house. The way in which our host went
the religious practice of saying 'graces,' ought not to be unrecorded. At
supper, when all the guests had taken their seats, he very abruptly deliv-
ers himself in one breath, of the forcible tho' simple prayer: 'Thank God
for supper!' after which he fell to without more ceremony. Breakfast in-
troduces no change in his religious habits, than the substitution of the
word 'breakfast' for supper. The same for dinner."[20]

The weather turned cold and rainy soon after Polignac's return to
Camden on October 31. Consequently, he spent much of his time in his
tent attending to administrative duties. On November 1 the Texas Bri-

gade bade farewell to its popular commander, Col. James E. Harrison. Harrison, having assumed command of the brigade after Polignac's promotion, was again replaced by Brig. Gen. W. H. King. Polignac joined with Kirby Smith and other officers in requesting Harrison's promotion to brigadier general and return to his brigade. Harrison left for Richmond with letters from Polignac and others addressed to various members of Congress, the War Department, and President Davis urging his advancement and reassignment to command.[21] While confined to his tent, Polignac spent much of his time writing letters and reading. He was particularly pleased with a new acquisition—the recently published journal of the English traveler, Lt. Col. Arthur Fremantle of the Cold Stream Guards. Fremantle's descriptions of the idiosyncrasies and humor of the Rebel troops he had encountered delighted the Frenchman, who found many parallels to his own experience.[22]

On November 4, after spending the day inspecting the various camps of his division, Polignac sought a bit of diversion by attending "a dancing party at the Court House at which General Officers & their staff were alone invited." Although impressed with the town's feminine residents, especially a Miss Helen Goddard, "the prettiest of the party," the general was somewhat taken aback by the other guests' seeming lack of propriety: "[I] Was invited to 'take a drink' & I complied out of courtesy, tho' not the least naturally inclined that way. Upon which I was led . . . out of the Court House, to a house across the square. The door was opened with precaution & we found ourselves in a dark passage. One of the party stooped & took up a bottle from behind the door, which he handed to me to drink out of! So much for ceremony.[23] Camden's citizenry insisted on maintaining a semblance of normalcy despite the exigencies of wartime. Although strong spirits had become a rare commodity so far from Shreveport, its social set made do without the previously indispensable staple. Polignac, who had taken an immediate interest in Miss Goddard, took every opportunity to join in the town's social activities. On November 7 he "Made several calls in the evening. Met a band of music in town that was going about a serenading. It is customary with the officers of the army to take the . . . 'serenade' in the shape of several national airs. In good times the serenaded parties responded with copious libations of whiskey; but now that this national wine has become a rarity those entertainments exhibit a more sedate character. The Confederate 'Euterpe' has to defray alone the expenses of the feast & retires out of breath, vainly sighing for the unfaithful american 'Bacchus.'"[24]

On the thirteenth Polignac "took leave of Helen Goddard." At eight o'clock the next morning he marched his division out of Camden; their destination was Walnut Hill near the Red River. The vicinity, Magruder had decided, would offer better opportunities for forage than the by now stripped countryside around Camden. Their four-day march carried the division over miserable roads churned into a muddy soup by frequent rains and wagon wheels. It was new territory for Polignac, and along the route he indulged his curiosity concerning its inhabitants.[25] Some, such as a Mr. Roberts who lived near Magnolia, seemed like the familiar Southern farmers Polignac had encountered on previous travels: "This old gentleman is from North Carolina & like most of the natives of that State of his class he is primitive in his manners, frank, open, hospitable."[26]

The division arrived at Walnut Hill on the nineteenth. Polignac discovered that his destination was "not a town, nor even a village—this name merely designates a house at which there is a post office." In any case, before his troops could begin establishing a more permanent camp, Polignac learned that Kirby Smith had countermanded Magruder. On the twenty-first he and Maj. Gen. John H. Forney, commanding Walker's former division, received new orders to march to Minden, Louisiana. Fifty miles away, Minden, the department commander had now decided, offered more accessible supplies and would make the division more readily available if needed. The six-day march took the two divisions through Rocky Mount, across Bayou Bodcau at Strange's Ferry and, despite a collapsed bridge, over the Dorcheat River.[27] Spirits ran high as they marched through Minden on the twenty-sixth. Polignac noted, "The neighborhood of Minden is said to be abundant in provisions & is looked upon by the soldiers as the land of milk and honey." For their part the town's residents greeted the soldiers as heroes. "As I entered the town at the head of my Division," Polignac recorded, "a lady sent me a bouquet with a slip of paper fastened to it, bearing the superscription—'All honour to General de Polignac, our gallant defender.'"[28] Two days later Minden's "gallant defender" wryly penned: "Today a lady attended by a gentleman drove up in a buggy to my H[eadquarters] & solicited an interview. I walked out to her buggy & learned from her own mouth, that the only object of her call was to gratify her intense desire of seeing a 'life General!' She thanked me most cordially for my politeness & promised to send me butter, vegetables, & home made wine. After she had left I resolved seriously in my mind the propriety of taking 'Barnum' on my staff & the profitable consequences which might result from such a step."[29]

Polignac's troops quickly went to work constructing "Camp Magruder," their new winter quarters three miles east of town. As the camp took shape, other details began repairs on the road linking Minden to

Shreveport. On December 7 the division performed well in a review for the benefit of an inspector sent by departmental headquarters in Shreveport.[30] Yet a mere change of locale could not dispel either Polignac's deepest anxieties or the basic problems plaguing his command. Always wearied by the monotony of camp life, Polignac offered another clue to his own deepening gloom in his November 29 diary entry: "I have for some time past felt that depression of spirits which hitherto has ever preceded some great event, as before the battle of Richmond Ky[.]—the battle of Mansfield etc. etc.—something like the clouds gathering before the lowering storm. Will this time the omen be justified???"[31]

All the while, the desertions continued. On December 2, under a darkening, lightning-streaked sky, Polignac watched as "Three men belonging to the Texas Brigade [15th Texas] were shot for desertion." By the middle of the month the weather turned cold and rainy. Polignac spent much of his time confined indoors, reading, writing, and attending to the mundane administrative chores.[32] As Christmas approached, a renewed wave of camp revivals offered some solace to the lonely, war-wearied soldiers. One Texan noted: "A revival of religion has commenced in camps. All take an interest [in] it. I never saw such a difference in men in my life." Yet the preachers had managed to spread only a thin veneer of reform on many of their new converts. On December 24 Polignac observed: "A concert was given at this place (Minden) the night before last, which I did not attend. As the Methodist Conference has adjourned, the Community is casting off the gloom which had spread over it, & is becoming quite lively. Numbers of females have joined the church—but the officers now hint at dancing parties & the joined young ladies seem perfectly willing to dance themselves out of the church."[33]

Polignac entered the new year of 1865 convinced that he would be of greater use to the Confederacy in a diplomatic rather than military capacity. As he later explained: "Letters which I received about that time having strengthened this opinion, I repaired to Shreveport . . . and suggested to General Kirby Smith the advisability of granting me a six month's leave of absence for the purpose of going abroad and availing myself of the curiosity and interest which the presence of an active participant in the great struggle now going on could not fail to awaken in foreign parts, in order to awaken sympathy to the Southern cause."[34] Kirby Smith was receptive to Polignac's proposal. Although France, like England, had balked at openly supporting the South, in part owing to its slavery system, the commanding general now believed the time was ripe for reopening negotiations. On January 9 he wrote Polignac's old acquaintance, the Confederate diplomat John Slidell, that "our cause has reached a crisis to call for foreign intervention." It would, he thought, be in France's interest to stabilize its position in Mexico "to restore peace and establish firmly the nationality of the Confederate States." To gain French recognition Kirby Smith was also certain that most of the planers in his department would "willingly accept any system of gradual emancipation to insure our independence as a people."[35]

On Monday, January 9, 1865, Polignac departed Shreveport for Europe. He was accompanied by his chief-of-staff, Maj. John C. Moncure, "to give more weight to my presence abroad," as he put it, and Col. Ernest Miltenberger. Miltenberger, Louisiana governor Henry W. Allen's aide-de-camp, carried a personal letter from the governor to Emperor Napoleon III. Neither time nor circumstances allowed for consultation with Richmond. Cut off by the Mississippi, Allen and Kirby Smith worked out the details of Polignac's mission independently and upon their own authority. Miltenberger, carrying Allen's letter, would be the party's official representative with Polignac acting in a liaison capacity.[36]

Before their departure Governor Allen drew Polignac aside. As the general recalled years later, the governor "imparted to me a scheme he was then revolving in his mind. . . . Seeing that the South could not replace its fallen combatants, whereas the North disposed of an ever-increasing army of foreign mercenaries; moreover, that whenever the Federals obtained temporary possession of Southern soil, they kidnapped the negroes and pressed them into military service, Governor Allen's idea was to arm the negroes, and as a consequence to give them their freedom. I remember his very words: 'Of course,' he said, 'We must give them their freedom.'"[37]

Allen obviously intended for Polignac to relate his plan to the emperor, but his letter, carried by Miltenberger, contained the formal proposal. Polignac never read the document, but Miltenberger later related that Allen "referred at length in the most pathetic manner to the strong and sacred ties that bound France and Louisiana. He also stated in very positive language, the imminent danger, in case the Confederate States should succumb, to the French occupation of Mexico and warned him that in such a contingency the immense Federal Army would beyond doubt be turned toward Mexico."[38]

The three men arrived at Marshall, Texas, at about 2:00 P.M. on January 9. They were graciously received by Maj. Gen. Benjamin Huger, who invited them to tea at his home. There they met the Confederate governor-in-exile of Missouri, Thomas C. Reynolds. Reynolds, caught up in the intrigue of the moment, took Polignac somewhat aback. As Polignac recounted, Reynolds conspiratorially "expressed himself upon political matters very categorically & rather imprudently considering his slight acquaintances with me. He must either have a great confidence in me or else not be afraid of assuming responsibilities?!" The next day Reynolds again accosted Polignac, pressing a rather bizarre document into his hand urging him to insist that the emperor "send to the Trans Mississippi Department some agent entirely in his confidence, perfectly *incognito*, but armed with full powers to meet any sudden event."[39]

They were greeted as guests of honor at every stop during their journey south through Texas. Traveling alternately by stagecoach and rail, their route carried them from Marshall, across the Sabine River to Henderson, and then on to Rusk. After a breakfast that featured the luxury of "genuine coffee or 'sure enough' coffee, as it is now generally called," the party moved on to Crockett. After Crockett they ferried the Trinity River, stopped for dinner at Huntsville, and passed through Anderson to Navasoto, where they boarded a train for Houston. From there they continued on through Richmond, Eagle Lake, Victoria, Texana, Lavaca, Goliad, San Patricio, Ranchos, King's Ranch, and Las Animas before arriving at Brownsville on the twenty-second.[40]

Polignac observed with intense interest that their stopping places between San Patricio and Brownsville were "mostly inhabited by Mexican peonens [*sic*].... I learnt that they received from their master six dollars a month, besides a few head of cattle or sheep every year & ration [of] Indian corn. In turn they raise stock (i.e. cattle, horses, sheep[,] etc.) which in Western Texas is a very abundant source of wealth. As their masters manage easily to keep them in debt, they are 'slaves' to all intents & purposes except that they are not provided for in old age."[41] Inclement weather delayed the three ambassadors' departure from Matamoros, Mexico, for approximately two weeks. Polignac, however, thoroughly enjoyed himself, attending a number of dinners, luncheons, and a concert.[42]

On Saturday, January 25, Polignac "Left Matamoros for Bagdad, an extemporised wooden village at the Mouth of the Rio Grande or La Bocca [*sic*] del Rio as it is called in Mexico. I went down in a steamer. As the Rio Grande is very shallow our steamer ran aground several times. Immediately on arriving I went on board of the steamer 'Mexico,' a screw steamship, sailing under the British flag." After waiting two days at anchor, the *Mexico* set sail for Havana, Cuba, arriving on the morning of February 18.[43] Ten days later they set out by steamship for Europe, arriving off Cádiz, Spain, on March 18 "after a stormy passage of at least fourteen days." Polignac was impressed by the city's architecture, but always the connoisseur, he could not resist critiquing the local music: "Another relic of the former Moorish intercourse with the Spanish race, is the national, or rather popular music, which is very monotonous & when sung more nasal than would be expected from an human voice. Men & women croon their old ditties in a drawling quivering tone to which they strum an accompaniment on the guitar with a stereotyped sameness. It reminds one of the national music of the Turks and negroes."[44] From Cádiz the group sailed to Seville, arriving on the evening of the twentieth. Traveling to Madrid "partly by stagecoach," they finally boarded a train for Paris. Upon his return to his native land, Polignac planned to exploit his acquaintance with the Duke de Morny, a close advisor to Napoleon III, to secure an interview with the emperor.[45]

However, "On the last day of our journey," as Polignac later recounted, "in looking over a newspaper, the first news that met my eye was that of the Duke de Morny's death. It seemed like the irony of fate that the fulcrum—so to speak—of my efforts should fail me just as I was reaching my destination." One hope remained. A Major de Vatry of the emperor's military staff offered to use his own influence to secure an interview.[46] Although Polignac attempted to put the best face upon it, the meeting between the small Confederate delegation and the emperor of France proved an uncomfortable affair for both parties. Although "guarded," Napoleon III received them "with the greatest courtesy" and listened attentively to Polignac's fervent defense of states' rights and the progress of the war. Yet Polignac could not ignore that the emperor skillfully manipulated the conversation so that "the political side of the contest was never touched upon." When pressed on the subject, "the Emperor," wrote the defeated petitioner, "made no reply." Colonel Miltenberger then handed Governor Allen's letter to the emperor, who, as Polignac remembered, "without opening it laid it on a table near him. He received us standing and our conversation lasted only a few minutes." Miltenberger recalled: "The Emperor listened attentively . . . [and he] informed us that he had at two different times, endeavored to get England to join France in taking action in behalf of the Confederate States, but without success, and France could not act independently of England. He then kindly said it was too late to take further action." The mission had proved a failure—a last desperate act of a dying nation. Polignac realized that the Confederacy was no more when "The news of General Lee's surrender reached us almost immediately afterward."[47]

Lee's surrender and President Davis's subsequent capture surprised many of those isolated in the remote Trans-Mississippi Department. At about the time of Polignac's departure for France, Kirby Smith began reorganizing and redistributing his forces. As a consequence, many of the troops of Polignac's old Texas Brigade were posted in their home state by mid-May, 1865. A few Confederate units remained defiant for some weeks, but eventually they too conceded the futility of continuing the struggle. Between May 20 and 24, the last of the Texas Brigade remaining with their colors were discharged and returned to their homes.[48]

Writing two years later, Polignac observed: "When I left the country on what I expected to be a six month's absence, I was unaware of the hopeless conditions of the affairs in the east. . . . I was glad in a manner to have been spared the sight of the last days of the Confederacy, altho' if the disaster could have been foreseen, I should not have left the country on a hopeless mission."[49]

In the spring of 1865, Polignac was suddenly a general without an army. Unlike his chief-of-staff John C. Moncure, he was at least in his native country. For his part Moncure was not only a man without a country but also far from his home and family. In April the two friends parted. Polignac, again with his own family and seeing no reason to return to America, chose to stay in Paris, while Moncure began his journey back to Louisiana. As the American waited in London for a steamer to carry him home, the two began what was to become a prolonged dialogue via the transatlantic mails.[50] The surviving letters do not, strictly speaking, reveal merely an extended conversation between separated friends. They do contain a tremendous amount of personal information and expressions of friendship, but as time passed, the nature of the letters subtly changed. Eventually, Polignac's correspondence assumed the nature of informal newsletters, intended to be passed around among his old comrades by his former chief-of-staff. Moncure's observations of the political scene during Reconstruction, in turn, served more and more as raw material for Polignac's pro-Southern propagandizing.

Polignac had begun his journalistic career during the war by publishing commentaries in the European press. In his attempts to sway public opinion in favor of the Confederacy, he astutely avoided the moral pitfalls of the slavery issue, instead concentrating on the question of states' rights. In all his writings he consistently championed the government of the cultivated Southern gentry against that of the Northern "mobocracy." His commitment had been, he asserted, to a "noble & just cause, hallowed by the most sacred rights." The actions of the Radical Republicans during Reconstruction further convinced him of the correctness of his position.[51]

Years after the war, in 1893, Polignac published a lengthy article in the *Nineteenth Century Review* defending "The Constitutional right of secession . . . and the doctrine of states' rights."[52] As for the slavery issue he rather simplistically denounced the North's position as a disingenuous political ploy. "The question of slavery," he declared, "was lugged in and used by the North as a blind to cover the injustice of their policy of coercion. Their logic was a mere piece of sophistry; for nothing can be more obvious than that abstract right of a state to secede."[53]

Polignac spent the five years immediately following the war readjusting to civilian life. He devoted much of his energy while living at his family's estate to his first love, mathematics. In 1870 he was vacationing on the Isle of Wight when he learned that Napoleon III had declared war on Prussia. Polignac immediately returned to Paris and offered his services to his country. The former Confederate general's experience in Louisiana served him well in the defense of his native soil. Polignac's unit was one of the few commands that managed to maintain cohesion and discipline in the face of the Prussian advance. As the French debacle unfolded, he quickly rose from the French Army rank of major to major general, commanding the 1st Brigade, 1st Division of Infantry, XX Army Corps. According to French records Polignac "gained great distinction" and displayed a "splendid calmness during action." However, the otherwise poorly led and trained French forces were no match for the well-organized Prussians. On March 25, 1871, after the fighting ended in French defeat, Polignac bade farewell to his troops and resigned his commission.[54]

A veteran of three wars under two flags, Camille de Polignac, at the age of thirty-nine, at last sheathed his sword. In 1873 he briefly considered P. G. T. Beauregard's proposal to accompany him to Egypt. The Khedive had offered the Creole the post of general-in-chief of his army, and Beauregard in turn offered Polignac the position of chief-of-staff. Beauregard, however, eventually declined the Khedive's offer and the matter was dropped.[55]

Many Confederate notables had remained abroad rather than return to a South under Northern rule. Among the expatriates, Polignac's old friend John Slidell had chosen to remain in Paris with his family. Mathilde, the Slidells' eldest daughter, eventually married Baron Emile Erlanger, an acquaintance of the Polignac family. While visiting the Slidells and their new in-laws, Polignac fell in love with and proposed to one of Erlanger's relatives, Marie Langenberger. They married on February 4, 1874, near Frankfurt, Germany, at Baron Wilhelm Erlanger's estate, Ingleheim. Marie shared her husband's love of music, and the two enjoyed a happy though tragically short marriage. Fourteen months after the wedding, twenty-four-year-old Marie died after giving birth to their daughter, Armande.[56] Although overjoyed with his new daughter,

Polignac was devastated by Marie's death. In 1863 his oldest brother, Alphonse, had died at the age of thirty-seven. The death of two people so close to him coupled with his own recurring headaches contributed to Polignac's near obsession with the health of himself and his family members. For reasons he never revealed to even his closest loved ones, he never again consumed either butter or milk. Two years after his wife's death, Polignac expressed his grief and hope in poetry:

> To My Daughter Age Two
> You who in your sky have
> a past without regrets,
> A present without fear,
> Who have at your table no empty seats,
> No lights turned out,
> Rejoice in the Lord![57]

Camille's second oldest brother, Ludovic, a professional soldier, remained for most of his life attached to the Arab Bureau of Algiers. Only Edmond, the youngest brother, remained in France, becoming Camille's closest friend and confidant. A professionally trained musician and composer, the educated Edmond helped his brother instill in Armande a love of music as well as languages.[58]

On May 5, 1883, fifty-one-year-old Camille de Polignac remarried. Although only eighteen, Margaret Elizabeth Knight had known the Polignac family most of her life. She was English and the couple were wed in Saint George Church, London.[59] Their marriage produced three children: Constance Mabel, born in 1885, Agnes in 1887, and Victor Mansfield—named after his father's most famous battle—in 1899. Shortly after Constance Mabel's birth, Polignac bought Podwein, a sprawling country estate in the Austrian mountains. The Polignacs enjoyed an idyllic life; he would often play his violin while Margaret accompanied on the piano. They also traveled extensively, but Polignac's most consuming passion continued to be mathematics. He joined the Société Mathématique de France and the Société Philomatique de Paris and spent many hours puzzling over complicated equations.[60]

Yet the American Civil War was never far from Polignac's thoughts. On October 6, 1913, surrounded by mementos of his Southern service, Polignac wrote to his friend, Gen. Marcus J. Wright: "As Time moves on, the origin and the purpose of the four-years-conflict . . . ceases to be a mere episode in the private history of a particular people, on a particular spot . . . it expands far beyond the narrow limits of the land upon which so many lives were sacrificed. It is an Object-lesson to the World, and must appeal to all sincere lovers of liberty wherever they may be found. Subsequent events have kept the world alive to the nefarious influence of political and administrative centralization, unless confined within well defined and narrow limits, and it is not unreasonable to expect that the much maligned Southern Cause will be, in future, more justly appreciated from being better understood."[61]

Just weeks later, on November 15, 1913, while working on a mathematical problem at his daughter Mabel's Parisian home, Polignac died of cerebral edema. His family interred his body in the family vault of his first wife, Marie, in Frankfurt, Germany. In 1925 Prince Victor Mansfield de Polignac accompanied his mother, Princess Camille de Polignac, to the dedication of a monument in honor of his father at Mansfield, Louisiana. "The monument," as described by a contemporary reporter, "stands near the center of the Mansfield Battle Field Park, some eighty feet on the other side of the Jefferson Davis Highway. The shaft, of Georgia granite, from Stone Mountain, is fourteen feet high, and above a base of concrete its full height is nineteen feet. On the monument, just above the wreath is inscribed: 'The LaFayette of the South.'"[62]

Union Casualties in the Battle of Richmond, Kentucky

August 30, 1862

———•◦•———

Command	Killed Officers	Killed Men	Wounded Officers	Wounded Men	Captured/ Missing Officers	Captured/ Missing Men	Total
General & Staff Officers	0	0	2	0	3	0	5
12th Indiana Infantry	0	25	6	142	22	586	781
16th Indiana Infantry	1	24	4	116	21	374	540
55th Indiana Infantry	1	10	4	43	4	425	487
66th Indiana Infantry	2	21	5	63	10	506	607
69th Indiana Infantry	1	16	3	108	22	476	626
71st Indiana Infantry	3	26	3	88	23	570	713
6th Kentucky Cavalry Batallion	0	0	0	1	1	61	63
7th Kentucky Cavalry	1	4	0	25	5	233	268
3rd Kentucky Infantry	0	1	1	13	7	66	88
18th Kentucky Infantry	3	36	7	104	7	230	387
Lamphere's Battery (improvised)	0	1	0	3	1	10	15
1st Michigan Light Artillery Battery F	0	6	0	9	0	54	69
95th Ohio Infantry	0	24	6	88	22	526	666
3rd Tennessee Infantry Battalion	0	0	0	0	11	27	38
Total	12	194	41	803	159	4,144	5,353

Total troops involved: 6,500

Source: U.S. War Department, *War of the Rebellion*, vol. 10, pt. 2, p. 909.

Confederate Casualties in the Battle of Richmond, Kentucky

August 30, 1862

———◆———

Army of Kentucky	Killed	Wounded	Missing	Total
2nd Brigade, 3rd Division:				
1st Arkansas Mounted Rifles	8	18	0	26
2nd Arkansas Mounted Rifles	1	10	0	11
4th Arkansas Infantry	6	17	0	23
30th Arkansas Infantry	1	9	0	10
4th Arkansas Infantry Battalion	0	6	0	6
Total	16	60	0	76
1st Brigade, 4th Division:				
154th Senior Tennessee Infantry	4	16	0	20
12th Tennessee Infantry	5	27	0	32
13th Tennessee Infantry	12	35	1	48
47th Tennessee Infantry	8	24	0	32
Total	29	102	1	132
2nd Brigade, 4th Division				
Staff	0	1	0	1
13th Arkansas Infantry	6	23	0	29
15th Arkansas Infantry	2	19	0	21
2nd Tennessee Infantry	17	95	0	112
5th Tennessee Infantry	2	23	0	25
48th Tennessee Infantry	4	42	0	46
Texas Battery	2	4	0	6
Company of Sharpshooters	0	3	0	3
Total	33	210	0	243
Total for Army	78	372	1	451
Total troops involved: 6,850				

Source: U.S. War Department, *War of the Rebellion*, vol. 10, pt. 2, p. 936.

Confederate and Union Losses in the Red River Campaign

March 10–May 22, 1864

—•—

	Confederate	Union
Men:		
Louisiana	4,275	5,412
Arkansas	est. 2,300	est. 2,750
Total	6,575	8,162
Guns:		
net loss	0	57 (including naval guns)
net gain	17–26	0
Wagons:		
gross loss	est. 50	822 (government-owned only)
net gain	est. 600	0
Cavalry mounts and draft animals (gross loss):	est. 700	est. 3,700
Vessels:	3	9 (including 3 gunboats)

Sources: U.S. Navy Department, *Official Records of the Union and Confederate Navies in the War of the Rebellion*, vol. 26, p. 172; Ludwell H. Johnson, *Red River Campaign*, p. 278.

Confederate Order Of Battle

Mansfield, April 8, 1864

———•••———

CONFEDERATE DISTRICT OF WEST LOUISIANA
Maj. Gen. Richard Taylor

1st Texas Infantry Division (Walker's)
Maj. Gen. John G. Walker

1st Brigade
Brig. Gen. Thomas N. Waul
12th Texas Infantry, Col. Overton C. Young
18th Texas Infantry, Col. Wilburn H. King
22nd Texas Infantry, Col. Richard B. Hubbard
13th Texas Cavalry (dismounted), Col. Anderson F. Crawford

2nd Brigade
Col. Horace Randal
11th Texas Infantry, Col. Oran M. Roberts
14th Texas Infantry, Col. Edward C. Clark
6th Texas Cavalry Battalion (dismounted), Lt. Col. Robert S. Gould
28th Texas Cavalry (dismounted), Lt. Col. Eli H. Baxter, Jr.

3rd Brigade
Brig. Gen. William R. Scurry
16th Texas Infantry, Col. George F. Flourney
17th Texas Infantry, Col. Robert T. P. Allen
19th Texas Infantry, Col. Richard W. Waterhouse, Jr.
16th Texas Cavalry (dismounted), Col. William Fitzhugh

French's Artillery Battalion
Maj. T. B. French
Texas 9th Field Artillery Battery (Lamar Artillery, Daniel's
Texas Battery), Capt. James M. Daniel
Haldeman's Texas Battery, Horace Haldeman

2nd Infantry Division (Mouton's) (Polignac's)
Brig. Gen. Alfred Mouton (killed, April 8, 1864),
Brig. Gen. Camille de Polignac

Louisiana Brigade
Col. Henry Gray
Crescent Consolidated Infantry, Col. James H. Beard
18th Consolidated Louisiana Infantry, Col. Leopold L. Armant (killed),
Lt. Col. Joseph Collins
28th Louisiana Infantry, Lt. Col. William Walker

2nd Texas Brigade
Brig. Gen. Camille de Polignac, Col. James R. Taylor (killed),
Col. James Harrison
15th Texas Infantry, Lt. Col. James E. Harrison
17th Texas Consolidated Cavalry (dismounted), Lt. Col. Sebron M. Noble
22nd Texas Cavalry (dismounted), Lt. Col. Robert D. Stone
31st Texas Cavalry (dismounted), Maj. Frederick Malone
34th Texas Cavalry (dismounted), Lt. Col. John H. Caudle

Faries's Artillery Battalion
Maj. Thomas A. Faries
1st Confederate Battery, Capt. E. T. M. Barnes
Bell (La.) Battery, Capt. Thomas Benton
St. Mary (La.) Cannoneers, Capt. Florian J. Cornay

Cavalry Division
Brig. Gen. Thomas Green (killed, April 12, 1864)

Bee's Cavalry Brigade
Brig. Gen. Hamilton P. Bee
26th Texas Cavalry, Col. Xavier B. DeBray

1st Texas Cavalry, Col. Augustus C. Buchel, (Lt. Col. William O. Yager)
Terrell's Texas Cavalry, Col. Alexander W. Terrell

Semmes's Artillery Battalion
Maj. O. J. Semmes

James Major Cavalry Division
Brig. Gen. James P. Major

Bagby Cavalry Brigade
Col. Arthur P. Bagby
7th Texas Cavalry, Lt. Col. Philemon T. Herbert, Jr.
5th Texas Cavalry, Maj. Hugh A. McPhaill
4th Texas Cavalry, Col. William P. Hardeman
13th Texas Cavalry Battalion, Lt. Col. Edward Waller, Jr.

Major's Cavalry Brigade
Col. Walter P. Lane
1st Texas Partisan Rangers, Lt. Col. R. P. Crump
2nd Texas Partisan Rangers, Col. Isham Chisum
2nd Cavalry Regiment, Arizona Brigade, Col. George W. Baylor
3rd Cavalry Regiment, Arizona Brigade, Lt. Col. George T. Madison

Unattached Cavalry
Vincent's Cavalry Brigade
Col. William G. Vincent
2nd Louisiana Cavalry, Col. William G. Vincent
4th Louisiana Cavalry (7th Louisiana Cavalry), Col. Louis Bush

Artillery Reserve Battalion
Maj. Charles W. Squires
West's Arkansas Battery, Capt. H. C. West
Pelican (La.) Battery, Capt. B. F. Winchester

Unattached Artillery
Nettle's Texas Battery
Capt. T. D. Nettles

Texas 12th Field Artillery Battery (Valverde Artillery)
McMahan's Texas Battery, Capt. M. V. McMahan
Texas 2nd Field Artillery Battery
West's Louisiana Battery, Capt. John A. A. West
Louisiana 6th Field Artillery Battery (Grosse Tete Flying Artillery)
Moseley's Texas Battery, Capt. W. G. Moseley

Sources: U.S. War Department, *The War of the Rebellion: A Compilation of the Official Records of the Union and Confederate Armies,* ser. 1, vol. 34, pt. 1, pp. 476–638; Stewart Sifakis, *Compendium of the Confederate Armies: Louisiana,* and *Compendium of the Confederate Armies: Texas;* Arthur W. Bergeron, Jr., *Guide to Louisiana Confederate Military Units, 1861–1865.*

Notes

———◦•◦———

CHAPTER 1

1. "Le Prince de Polignac," obituary translated from *Le Figaro* (Paris), Nov. 19, 1913, in Marcus J. Wright Papers, Southern Historical Collection, University of North Carolina, Chapel Hill.

2. Camille Armand Jules Marie, Prince de Polignac diary, Feb. 1, 1864, (microfilm, Russell Library, Northwestern Louisiana State University, Natchitoches, Louisiana; original diary, letters, and papers are in the Polignac family archives, Paris, France).

3. Ibid.

4. Frederick B. Artz, *France under the Bourbon Restoration*, p. 26; Daniel J. Frankignoul, *Prince Camille de Polignac Major General, C.S.A.*, p. 19; Roy O. Hatton, "A Soldier's Life," pp. 9, 12, 21, 23, 25; Hedwige de Polignac, *Les Polignac*, pp. 161–62, 169, 228, 252; John B. Wolf, *France: 1814–1919*, pp. 66–68.

5. Denise Folliot, *Queen of France*, trans. Andre Castelot, pp. 106–108, 111, 146, 171; Phillip Gibbs, *Men and Women of the French Revolution*, p. 28; Hatton, "Soldier's Life," pp. 3–6.

6. Artz, *Bourbon Restoration*, p. 26; Hatton, "Soldier's Life," pp. 9–10, 12; Polignac, *Les Polignac*, pp. 161–65.

7. Artz, *Bourbon Restoration*, p. 32; Frederick B. Artz, *Reaction and Revolution*, p. 267; Hatton, "Soldier's Life," pp. 12–20; Polignac, *Les Polignac*, pp. 224–26; Wolf, *France: 1814–1919*, pp. 67–68; Gordon Wright, *France in Modern Times*, p. 244.

8. Hatton, "Soldier's Life," p. 20; Polignac, *Les Polignac*, pp. 236–37.

9. Hatton, "Soldier's Life," pp. 21–22; Polignac, *Les Polignac*, pp. 228, 239–40, 252.

10. Denys Cochin, "Strategie," *Le Figaro* (Paris), Aug. 31, 1920; Hatton, "Soldier's Life," pp. 23–24.

11. Hatton, "Soldier's Life," pp. 26–29; Polignac, *Les Polignac*, pp. 247–48.

12. Hatton, "Soldier's Life," pp. 29–33; "Major General Prince Camille de Polignac, C.S.A.," *United Daughters of the Confederacy Magazine* 20 (Jan., 1957): p. 14.

13. Hatton, "Soldier's Life," p. 33; French Military Discharge, Feb. 15, 1859, C. A. J. M. Polignac Letters, 1844–67, (microfilm, Hill Memorial Library, Louisiana State University, Baton Rouge).

14. Hatton, "Soldier's Life," p. 34; Camille de Polignac to P. G. T. Beauregard, Mar. 22, 1861, Mansfield Museum, Mansfield, Louisiana, typescript.

15. Hatton, "Soldier's Life," p. 34; Polignac to Beauregard, Mar. 22, 1861.

16. Hatton, "Soldier's Life," p. 34.

17. Camille de Polignac to Alphonse de Polignac, Oct. 14, 1859, Polignac Letters.

18. Eli N. Evans, *Judah P. Benjamin, The Jewish Confederate*, pp. 194, 199, 393; Hatton, "Soldier's Life," p. 33.

19. Evans, *Judah P. Benjamin*, p. 27.

20. Ibid., pp. vii, viii, 1, 4, 5, 16, 17, 19, 23, 25–27, 138, 333.

21. Ibid; Polignac to Beauregard, Mar. 22, 1861.

22. Evans, *Judah P. Benjamin*, pp. vii, viii, 1, 4, 5, 16, 17, 19, 23, 25–27, 138, 333; Polignac to Beauregard, Mar. 22, 1861; T. Harry Williams, *P. G. T. Beauregard: Napoleon in Gray*, p. 42.

23. Polignac to Beauregard, Mar. 22, 1861; Williams, *Napoleon in Gray*, pp. 35–36.

24. Polignac to Beauregard, Mar. 22, 1861.

25. Judah P. Benjamin to Camille de Polignac, Mar. 9, 1861, Polignac letters; Hatton, "Soldier's Life," p. 37.

26. Polignac to Beauregard, Mar. 22, 1861.

27. Ibid.

28. Ibid.

29. J. C. Moncure to Camille de Polignac, July 27, 1865, J. C. Moncure Papers, J. J. Fair Hardin Collection, Hill Memorial Library, Louisiana State University, Baton Rouge.

30. Hatton, "Soldier's Life," p. 41.

31. Frankignoul, *Prince Camille de Polignac*, pp. 25–26; Williams, *Napoleon in Gray*, pp. 50, 53, 58; Polignac diary, Apr. 3, 1862.

32. Mike Wright, *City under Siege, Richmond in the Civil War*, pp. 3, 13, 15; John B. Jones, *A Rebel War Clerk's Diary*, ed. Earl Schenck Miers, pp. 7, 29, 30.

33. Jones, *Diary*, pp. 10, 14, 31; Emory M. Thomas, *The Confederate State of Richmond: A Biography of the Capital*, p. 36.

34. Mark Mayo Boatner III, *Civil War Dictionary*, pp. 54, 55, 59; Walter Lord, ed., *The Fremantle Diary, Being the Journal of Lieutenant Colonel James Arthur Lyon Fremantle, Coldstream Guards on His Three Months in the Southern States*, pp. 260, 261; Ella Lonn, *Foreigners in the Confederacy*, p. 56.

35. Thomas, *Confederate State of Richmond*, p. 45.

36. Jones, *Diary*, pp. 31–32; Thomas, *Confederate State of Richmond*, pp. 42–43.

37. Sen. Doc. 234, 58th Cong., 2nd sess., *Journal of the Congress of the Confederate States of America, 1861–1865*, 1:424, 842–43; Register of Appointments, Confederate States Army, Confederate Archives, National Archives, Washington, D.C.; Letters Received by the Confederate Adjutant and Inspector General, Jan.–Apr., 1862, National Archives.

38. Frankignoul, *Prince Camille de Polignac*, p. 25; Jones, *Diary*, p. 32.

39. Polignac diary, June 12, 1862.

40. Basil Wilson Duke, *Reminiscences of General Basil W. Duke* (Garden City, N.Y.: Doubleday, 1911), p. 132; Lonn, *Foreigners in the Confederacy*, p. 213.

41. Williams, *Napoleon in Gray*, p. 35.

42. Thomas Cooper DeLeon, *Belles, Beaux, and Brains of the '60s*, pp. 331–32; Lonn, *Foreigners in the Confederacy*, p. 213.

43. Williams, *Napoleon in Gray*, p. 67.

44. Ibid., pp. 81–91; Jones, *Diary*, p. 35.

45. Williams, *Napoleon in Gray*, pp. 92–101.

46. Ibid., pp. 70, 96, 98.

47. Camille de Polignac to Sir, Oct. 30, 1861, Camillus J. Polignac File, War Department Collection of Confederate Records, National Archives.

48. Ibid.; Hatton, "Soldier's Life," pp. 28–29.

49. Polignac to Sir, Oct. 30, 1861.

50. Ibid.

51. Paul F. Hammond, "General Kirby Smith's Campaign in Kentucky in 1862," *Southern Historical Society Papers* 9 (Aug., 1881; reprint, Wilmington, N.C.: Broadfoot, 1990): pp. 246–47; Lonn, *Foreigners in the Confederacy*, p. 213.

52. Hammond, "General Kirby Smith's Campaign in Kentucky," pp. 246–47; Lonn, *Foreigners in the Confederacy*, p. 213.

53. Polignac to Sir, Oct. 30, 1861.
54. Williams, *Napoleon in Gray*, p. 109.
55. Ibid., pp. 69, 109.
56. Polignac to Sir, Oct. 30, 1861.
57. Boatner, *Civil War Dictionary*, pp. 552–53.
58. Ibid., p. 736.
59. Polignac to Sir, Oct. 30, 1861.

Chapter 2

1. Jones, *Diary*, 62–65.
2. Ibid., p. 63.
3. Evans, *Judah P. Benjamin*, pp. 123–25.
4. Williams, *Napoleon in Gray*, pp. 114–15.
5. Ibid.; Jones, *Diary*, p. 65.
6. Polignac diary, Mar. 27, 1862; C. Vann Woodward, ed., *Mary Chesnut's Civil War*, pp. 88, 433.
7. Bell Irvin Wiley, *Confederate Women*, pp. 7, 11, 14, 21.
8. Woodward, *Mary Chesnut's Civil War*, pp. 88, 206.
9. Ibid., p. 88.
10. Lonn, *Foreigners in the Confederacy*, p. 170; Woodward, *Mary Chesnut's Civil War*, pp. 88, 136–37.
11. Wiley, *Confederate Women*, pp. 93, 94, 97, 98, 100, 101, 118.
12. Polignac diary, Apr. 17, 1862.
13. Williams, *Napoleon in Gray*, pp. 120–21, 150.
14. Thomas L. Livermore, *Numbers and Losses in the Civil War in America: 1861–1865*, pp. 79, 80; Williams, *Napoleon in Gray*, pp. 138, 145, 146.
15. Grady McWhiney, *Braxton Bragg and Confederate Defeat*, pp. 153–54, 214, 236; Williams, *Napoleon in Gray*, pp. 145, 147, 205.
16. McWhiney, *Braxton Bragg*, pp. 198, 256.
17. Ibid., pp. 250, 253.
18. Sam R. Watkins, *"Co. Aytch": A Side Show of the Big Show*, ed. Bell Irvin Wiley, pp. 69, 71.
19. Polignac diary, Apr. 17, 20, 22, 1862.
20. Ibid., Apr. 23, 24, 1862.
21. Ibid., Apr. 27, 1862.
22. McWhiney, *Braxton Bragg*, pp. 192, 206, 211.
23. Polignac diary, Apr. 26, 28, 1862.
24. Ibid., Apr. 29, 1862; Watkins, *Co. Aytch*, p. 70.
25. Polignac diary, Apr. 29, 1862.
26. Ibid., May 1, 6, 1862.
27. McWhiney, *Braxton Bragg*, p. 256; Polignac diary, May 17, 1862; Williams, *Napoleon in Gray*, pp. 150–52.
28. Polignac diary, May 17, 1862; Watkins, *Co. Aytch*, p. 71; Williams, *Napoleon in Gray*, p. 152.
29. McWhiney, *Braxton Bragg*, p. 96; Polignac diary, May 11, 1862; Williams, *Napoleon in Gray*, p. 151.
30. McWhiney, *Braxton Bragg*, p. 96; Polignac diary, May 1, 9, 10, 1862.
31. Polignac diary, May 3, 1862.
32. Ibid.
33. Ibid.
34. Ibid., May 4, 1862.

35. McWhiney, *Braxton Bragg*, p. 96; Williams, *Napoleon in Gray*, p. 151.
36. McWhiney, *Braxton Bragg*, p. 256; Williams, *Napoleon in Gray*, p. 151.
37. Polignac diary, May 8, 1862.
38. Polignac diary, May 8, 9, 10, 1862.
39. Ibid., May 12, 1862; Williams, *Napoleon in Gray*, p. 151.
40. Polignac diary, May 12, 1862; Williams, *Napoleon in Gray*, p. 151.
41. Polignac diary, May 12, 1862, Williams, *Napoleon in Gray*, p. 151.
42. Polignac diary, May 4, 1862.
43. McWhiney, *Braxton Bragg*, p. 96; Williams, *Napoleon in Gray*, p. 151.
44. McWhiney, *Braxton Bragg*, p. 256; Williams, *Napoleon in Gray*, p. 151.
45. McWhiney, *Braxton Bragg*, p. 256; Williams, *Napoleon in Gray*, p. 151; Polignac diary, May 8, 1862.
46. Polignac diary, May 8, 9, 10, 1862.
47. Ibid., May 12, 1862; Williams, *Napoleon in Gray*, p. 151.

CHAPTER 3

1. Polignac diary, May 18, 1862.
2. Ibid.
3. Ibid., May 11, 14, 1862.
4. Ibid., May 11, 24, 1862.
5. Ibid., May 25, 1862.
6. Ibid.
7. Ibid., May 12, 1862; Williams, *Napoleon in Gray*, p. 257.
8. Polignac diary, May 17, 1862.
9. Ibid., May 16, 17, 20, 1862.
10. Thomas Lawrence Connelly, *Army of the Heartland: The Army of Tennessee, 1862–1862*, pp. 191, 198; Williams, *Napoleon in Gray*, p. 152; Polignac diary, May 19, 1862.
11. Connelly, *Army of the Heartland*, pp. 191, 198; Williams, *Napoleon in Gray*, p. 152.
12. Polignac diary, May 19, 1862.
13. Ibid.
14. Ibid., May 21, 1862.
15. Connelly, *Army of the Heartland*, p. 176; Polignac diary, May 22, 1861; *The War of the Rebellion: A Compilation of the Official Records of the Union and Confederate Armies*, ser. 1, vol. 10, pt. 2, pp. 403, 423, 440, 463, 465, 487, 516517, 524, 538. (Hereafter cited as *O.R.*, with reference to series 1 unless otherwise stated.)
16. Polignac diary, May 23, 1862.
17. Ibid.; Connelly, *Army of the Heartland*, p. 176.
18. Polignac diary, Apr. 22, 1862.
19. Ibid., May 25, 1862.
20. Connelly, *Army of the Heartland*, p. 177.
21. Polignac diary, May 28, 1862.
22. Connelly, *Army of the Heartland*, p. 177; McWhiney, *Braxton Bragg*, pp. 257–58; Polignac diary, May 29, 1862; *O.R.*, vol. 10, pt. 2, pp. 545, 555–58, 560.
23. Connelly, *Army of the Heartland*, p. 177; McWhiney, *Braxton Bragg*, pp. 257–58; *O.R.*, vol. 10, pt. 1, pp. 762–73; pt. 2, p. 557.
24. Polignac diary, May 28, June 11, 1862.
25. Ibid., May 28–29, 1862.
26. Ibid., June 1, 1862; McWhiney, *Braxton Bragg*, p. 258; *O.R.*, vol. 10, pt. 2, pp. 563, 570, 574, 576, 580, 588, 601.
27. McWhiney, *Braxton Bragg*, p. 258; Polignac diary, May 30, 1861, June 1, 1862.
28. Polignac diary, May 30, 1862.

29. Ibid., June 1–7, 11, 1862; Connelly, *Army of the Heartland*, p. 177.

30. Polignac diary, June 1–7, 11, 1862; Connelly, *Army of the Heartland*, p. 177.

31. Connelly, *Army of the Heartland*, p. 177.

32. Ibid.; Polignac diary, June 11, 1862.

33. Polignac diary, June 11, 1862.

34. Ibid.

35. Ibid.

36. Ibid., June 13, 1862.

37. Ibid., June 14, 1862.

38. Connelly, *Army of the Heartland*, pp. 180–81.

39. Ibid.; McWhiney, *Braxton Bragg*, pp. 260–61; Polignac diary, June 11, 1862.

40. Polignac diary, June 21–22, 1862.

41. Ibid., June 23, 1862.

42. McWhiney, *Braxton Bragg*, pp. 262–64.

43. Ibid., p. 263; Polignac diary, June 21–24, 1862; Ezra J. Warner, *Generals in Gray: Lives of the Confederate Commanders*, pp. 242–43.

44. Polignac diary, June 24, 1862.

45. Ibid., June 20, 1862; Connelly, *Army of the Heartland*, pp. 189–90; McWhiney, *Braxton Bragg*, pp. 266–67.

46. Connelly, *Army of the Heartland*, p. 190; McWhiney, *Braxton Bragg*, pp. 266–69; Polignac diary, June 21–23, 1862.

47. McWhiney, *Braxton Bragg*, pp. 268–70.

48. Polignac diary, July 21–22, 1862.

49. Ibid., July 19, 22, 24, 1862.

50. Ibid., July 24, Aug. 1, 1862; McWhiney, *Braxton Bragg*, pp. 268–70.

51. Polignac diary, Aug. 1, 1862; McWhiney, *Braxton Bragg*, pp. 268–71.

52. Polignac diary, July 6, Aug. 1, 1862, 1862.

53. Ibid., July 9, 20, Aug. 6–7, 1862.

54. Ibid., Aug. 6, 1862.

55. Connelly, *Army of the Heartland*, pp. 206–207; James Lee McDonough, *War in Kentucky: From Shiloh to Perryville*, pp. 193, 277–78; McWhiney, *Braxton Bragg*, p. 273.

56. Connelly, *Army of the Heartland*, pp. 187–93, 206–207; McDonough, *War in Kentucky*, pp. 76–78; McWhiney, *Braxton Bragg*, pp. 272–74.

57. Connelly, *Army of the Heartland*, pp. 193, 205–10; McWhiney, *Braxton Bragg*, pp. 272–74; Polignac diary, Aug. 6–7, 1862.

Chapter 4

1. Polignac diary, Aug. 11, 1862.

2. Ibid., Aug. 11, 1862; Hammond, "General Kirby Smith's Campaign in Kentucky," pp. 246–47; Warner, *Generals in Gray*, pp. 241–42, 279–80.

3. Polignac diary, Aug. 11, 1862; Joseph Howard Parks, *General Edmund Kirby Smith, C.S.A.*, p. 202.

4. Polignac diary, Aug. 11, 1862; Parks, *Kirby Smith*, p. 202.

5. Polignac diary, Aug. 11, 1862.

6. Ibid.

7. Ibid., Aug. 12, 1862.

8. Ibid., Aug. 14, 1862.

9. Parks, *Kirby Smith*, p. 206.

10. Polignac diary, Aug. 15–16, 1862.

11. Ibid., Aug. 17, 1862; Parks, *Kirby Smith*, pp. 206–207.

12. Polignac diary, Aug. 17, 1862.

13. Ibid.

14. Ibid., Aug. 18, 1862; Parks, *Kirby Smith*, pp. 205–206.

15. Polignac diary, Aug. 18, 1862; Parks, *Kirby Smith*, p. 206.

16. Parks, *Kirby Smith*, pp. 205–206.

17. Polignac diary, Aug. 19–24, 1862; *O.R.*, vol. 16, pt. 1, pp. 937–38.

18. Parks, *Kirby Smith*, p. 206; *O.R.*, vol. 16, pt. 1, p. 938.

19. Parks, *Kirby Smith*, p. 207.

20. Polignac diary, Aug. 19–24, 1862; Parks, *Kirby Smith*, p. 207.

21. Polignac diary, Aug. 24–28, 1862.

22. Hammond, "Kirby Smith's Campaign in Kentucky," pp. 251–52.

23. Lonn, *Foreigners in the Confederacy*, p. 170.

24. Hammond, "Kirby Smith's Campaign in Kentucky," pp. 251–52.

25. Polignac diary, Aug. 29, 1862.

26. *O.R.*, vol. 16, pt. 1, pp. 918–19.

27. Ibid., pp. 908, 911, 918; Hammond, "Kirby Smith's Campaign in Kentucky," p. 249; Ezra J. Warner, *Generals in Blue: Lives of the Union Commanders*, pp. 310, 343–44.

28. Polignac diary, Aug. 29, 1862; *O.R.*, vol. 16, pt. 1, pp. 908, 911, 916, 918–19.

29. Polignac diary, Aug. 29, 1862; *O.R.*, vol. 16, pt. 1, pp. 949, 945.

30. Polignac diary, Aug. 29, 1862; *O.R.*, vol. 16, pt. 1, pp. 949, 945.

31. Polignac diary, Aug. 29, 1862; *O.R.*, vol. 16, pt. 1, pp. 944, 949; Hammond, "Kirby Smith's Campaign in Kentucky," p. 949; Parks, *Kirby Smith*, pp. 211–12.

32. Parks, *Kirby Smith*, pp. 212–13; *O.R.*, vol. 16, pt. 1, pp. 908–909.

33. Polignac diary, Aug. 30, 1862; Hammond, "Kirby Smith's Campaign in Kentucky," p. 250; *O.R.*, vol. 16, pt. 1, pp. 912, 945, 949, 951.

34. Polignac diary, Aug. 30, 1862; *O.R.*, vol. 16, pt. 1, p. 945.

35. Polignac diary, Aug. 30, 1862; *O.R.*, vol. 16, pt. 1, pp. 912, 945.

36. *O.R.*, vol. 16, pt. 1, pp. 912, 945.

37. Polignac diary, Aug. 30, 1862; *O.R.*, vol. 16, pt. 1, pp. 912, 945, 949; Hammond, "Kirby Smith's Campaign in Kentucky," p. 250.

38. *O.R.*, vol. 16, pt. 1, pp. 912, 918, 920, 940.

39. Ibid., pp. 920, 941–42.

40. Ibid., p. 947; Polignac diary, Aug. 30, 1862.

41. *O.R.*, vol. 16, pt. 1, pp. 934, 946, 947; Hammond, "Kirby Smith's Campaign in Kentucky," p. 250.

42. *O.R.*, vol. 16, pt. 1, pp. 926, 927, 947.

43. Ibid., p. 927.

44. Ibid., pp. 947, 951; Polignac diary, Aug. 30, 1862; Hammond, "Kirby Smith's Campaign in Kentucky," pp. 250, 251.

45. Hammond, "Kirby Smith's Campaign in Kentucky," pp. 250, 251; *O.R.*, vol. 16, pt. 1, p. 938.

46. *O.R.*, vol. 16, pt. 1, pp. 913, 917, 920, 921.

47. Ibid., pp. 934, 940; Hammond, "Kirby Smith's Campaign in Kentucky," p. 251.

48. Polignac diary, Aug. 30, 1862.

49. *O.R.*, vol. 16, pt. 1, p. 934; Hammond, "Kirby Smith's Campaign in Kentucky," pp. 251, 252.

50. *O.R.*, vol. 16, pt. 1, pp. 909, 913, 914; Hammond, "Kirby Smith's Campaign in Kentucky," p. 253.

51. *O.R.*, vol. 16, pt. 1, pp. 909, 914, 921; Polignac diary, Aug. 30, 1862.

52. *O.R.*, vol. 16, pt. 1, pp. 909, 914, 931, 932, 941, 947.

53. Ibid., pp. 938, 939.

54. Ibid., p. 914.

55. Ibid., pp. 907, 908, 914, 922; Livermore, *Numbers and Losses*, pp. 89, 90.

56. Polignac diary, Aug. 30, 1862.

57. Ibid; *O.R.*, vol. 16, pt. 1, pp. 948, 952.
58. Polignac diary, Sept. 1–13, 1862.
59. Ibid.; *O.R.*, vol. 16, pt. 1, p. 952.
60. Polignac diary, Sept. 1–13, 1862.

CHAPTER 5

1. Grady McWhiney and Perry Jamieson, *Attack and Die: Civil War Military Tactics and the Southern Heritage*, pp. 150–51; Polignac diary, Oct. 5, 1862.
2. Polignac diary, Oct. 6, 1862.
3. McWhiney and Jamieson, *Attack and Die*, p. 8; Polignac diary, Oct. 21, 1862.
4. Polignac diary, Oct. 21, 1862.
5. Ibid., Nov. 11–13, 16, 1862.
6. Ibid., June 14, Nov. 13, 1862.
7. Hatton, "Soldier's Life," p. 77; Polignac diary, Nov. 16, 1862; Daniel J. Frankignoul, letter to author, Sept. 27, 1997.
8. Hatton, "Soldier's Life," p. 77; James I. Robertson, Jr., *The Civil War: Tenting Tonight* (Alexandria, Va.: Time-Life Books, 1984), p. 97.
9. Polignac diary, Dec. 4, 19,1862; H. H. Cunningham, ed., *Doctors in Gray: The Confederate Medical Service* (Baton Rouge: Louisiana State University Press, 1960), pp. 199, 215, 225, 306.
10. Hatton, "Soldier's Life," p. 83; Polignac diary, Dec. 18, 1862.
11. Polignac diary, Nov. 16, 25, 1862.
12. Ibid., Nov. 26, 30, Dec. 1, 7, 9, 11, 14, 16, 18–19, 21, 1862; Frankignoul, letter to author, Sept. 27, 1997.
13. Polignac diary, Nov. 25–26, 1862.
14. Ibid., Nov. 27, Dec. 18, 1862.
15. Ibid., Nov. 21, 1862.
16. Ibid., Nov. 16, 24, 30, 1862.
17. John Pegram to Camille de Polignac, Nov. 26, 1862, Polignac Letters.
18. Ibid.
19. Polignac diary, Nov. 26–28, Dec. 4, 1862.
20. Alfred Hoyt Bell, *The Beleaguered City: Richmond, 1861–1865*, p. 161; Polignac diary, Nov. 19, 23, Dec. 6, 8–10, 13, 1862.
21. Polignac diary, Dec. 6, 1862.
22. Ibid., Dec. 9, 1862.
23. Ibid., Dec. 17, 1862.
24. Ibid., May 23, Dec. 5, 27, 30, 1862.
25. Ibid., May 19, July 19, Dec. 24, 1862.
26. Ibid., Dec. 25, 31, 1862.
27. Jones, *Diary*, p. 144; Polignac diary, Jan. 1, 1863; Thomas Cooper DeLeon, *Four Years in the Rebel Capitals*, p. 269.
28. Polignac diary, May 26–27, 1862, Jan. 2,1863.
29. Ibid., Jan. 10–12, 1863.
30. Ibid., June 6, 1862, Jan. 13, 22, 30, Feb. 5,1863.
31. Mary Boykin Chesnut, *A Diary from Dixie*, ed. Ben Ames Williams (Boston: Houghton Mifflin Company, 1949), p. 285; Polignac diary, Feb. 7, 1863; Woodward, *Mary Chesnut's Civil War*, pp. 87, 134.
32. Polignac diary, Feb. 7, 1863.
33. Jones, *Diary*, p. 152.
34. Polignac diary, Mar. 6, 1863.
35. Jones, *Diary*, p. 164.

36. Polignac diary, Feb. 28, Mar. 3, 1863.

37. Ibid., Jan. 3, Feb. 15, 1863; Woodward, *Mary Chesnut's Civil War*, p. 503.

38. Jones, *Diary*, pp. 144–45; Polignac diary, Jan. 10–12, 1863.

39. Polignac diary, Jan. 10–12, 15, 1863.

40. Ibid., Feb. 26, Mar. 1–3, 1863.

41. Ibid., Mar. 6, 1863.

42. Ibid., Mar. 9, 1863; Woodward, *Mary Chesnut's Civil War*, p. 110.

43. Polignac diary, Mar. 9, 1863.

44. Ibid., Mar. 16, 1863.

45. Ibid., Mar. 19–21, 28, 1863.

46. Jones, *Diary*, p. 183.

47. Joseph H. Crute, *Confederate Staff Officers* (Powhatan, Va.: Derwent Books, 1982), p. 153; Jones, *Diary*, p. 163; Polignac diary, Mar. 31, Apr. 3, 1863. Cuculler often spelled his name "Cucullu" on official documents.

Chapter 6

1. Polignac diary, Apr. 3, 6, 12, 1863; Frankignoul, *Prince Camille de Polignac*, p. 40; *O.R.*, vol. 15, p. 1023.

2. Polignac diary, Apr. 3, 1863.

3. Polignac diary, Apr. 3, 6, May 7–11, 1863.

4. Ibid.; Thomas S. Dickey and Peter C. George, *Field Artillery Projectiles of the American Civil War*, p. 372; Polignac diary, May 7–11, 1863.

5. Polignac diary, May 7–11, 1863.

6. Ibid., May 5–13, 1863.

7. Ibid., May 11–21, 1863.

8. Ibid., May 16, 1863.

9. Ibid., May 19–23, 1863.

10. Ibid., May 25, 1863.

11. Ibid., May 30, 1863; Alwyn Barr, *Polignac's Texas Brigade*, pp. 19–21, 40, 41; *O.R.*, vol. 22, pt. 2, 839–40; Polignac diary, May 31, 1863.

12. Polignac diary, May 30, June 3, 1863; Barr, *Polignac's Texas Brigade*, pp. 1921.

13. Polignac diary, June 4, 10, 12, 1863.

14. Ibid., June 15, 1863; *O.R.*, vol. 15, pt. 1, p. 590.

15. John D. Winters, *The Civil War in Louisiana*, p. 212.

16. Polignac diary, June 19–20, 23, 1863; *O.R.*, vol. 22, pt. 1, p. 933.

17. Polignac diary, June 20–21, 1863.

18. Ibid., June 28, 1863.

19. Ibid., July 1–4, 1863.

20. Ibid., July 5, 1863.

21. Ibid., July 6, 1863.

22. Ibid., July 7–8, 1863.

23. Ibid., July 15, 17, 1863; *O.R.*, vol. 22, pt. 1, p. 933.

24. Barr, *Polignac's Texas Brigade*, pp. 1, 21; Rebecca W. Smith and Marion Mullins, eds., "The Diary of H. C. Medford, Confederate Soldier, 1864," *Southwestern Historical Quarterly* 34 (Jan., 1931): 219; Marcus J. Wright, comp., *Texas in the War 1861–1865*, pp. 120–21; *O.R.*, vol. 17, pt. 2, p. 16; vol. 22, pt. 1, p. 933; vol. 26, pt. 2, p. 113.

25. Polignac diary, July 20, 1863; Robert S. Weddle, *Plow-Horse Cavalry: The Caney Creek boys in the Thirty-fourth Texas*, p. 91.

26. Polignac diary, July 20, 1863.

27. Ibid.

28. Ibid.

29. Ibid., July 21–27, 1863; *O.R.*, vol. 26, pt. 2, p. 109.

30. Polignac diary, July 28, 1863.

31. Ibid.

32. Ibid., July 30, 1863.

33. Ibid., Aug. 1, 1863.

34. Ibid., Aug. 1, 2–7, 1863; Warner, *Generals in Gray*, pp. 299–300.

35. Polignac diary, Aug. 8–16, 1863.

36. Ibid., Aug. 19, 1863.

37. Ibid., Aug. 17, 25, 1863; T. Michael Parrish, *Richard Taylor: Soldier Prince of Dixie*, p. 267; *O.R.*, vol. 15, pt. 1, pp. 1093–95.

38. Polignac diary, Aug. 27, 29, Sept. 10, 11, 1863.

39. Ibid., Aug. 30, Sept. 4, 1863.

40. Ibid., Sept. 13–17, 1863.

41. Ibid., Sept. 22, 1863.

42. Ibid.

43. Ibid.

44. Ibid., Sept. 21–22, 1863.

45. Ibid.

46. Ibid.

47. Ibid.

48. Ibid., Sept. 23, 1863; Parrish, *Richard Taylor*, pp. 307–309.

49. Polignac diary, Sept. 25, 27–28, 1863; Parrish, *Richard Taylor*, p. 308.

50. Polignac diary, Sept. 29, 1863.

51. Parrish, *Richard Taylor*, pp. 308–12; Richard Taylor, *Destruction and Reconstruction: Personal Experiences of the Late War*, ed. Richard B. Harwell, pp. 179–80; *O.R.*, vol. 26, pt. 1, pp. 328–32; Winters, *Civil War in Louisiana*, pp. 296–97.

52. Polignac diary, Oct. 14, 18, 1863.

53. Taylor, *Destruction and Reconstruction*, pp. 183, 352–53.

54. Edwin C. Bearss, ed., *A Louisiana Confederate: Diary of Felix Pierre Poché*, p. 32.

55. Taylor, *Destruction and Reconstruction*, p. 183; Mrs. B. Girard Wright, *A Southern Girl in '61: The Wartime Memories of a Confederate Senator's Daughter*, pp. 92–93.

56. John S. Bowman, ed., *Who Was Who in the Civil War*, p. 204; Parrish, *Richard Taylor*, pp. 1–3; Warner, *Generals in Gray*, pp. 299–300.

57. Lonn, *Foreigners in the Confederacy*, p. 166.

58. Taylor, *Destruction and Reconstruction*, p. 183.

59. Barr, *Polignac's Texas Brigade*, p. 129; Polignac diary, Oct. 18, 27, 1863.

60. Polignac diary, Oct. 27, 1863.

61. J. P. Blessington, *The Campaigns of Walker's Texas Division*, p. 153; Jefferson Davis Bragg, *Louisiana in the Confederacy*, pp. 158–59.

62. Polignac diary, Dec. 9, 1863.

63. Barr, *Polignac's Texas Brigade*, p. 33; Polignac diary, Nov. 10, 1863.

64. Polignac diary, Nov. 19, 1863.

65. Bearss, *A Louisiana Confederate*, pp. 63, 66; Polignac diary, Dec. 23, 1863.

66. Barr, *Polignac's Texas Brigade*, p. 33; Bearss, *A Louisiana Confederate*, p. 63; Cooper K. Ragan, ed., "The Diary of Captain George W. O'Brien, 1863," *Southwestern Historical Quarterly* 67 (Jan., 1964): 364–66; Polignac diary, Dec. 12, 23, 1863.

67. Maj. Silas T. Grisamore, "Reminiscences," *Weekly Thibodaux (Louisiana) Sentinel*, July 17, 1869, cited in Hatton, "Soldier's life," p. 132.

68. Barr, *Polignac's Texas Brigade*, pp. 33–34; Bearss, *A Louisiana Confederate*, p. 66, 68.

69. Blessington, *Walker's Texas Division*, p. 163; Polignac diary, Dec. 24, 1863.

CHAPTER 7

1. Polignac diary, Jan. 1, 1864.

2. Barr, *Polignac's Texas Brigade*, p. 35; Bearss, ed., *A Louisiana Confederate*, pp. 68, 69; Polignac diary, Jan. 10, 1864.

3. Polignac diary, Jan. 10, 1864.

4. Ibid., Jan. 16, 1864; *O.R.*, vol. 34, pt. 2, pp. 914, 929–30.

5. Polignac diary, Jan. 16, 1864.

6. Bearss, *A Louisiana Confederate*, p. 74; Polignac diary, Jan. 20–22, 24, 1864.

7. Bearss, *A Louisiana Confederate*, p. 74; Polignac diary, Jan. 25–26, 30, 1864; Barr, *Polignac's Texas Brigade*, p. 35; *O.R.*, vol. 34, pt. 2, p. 914; Winters, *Civil War in Louisiana*, pp. 141, 158.

8. Polignac diary, Feb. 3, 5, 1864; *O.R.*, vol. 34, pt. 2, p. 944.

9. *O.R.*, vol. 34, pt. 2, p. 944.

10. Ibid., pp. 952–53.

11. Barr, *Polignac's Texas Brigade*, p. 36; Polignac diary, Feb. 6–7, 1864; *O.R.*, vol. 34, pt. 2, pp. 934–35, 977.

12. Polignac diary, Feb. 6, 1864.

13. Taylor, *Destruction and Reconstruction*, pp. 352–53; Wright, *A Southern Girl*, pp. 92–93.

14. Barr, *Polignac's Texas Brigade*, p. 36; *O.R.*, vol. 34, pt. 2, p. 130.

15. Barr, *Polignac's Texas Brigade*, pp. 36–37; Polignac diary, Feb. 25, 1864.

16. Taylor, *Destruction and Reconstruction*, pp. 183, 352–53; Winters, *Civil War in Louisiana*, pp. 320, 323; Wright, *A Southern Girl*, pp. 92–93.

17. Polignac diary, Feb. 23, 1864.

18. Ibid., Mar. 1, 1864; *O.R.*, vol. 34, pt. 2, p. 155.

19. *O.R.*, vol. 34, pt. 2, p. 155; *Official Records of the Union and Confederate Navies in the War of the Rebellion*, ser. 1, vol. 25, pp. 787–88. (Hereafter cited as *O.R.N.*, with reference to series 1 unless otherwise stated.)

20. Billy Flinn to Mrs. Cockrell, Mar. 6, 1864, George W. Guess Letters, 1861–65, Louisiana Vertical File, Louisiana Room, Louisiana State University Library, Baton Rouge; Polignac diary, Mar. 1–7, 1864; *O.R.*, vol. 24, pt. 2, pp. 1555–58; *O.R. N.*, vol. 25, pp. 787–89.

21. *O.R.*, vol. 34, pt. 2, pp. 159–60; Tony Gibbons, *Warships and Naval Battles of the U.S. Civil War*, p. 57.

22. *O.R.*, vol. 34, pt. 2, pp. 159–60; Gibbons, *Warships and Naval Battles*, p. 57.

23. *O.R.*, vol. 34, pt. 2, pp. 155–56; Flinn to Cockrell, Mar. 6, 1864.

24. *O.R.*, vol. 34, pt. 2, pp. 158–60.

25. Ibid., pp. 155–56, 158–59; Flinn to Cockrell, Mar. 6, 1864; Gibbons, *Warships and Naval Battles*, p. 57.

26. *O.R.*, vol. 34, pt. 2, pp. 156–57, 158–59.

27. Ibid., pp. 156–59; Flinn to Cockrell, Mar. 6, 1864.

28. *O.R.*, vol. 34, pt. 2, pp. 155–57; Polignac diary, Mar. 4, 1864.

29. *O.R.*, vol. 34, pt. 2, pp. 157, 488, 1015; St. John R. Liddell, *Liddell's Record*, ed. Nathaniel C. Hughes (Dayton, Ohio: Morningside Press, 1985), pp. 175–78.

30. *O.R.N.*, vol. 15, p. 787.

31. *O.R.*, vol. 34, pt. 2, p. 158; Taylor, *Destruction and Reconstruction*, p. 184; Liddell, *Liddell's Record*, pp. 175–78.

32. Ludwell H. Johnson, *Red River Campaign: Politics and Cotton in the Civil War*, pp. 34–35; Winters, *Civil War in Louisiana*, p. 325.

33. *O.R.*, vol. 34, pt. 2, pp. 895–96; Parrish, *Richard Taylor*, p. 317; Winters, *Civil War in Louisiana*, p. 327.

34. *O.R.*, vol. 34, pt. 2, p. 1024; Taylor, *Destruction and Reconstruction*, p. 184.

35. Barr, *Polignac's Texas Brigade*, p. 38; *O.R.*, vol. 34, pt. 2, pp. 492–96, 573–75; Taylor, *Destruction and Reconstruction*, p. 185.

36. Parrish, *Richard Taylor*, p. 320; Taylor, *Destruction and Reconstruction*, p. 183.

37. Johnson, *Red River Campaign*, p. 94; *O.R.*, vol. 34, pt. 2, pp. 255–56; Polignac diary, Apr. 7, 1864.

38. *O.R.*, vol. 34, pt. 2, pp. 255–56; Winters, *Civil War in Louisiana*, p. 325.

39. Polignac diary, Apr. 7, 1864.

40. Barr, *Polignac's Texas Brigade*, p. 38; Parrish, *Richard Taylor*, pp. 327–29; Taylor, *Destruction and Reconstruction*, p. 187.

41. William Arceneaux, *Acadian General: Alfred Mouton and the Civil War*, p. 118; Parrish, *Richard Taylor*, pp. 327–28; Warner, *Generals in Gray*, p. 222.

42. Johnson, *Red River Campaign*, p. 96–97; *O.R.*, vol. 34, pt. 1, pp. 496, 500, 562, 578; Parrish, *Richard Taylor*, pp. 188, 327, 330; Taylor, *Destruction and Reconstruction*, p. 188.

43. Johnson, *Red River Campaign*, pp. 99–100; Rear Adm. David D. Porter, "The Mississippi Flotilla in the Red River Expedition," in *Battles and Leaders of the Civil War*, eds. Robert U. Johnson and Clarence C. Buel, 4:366; *O.R.*, vol. 34, pt. 1, pp. 168–203, 426–27.

44. Barr, *Polignac's Texas Brigade*, p. 38; Johnson, *Red River Campaign*, pp. 111–12; Polignac diary, Apr. 7, 1864; Winters, *Civil War in Louisiana*, p. 335.

45. Barr, *Polignac's Texas Brigade*, pp. 38–39; Polignac diary, Apr. 7, 1864; Taylor, *Destruction and Reconstruction*, p. 189; Johnson, *Red River Campaign*, pp. 117–18; *O.R.*, vol. 34, pt. 1, pp. 181, 566; Winters, *Civil War in Louisiana*, pp. 337–38.

CHAPTER 8

1. Johnson, *Red River Campaign*, pp. 120–21; Taylor, *Destruction and Reconstruction*, p. 190; *O.R.*, vol. 34, pt. 1, p. 515.

2. Johnson, *Red River Campaign*, pp. 122–23; Robert L. Kerby, *Kirby Smith's Confederacy: The Trans-Mississippi South, 1863–1865*, pp. 381–85.

3. Kerby, *Kirby Smith's Confederacy*, p. 303; Parrish, *Richard Taylor*, p. 338; Edmund Kirby Smith, "The Defense of the Red River," in *Battles and Leaders*, eds. Johnson and Buel, 4:369–71; Taylor, *Destruction and Reconstruction*, p. 191.

4. Barr, *Polignac's Texas Brigade*, p. 39; Parrish, *Richard Taylor*, p. 339; Rebecca W. Smith and Marion Mullins, eds., "The Diary of H. C. Medford, Confederate Soldier, 1864," *Southwestern Historical Quarterly* 34 (Jan., 1931): 215.

5. William R. Boggs, *Military Reminiscences of Gen. Wm. R. Boggs, C.S.A.*, ed. William K. Boyd, p. 76; Parrish, *Richard Taylor*, p. 339; Taylor, *Destruction and Reconstruction*, pp. 193–94.

6. Parrish, *Richard Taylor*, p. 340.

7. Barr, *Polignac's Texas Brigade*, p. 39; Edwin C. Bearss, ed., *A Louisiana Confederate: Diary of Felix Pierre Poché*, p. 105; Norman D. Brown, ed., *Journey to Pleasant Hill: The Civil War Letters of Captain Elijah P. Petty, Walker's Texas Division, C.S.A.*, pp. 391–92; Parrish, *Richard Taylor*, p. 344; Polignac diary, Apr. 8, 1864; Smith and Mullins, "Diary of H. C. Medford," p. 215.

8. Barr, *Polignac's Texas Brigade*, p. 39; Bearss, *A Louisiana Confederate*, p. 105; Parrish, *Richard Taylor*, p. 341; Taylor, *Destruction and Reconstruction*, p. 193.

9. Bearss, *A Louisiana Confederate*, p. 105; Parrish, *Richard Taylor*, p. 341; Polignac diary, Apr. 8, 1864; Taylor, *Destruction and Reconstruction*, pp. 194–95; Ralph A. Wooster, *Texas and Texans in the Civil War*, pp. 140–41.

10. Johnson, *Red River Campaign*, pp. 124–27; Parrish, *Richard Taylor*, pp. 337–38, 342.

11. Johnson, *Red River Campaign*, pp. 124–27; Alvin M. Josephy, Jr., *The Civil War in the American West*, p. 200; Parrish, *Richard Taylor*, pp. 337–38, 342–43.

12. Smith and Mullins, "Diary of H. C. Medford," p. 316.

13. Bearss, *A Louisiana Confederate*, p. 106.

14. *O.R.*, vol. 34, pt. 1, p. 526; Parrish, *Richard Taylor*, pp. 341–42.

15. Bearss, *A Louisiana Confederate*, p. 106; Johnson, *Red River Campaign*, pp. 128–29.

16. Bearss, *A Louisiana Confederate*, p. 106; Johnson, *Red River Campaign*, p. 133; Taylor, *Destruction and Reconstruction*, pp. 195–96.

17. Bearss, *A Louisiana Confederate*, p. 106; J. E. Hewitt, "The Battle of Mansfield Louisiana," *Confederate Veteran* 33 (May, 1925): 172.

18. Parrish, *Richard Taylor*, pp. 343–44; Taylor, *Destruction and Reconstruction*, p. 194.

19. Blessington, *Walker's Texas Division*, p. 186; Brown, *Journey to Pleasant Hill*, pp. 393–94; Kerby, *Kirby Smith's Confederacy*, p. 304; Parrish, *Richard Taylor*, p. 344; Taylor, *Destruction and Reconstruction*, p. 196.

20. Bearss, *A Louisiana Confederate*, pp. 106–107; *O.R.*, vol. 34, pt. 1, p. 564; Parrish, *Richard Taylor*, p. 344; Smith and Mullins, "Diary of H. C. Medford," p. 217; Taylor, *Destruction and Reconstruction*, p. 196.

21. Bearss, *A Louisiana Confederate*, pp. 106–107; Parrish, *Richard Taylor*, p. 346.

22. Arceneaux, *Acadian General*, p. 132; Parrish, *Richard Taylor*, p. 347; Robert S. Weddle, *Plow-Horse Cavalry: The Caney Creek Boys of the Thirty-fourth Texas*, p. 36.

23. Hewitt, "Battle of Mansfield," pp. 172–73.

24. Ibid.; *O.R.*, vol. 34, pt. 1, p. 564; Parrish, *Richard Taylor*, pp. 346–48.

25. Barr, *Polignac's Texas Brigade*, p. 39; Hewitt, "Battle of Mansfield," p. 173; *O.R.*, vol. 34, pt. 1, p. 564; Taylor, *Destruction and Reconstruction*, p. 196.

26. Arceneaux, *Acadian General*, p. 132; Bearss, *A Louisiana Confederate*, p. 107; Hewitt, "Battle of Mansfield," p. 173; Johnson, *Red River Campaign*, pp. 135–36; Parrish, *Richard Taylor*, p. 346.

27. Bearss, *A Louisiana Confederate*, p. 107; Hewitt, "Battle of Mansfield," p. 173.

28. Jefferson Davis Bragg, *Louisiana in the Confederacy*, p. 265; *O.R.*, vol. 34, pt. 1, p. 564.

29. Arceneaux, *Acadian General*, p. 132; Taylor, *Destruction and Reconstruction*, p. 196.

30. Bearss, *A Louisiana Confederate*, pp. 106–107; Hewitt, "Battle of Mansfield," p. 173; Johnson, *Red River Campaign*, pp. 135–36.

31. Josephy, *Civil War in the American West*, p. 204; Fredericka Meiners, "Hamilton P. Bee in the Red River Campaign of 1864," in *Lone Star Blue and Gray: Essays on Texas in the Civil War*, ed. Ralph A. Wooster, pp. 294–95; *O.R.*, vol. 34, pt. 1, pp. 564–65; Smith and Mullins, "Diary of H. C. Medford," p. 218; Taylor, *Destruction and Reconstruction*, pp. 196–97.

32. Bearss, *A Louisiana Confederate*, pp. 106–107; Frank M. Flinn, *Campaigning with Banks in Louisiana*, p. 108; Johnson, *Red River Campaign*, p. 135; *O.R.*, vol. 34, pt. 1, p. 462.

33. Johnson, *Red River Campaign*, pp. 136–37; Josephy, *Civil War in the American West*, p. 205; Frank Moore, ed., *The Rebellion Record: A Diary of American Events*, 8:548; Parrish, *Richard Taylor*, p. 349.

34. Hewitt, "Battle of Mansfield," p. 197; Polignac diary, Apr. 8, 1864.

35. Bearss, *A Louisiana Confederate*, p. 108; Blessington, *Walker's Texas Division*, p. 189; Johnson, *Red River Campaign*, p. 137; Josephy, *Civil War in the American West*, p. 205; Parrish, *Richard Taylor*, pp. 348–49; Smith and Mullins, "Diary of H. C. Medford," p. 218.

36. Johnson, *Red River Campaign*, p. 139; Josephy, *Civil War in the American West*, p. 205; Parrish, *Richard Taylor*, pp. 348–50.

37. Hewitt, "Battle of Mansfield," p. 198; Johnson, *Red River Campaign*, pp. 138–39; Josephy, *Civil War in the American West*, p. 205; Parrish, *Richard Taylor*, pp. 350–51.

38. Taylor, *Destruction and Reconstruction*, p. 197.

39. *O.R.*, vol. 34, pt. 1, p. 417; Parrish, *Richard Taylor*, p. 351; Taylor, *Destruction and Reconstruction*, p. 198.

40. Barr, *Polignac's Texas Brigade*, p. 40; Johnson, *Red River Campaign*, p. 139; Josephy, *Civil War in the American West*, pp. 205–206; Parrish, *Richard Taylor*, p. 351; Smith and Mullins, "Diary of H. C. Medford," p. 219.

41. *O.R.*, vol. 34, pt. 1, pp. 200–201; Parrish, *Richard Taylor*, p. 352; Taylor, *Destruction and Reconstruction*, p. 197.

42. Johnson, *Red River Campaign*, pp. 139–41; Livermore, *Numbers and Losses*, pp. 6670; Wooster, *Texas and Texans*, p. 142.

43. Taylor, *Destruction and Reconstruction*, p. 198.

44. Hewitt, "Battle of Mansfield," p. 173; Weddle, *Plow-Horse Cavalry*, pp. 115–17; Wooster, *Texas and Texans*, p. 142.

45. Johnson, *Red River Campaign*, p. 146; Josephy, *Civil War in the American West*, p. 206.

46. Johnson, *Red River Campaign*, pp. 153–54; Josephy, *Civil War in the American West*, p. 206; *O.R.*, vol. 34, pt. 1, p. 565; Taylor, *Destruction and Reconstruction*, p. 199.

47. Johnson, *Red River Campaign*, p. 153; Josephy, *Civil War in the American West*, p. 206; Smith and Mullins, "Diary of H. C. Medford," p. 220.

48. Josephy, *Civil War in the American West*, p. 197; Parrish, *Richard Taylor*, p. 356; Smith and Mullins, "Diary of H. C. Medford," pp. 220–21; Mamie Yeary, comp., *Reminiscences of the Boys in Gray, 1861–1865*, p. 627.

49. Brown, *Journey to Pleasant Hill*, p. 404; Johnson, *Red River Campaign*, pp. 153–54; Josephy, *Civil War in the American West*, p. 206; Parrish, *Richard Taylor*, p. 356.

50. Johnson, *Red River Campaign*, p. 154; Parrish, *Richard Taylor*, pp. 356–57; Taylor, *Destruction and Reconstruction*, p. 199.

51. Taylor, *Destruction and Reconstruction*, pp. 199–200.

52. Johnson, *Red River Campaign*, p. 155; Josephy, *Civil War in the American West*, p. 207; Parrish, *Richard Taylor*, p. 357.

53. Johnson, *Red River Campaign*, p. 154; Josephy, *Civil War in the American West*, p. 207; *O.R.*, vol. 34, pt. 1, pp. 566–67; Parrish, *Richard Taylor*, p. 357; Taylor, *Destruction and Reconstruction*, p. 200.

54. Thomas Reuben Bonner, "Sketches of the Campaign of 1864," *The Land We Love* 5 (Oct., 1868): 459–66, 6 (Nov., 1868): 7–12; *Harper's Weekly*, May 7, 1864; Johnson, *Red River Campaign*, pp. 155–56; Josephy, *Civil War in the American West*, pp. 207–208; *O.R.*, vol. 34, pt. 1, pp. 567, 608, 617; Parrish, *Richard Taylor*, pp. 358–59; Taylor, *Destruction and Reconstruction*, p. 201; Wooster, *Texas and Texans*, pp. 42–43.

55. Barr, *Polignac's Texas Brigade*, p. 40; Johnson, *Red River Campaign*, p. 168; Parrish, *Richard Taylor*, p. 362.

56. Blessington, *Walker's Texas Division*, pp. 197–98; Josephy, *Civil War in the American West*, p. 208; Polignac diary, Apr. 9, 1864.

57. Johnson, *Red River Campaign*, p. 147; Parrish, *Richard Taylor*, pp. 362, 364.

58. Johnson, *Red River Campaign*, pp. 158–59; Josephy, *Civil War in the American West*, p. 208; *O.R.*, vol. 34, pt. 1, pp. 317, 328, 350, 367–68, 373; Parrish, *Richard Taylor*, pp. 362–63; Polignac diary, Apr. 9, 1864.

59. Polignac diary, Apr. 9, 1864.

60. Bearss, *A Louisiana Confederate*, p. 110; *O.R.*, vol. 34, pt. 1, pp. 616–18; Polignac diary, Apr. 9, 1864.

61. Kirby Smith, "Defense of the Red River," p. 372; *O.R.*, vol. 34, pt. 1, p. 554; Taylor, *Destruction and Reconstruction*, pp. 203–204.

62. Kirby Smith, "Defense of the Red River," p. 372.

63. Livermore, *Numbers and Losses*, pp. 109–10; Taylor, *Destruction and Reconstruction*, 203–204.

64. Bearss, *A Louisiana Confederate*, p. 111.

CHAPTER 9

1. Fred Harvey Harrington, *Fighting Politician: Major General N. P. Banks*, pp. 157–58; Johnson, *Red River Campaign*, pp. 162–65; Parrish, *Richard Taylor*, p. 369; Kirby Smith, "De-

fense of the Red River," p. 372; Taylor, *Destruction and Reconstruction*, p. 206; Winters, *Civil War in Louisiana*, pp. 348–55.

2. Barr, *Polignac's Texas Brigade*, p. 41; Johnson, *Red River Campaign*, pp. 211–12; Parrish, *Richard Taylor*, pp. 370–73; Smith, "Defense of the Red River," p. 372; Taylor, *Destruction and Reconstruction*, pp. 205, 213–14.

3. Polignac diary, Apr. 13, 1864; Taylor, *Destruction and Reconstruction*, p. 218.

4. Barr, *Polignac's Texas Brigade*, p. 41.

5. Ibid.; Bearss, *A Louisiana Confederate*, p. 108; Weddle, *Plow-Horse Cavalry*, p. 117.

6. Bearss, *A Louisiana Confederate*, p. 108.

7. Barr, *Polignac's Texas Brigade*, p. 41.

8. Hatton, "Soldier's Life," p. 160.

9. Barr, *Polignac's Texas Brigade*, pp. 41–42.

10. Johnson, *Red River Campaign*, pp. 211–23; Parrish, *Richard Taylor*, p. 376; David D. Porter, *The Naval History of the Civil War*, pp. 517–19; Taylor, *Destruction and Reconstruction*, pp. 218–20.

11. Parrish, *Richard Taylor*, p. 372; Polignac diary, Apr. 18, 1864.

12. Polignac diary, Apr. 20, 1864.

13. Ibid.

14. Barr, *Polignac's Texas Brigade*, p. 42; O.R., vol. 34, pt. 1, p. 190; Polignac diary, Apr. 26, 1864.

15. Johnson, *Red River Campaign*, pp. 225–26; O.R., vol. 34, pt. 1, pp. 262, 394–95, 460; Taylor, *Destruction and Reconstruction*, p. 220.

16. Johnson, *Red River Campaign*, pp. 225–26; O.R., vol. 34, pt. 1, pp. 262, 394–95, 460; Taylor, *Destruction and Reconstruction*, p. 220.

17. Johnson, *Red River Campaign*, pp. 226–34; O.R., vol. 34, pt. 1, pp. 580–81, 590, 611; Parrish, *Richard Taylor*, pp. 376–78; Richard Taylor to W. R. Boggs, June 1, 1864, Joseph L. Brent Papers, Tulane University, New Orleans; Taylor, *Destruction and Reconstruction*, p. 220.

18. Barr, *Polignac's Texas Brigade*, pp. 42–43; J. E. Harrison to "Dear Ballinger," Apr. 27, 1864, William Pitt Barringer Collection, University of Texas Library Archives, Austin.

19. Barr, *Polignac's Texas Brigade*, p. 43; Johnson, *Red River Campaign*, pp. 237–38; O.R.N., vol. 26, pp. 72, 74, 79, 167, 169,176, 781–82, 786.

20. Barr, *Polignac's Texas Brigade*, p. 43; Johnson, *Red River Campaign*, p. 238; O.R.N., vol. 26, pp. 74, 167, 169, 176, 781–82, 786; Polignac diary, Apr. 28, 1864.

21. Johnson, *Red River Campaign*, pp. 238–39; O.R.N., vol. 26, pp. 74–75.

22. Johnson, *Red River Campaign*, p. 239; Polignac diary, Apr. 28, 1864; Taylor, *Destruction and Reconstruction*, pp. 221–23; Weddle, *Plow-Horse Cavalry*, p. 119.

23. Johnson, *Red River Campaign*, pp. 239–40.

24. Ibid., pp. 240–41.

25. Barr, *Polignac's Texas Brigade*, p. 42; Johnson, *Red River Campaign*, p. 241; Polignac diary, Apr. 28, 1864.

26. Barr, *Polignac's Texas Brigade*, p. 42; Johnson, *Red River Campaign*, p. 241; O.R.N., vol. 26, pp. 76, 82–84, 176; Polignac diary, Apr. 28, 1864.

27. Johnson, *Red River Campaign*, pp. 248–49; Robert L. Kerby, *Kirby Smith's Confederacy*, p. 316; Edward G. Longacre, "Rescue on Red River," *Civil War Times Illustrated* 14, no. 6 (Oct., 1975): 9, 42; Parrish, *Richard Taylor*, p. 383; Taylor, *Destruction and Reconstruction*, pp. 226–27.

28. Barr, *Polignac's Texas Brigade*, pp. 43–44; Johnson, *Red River Campaign*, p. 254; Parrish, *Richard Taylor*, p. 382; Polignac diary, May 3, 1864; O.R., vol. 34, pt. 1, pp. 168, 443, 588–89; pt. 3, pp. 294, 296.

29. Taylor, *Destruction and Reconstruction*, p. 225.

30. Johnson, *Red River Campaign*, pp. 258–59; O.R., vol. 34, pt. 1, pp. 588, 590; Parrish, *Richard Taylor*, pp. 383–84.

31. Barr, *Polignac's Texas Brigade*, pp. 43–44; *O.R.*, vol. 34, pt. 1, pp. 588–89; pt. 3, pp. 811–12; Polignac diary, May 3, 14, 1864.

32. Johnson, *Red River Campaign*, pp. 267–72; Longacre, "Rescue on Red River," pp. 8–9, 39–42; *O.R.*, vol. 34, pt. 1, pp. 191–93, 209–10, 402–404, 591; *O.R.N.*, vol. 26, pp. 130–35, 173; Parrish, *Richard Taylor*, pp. 385, 389.

33. Barr, *Polignac's Texas Brigade*, p. 44; *O.R.*, vol. 34, p. 593; Taylor, *Destruction and Reconstruction*, p. 232.

34. Barr, *Polignac's Texas Brigade*, pp. 44–45; *O.R.*, vol. 34, pp. 193, 211–12, 593.

35. Johnson, *Red River Campaign*, pp. 273–74; *O.R.*, vol. 34, pp. 193, 211–12, 591, 593.

36. Johnson, *Red River Campaign*, p. 274; *O.R.*, vol. 34, pp. 193, 211–12, 591, 593; Polignac diary, May 19, 1864.

37. Barr, *Polignac's Texas Brigade*, p. 45; Johnson, *Red River Campaign*, pp. 274–75; *O.R.*, vol. 34, pp. 193, 212, 593–95; Polignac diary, May 19, 1864.

38. Barr, *Polignac's Texas Brigade*, p. 45; Polignac diary, May 19, 1864.

39. Barr, *Polignac's Texas Brigade*, p. 44; Bearss, *A Louisiana Confederate*, pp. 122–23; *O.R.*, vol. 34, pp. 193, 212, 593–95; Winters, *Civil War in Louisiana*, p. 376.

40. Barr, *Polignac's Texas Brigade*, pp. 45–46.

41. Johnson, *Red River Campaign*, p. 275; *O.R.*, vol. 34, pp. 304, 320, 329, 337, 347–48, 357, 364, 367, 594, 624, 631; Taylor, *Destruction and Reconstruction*, p. 191.

42. Arthur W. Bergeron, Jr., *Guide to Louisiana Confederate Military Units, 1861–1865*, p. 18; Johnson, *Red River Campaign*, p. 275; Polignac diary, May 19, 1864; John Scott, *Story of the Thirty-second Iowa Infantry Volunteers*, p. 278.

43. Bearss, *A Louisiana Confederate*, p. 123.

44. Barr, *Polignac's Texas Brigade*, pp. 46, 47; Bearss, *A Louisiana Confederate*, pp. 123, 127; Johnson, *Red River Campaign*, p. 275; *O.R.*, vol. 34, pp. 304, 320, 329, 337, 347–48, 357, 364, 367, 370, 467, 594, 624, 631.

45. Johnson, *Red River Campaign*, p. 276; *O.R.*, vol. 34, pt. 1, p. 594; pt. 3, p. 644; Kirby Smith, "Defense of the Red River," p. 360; Taylor, *Destruction and Reconstruction*, p. 232.

46. Kerby, *Kirby Smith's Confederacy*, p. 319.

47. Taylor, *Destruction and Reconstruction*, pp. 229–30.

48. Johnson, *Red River Campaign*, pp. 277–78, Grady McWhiney and Perry Jamison, *Attack and Die*, pp. 77, 144.

49. Johnson, *Red River Campaign*, pp. 277–78.

50. Johnson, *Red River Campaign*, pp. 283–84; S. C. Jones, *Reminiscences of the Twenty-second Iowa Volunteer Infantry*, p. 69; *O.R.*, vol. 34, p. 595.

51. Barr, *Polignac's Texas Brigade*, p. 47; "Reply of Maj. Gen. Polignac," Louisiana Historical Collection, Confederate Personnel, Manuscripts Section, Tulane University Library, New Orleans; Polignac diary, June 1, 1864.

52. Barr, *Polignac's Texas Brigade*, p. 47; Bearss, *A Louisiana Confederate*, pp. 127–28, 294.

53. Barr, *Polignac's Texas Brigade*, p. 47; Bearss, *A Louisiana Confederate*, p. 129; *O.R.N.*, vol. 26, pp. 369–70, 779–80.

54. Barr, *Polignac's Texas Brigade*, p. 47; Bearss, *A Louisiana Confederate*, p. 129; *O.R.N.*, vol. 26, pp. 369–70, 779–80; Polignac diary, July 28, 1864.

CHAPTER 10

1. Barr, *Polignac's Texas Brigade*, pp. 47–48.

2. Ibid., p. 48; Parks, *Kirby Smith*, p. 420; Parrish, *Richard Taylor*, p. 406; *O.R.*, vol. 34, pt. 1, p. 548; vol. 41, pt. 1, p. 90.

3. Barr, *Polignac's Texas Brigade*, p. 48; Parks, *Kirby Smith*, p. 420; Parrish, *Richard Taylor*, p. 406; *O.R.*, vol. 34, pt. 1, p. 548; vol. 41, pt. 1, p. 90; Polignac diary, Aug. 1–9, 1864.

4. Brown, *Journey to Pleasant Hill*, p. 436; Winters, *Civil War in Louisiana*, p. 381.

5. Bearss, *A Louisiana Confederate*, pp. 155, 156, 304; Kerby, *Kirby Smith's Confederacy*, pp. 327–29; *O.R.*, vol. 41, pt. 1, p. 112.

6. Polignac diary, Aug. 10–11, 1864.

7. Barr, *Polignac's Texas Brigade*, p. 49; Bearss, *A Louisiana Confederate*, pp. 155–56, 304; Blessington, *Walker's Texas Division*, p. 275; Kerby, *Kirby Smith's Confederacy*, pp. 337–39; Parks, *Kirby Smith*, p. 429.

8. Barr, *Polignac's Texas Brigade*, p. 49; Polignac diary, Aug. 31, Sept. 1–6, 1864.

9. Barr, *Polignac's Texas Brigade*, p. 49; Polignac diary, Sept. 9, 1864.

10. Polignac diary, Sept. 18, 1864.

11. Barr, *Polignac's Texas Brigade*, p. 50; Bearss, *A Louisiana Confederate*, p. 166; Blessington, *Walker's Texas Division*, pp. 277–78; Polignac diary, Sept. 26, 1864.

12. Polignac diary, Sept. 27, 1864.

13. Barr, *Polignac's Texas Brigade*, p. 50; L. David Norris, ed., *With the 18th Texas Infantry: The Autobiography of Wilburn Hill King*, p. 81; Parks, *Kirby Smith*, pp. 438–39; Polignac diary, Oct. 30, 1864.

14. Barr, *Polignac's Texas Brigade*, p. 50; *O.R.*, series 1, vol. 3, p. 961; Polignac diary, Sept. 28–29, Oct. 1–5, 8, 1864.

15. Barr, *Polignac's Texas Brigade*, p. 51; *O.R.*, series 1, vol. 41, pt. 3, p. 967; pt. 4, p. 1002; ser. 4, vol. 3, p. 961; Polignac diary, Oct. 9–10, 1864.

16. Polignac diary, Oct. 12–13, 1864.

17. Ibid., Oct. 13–16, 1864.

18. Ibid., Oct. 18, 1864.

19. Ibid., Oct. 20, 24, 1864.

20. Ibid., Nov. 3, 1864.

21. Ibid., Oct. 31, Nov. 1–2, 1864; Barr, *Polignac's Texas Brigade*, pp. 50–51; C. J. Polignac to William P. Miles, Nov. 1, 1864, William P. Miles Papers, Southern Historical Collection, University of North Carolina, Chapel Hill.

22. Polignac diary, Nov. 3, 1864.

23. Ibid., Nov. 4, 1864.

24. Ibid., Nov. 7, 1864.

25. Barr, *Polignac's Texas Brigade*, p. 51; Polignac diary, Nov. 13–14, 1864.

26. Polignac diary, Nov. 15–16, 1864.

27. Ibid., Nov. 18, 21, 24–26, 1864; Barr, *Polignac's Texas Brigade*, p. 51; *O.R.*, vol. 41, pt. 3, p. 967; pt. 4, p. 1002.

28. Polignac diary, Nov. 26, 1864.

29. Ibid., Nov. 28, 1864.

30. Barr, *Polignac's Texas Brigade*, p. 51; Norris, *With the 18th Texas*, p. 82; Polignac diary, Dec. 1, 7, 1864.

31. Polignac diary, Nov. 29, 1864.

32. Barr, *Polignac's Texas Brigade*, p. 52; Polignac diary, Dec. 2, 1864.

33. Blessington, *Walker's Texas Division*, pp. 282–83; Norris, *With the 18th Texas*, p. 82.

34. Barr, *Polignac's Texas Brigade*, p. 52; Polignac diary, Dec. 24, 1864.

35. C. J. Polignac, "Polignac's Mission," *Southern Historical Society Papers* 32 (Jan.–Dec., 1904): 365.

36. Kerby, *Kirby Smith's Confederacy*, p. 373; *O.R.*, vol. 48, pt. 1, pp. 1319–20; Parks, *Kirby Smith*, p. 451.

37. Polignac, "Polignac's Mission," pp. 364–71.

38. Ibid., p. 370.

39. Alcee Fortier, *A History of Louisiana*, 4:60.

40. Polignac diary, Jan. 10–11, 1865; Thomas C. Reynolds to Maj. Gen. C. J. Polignac, Jan. 10, 1865, C. A. J. M. Polignac Letters, 1844–67 (microfilm, Special Collections, Hill Memorial Library, Louisiana State University, Baton Rouge).

41. Polignac diary, Jan. 12, 15, 17, 22, Feb. 1, 1865.

42. Ibid., Jan. 22, 1865.

43. Ibid., Feb. 25, 1865.

44. Ibid., Feb. 25, 1865; Polignac, "Polignac's Mission," p. 368.

45. Polignac diary, Mar. 18, 1865.

46. Ibid., Mar. 21, 1865; Polignac, "Polignac's Mission," p. 368.

47. Polignac, "Polignac's Mission," p. 368–69; Fortier, *A History of Louisiana*, vol. 4, p. 60.

48. Barr, *Polignac's Texas Brigade*, pp. 53–56; Blessington, *Walker's Texas Division*, pp. 291–92, 294, 297, 302.

49. Camille de Polignac to Gen. J. H. Harrison, Aug. 20, 1867, in Polignac diary, Aug. 20, 1867.

50. Polignac, "Polignac's Mission," pp. 365–71; J. C. Moncure to Gen. C. J. Polignac, May 16, June 23, July 27, 1865, J. C. Moncure Papers, Hill Memorial Library, Louisiana State University.

51. Polignac to Harrison, Aug. 20, 1867; Polignac diary, Aug. 20, 1867, C. J. Polignac to J. C. Moncure, Jan. 27, 1868, Moncure Papers.

52. Camille de Polignac, "Ulster and the Confederate States," *Nineteenth Century Review* 33 (June, 1893): 929–31.

53. Ibid., pp. 927–28.

54. The Marquise de Crequi Montfort de Courtivron, "le General Prince Camille de Polignac" (Paris, France, 1962) C. A. J. M. de Polignac Papers (microfilm, Louisiana State University Library, Baton Rouge), pp. 1–8; C. A. J. M. de Polignac, "Journal Militaire," Polignac Papers.

55. [P.] G. T. Beauregard to Prince Camille de Polignac, June 11, 1870, Apr. 7, 1873, Polignac Letters, 1844–67.

56. The Marquise de Crequi Montfort de Courtivron, "Notes on Prince Camille de Polignac," (Paris, France, 1966), Polignac Papers, pp. 1–2; Hatton, "Soldier's Life," pp. 210–11.

57. Hatton, "Soldier's Life," p. 211.

58. Ibid., pp. 22–23, 211.

59. Ibid., p. 212.

60. Ibid., pp. 212–16; "Major General Prince Camille de Polignac, C.S.A.," *United Daughters of the Confederacy Magazine* 20 (Jan., 1957): 22.

61. C. J. Polignac to Gen. Marcus J. Wright, Oct. 6, 1913, Marcus J. Wright Papers, Southern Historical Collection, University of North Carolina, Chapel Hill.

62. Hatton, "Soldier's Life," p. 218; Mrs. F. C. Kolman, "Confederate Monuments at Mansfield, La." *Confederate Veteran* 33 (1925): 170–72.

Bibliography

ARCHIVES AND MANUSCRIPT COLLECTIONS

Confederate Research Center, Hill College, Hillsboro, Texas. United Daughters of the Confederacy Collection: Wilburn Hill King Papers. Walter, John S., "Histories of Texas Units in the Civil War," 1981.

Hill Memorial Library, Louisiana State University, Baton Rouge. Nathaniel P. Banks Letterbook. "Notes on the Red River Campaign," J. Fair Hardin Papers. Arthur W. Hyatt Diary (typescript). Special Collections: John C. Moncure Papers, J. Fair Hardin Collection; J. D. Garland Papers.

Historic New Orleans Collection, New Orleans. Miscellaneous Manuscript Collection.

Howard-Tilton Memorial Library, Tulane University, New Orleans. Joseph L. Brent Papers. Louisiana Historical Association Collections: Civil War Papers.

Louisiana State University Library, Baton Rouge. Louisiana Vertical File: George W. Guess Letters, 1861–65. C. A. J. M. Polignac Letters, 1844–67 (microfilm).

Mansfield Museum, Mansfield, Louisiana. Camille de Polignac, "Appeal to the People" (photocopy). Prince Camille de Polignac to P. G. T. Beauregard, March 22, 1861 (typescript).

National Archives, Washington, D.C. Confederate Archives: Register of Appointments, Confederate States Army. Confederate Service Record Files: Richard Taylor Papers. Letters Received by the Confederate Adjutant and Inspector General, January–April, 1862, and October–December, 1863. War Department Collection of Confederate Records: General and Staff Officers File, Confederate States of America; Camillus J. Polignac File.

Russell Library, Northwestern Louisiana State University, Natchitoches. C. E. Cloutier Manuscript Collection. Camille de Polignac
Diary of the War between the States (microfilm).

Southern Historical Collection, University of North Carolina, Chapel
Hill. Felix Pierre Poché Diary. Edmund Kirby Smith Papers. John
G. Walker Papers. Marcus J. Wright Papers.

Texas State Archives, Austin. Hamilton P. Bee Papers.

Tulane University Library, New Orleans. Louisiana Historical Collection. Manuscripts Section: Camille de Polignac, "Reply of Maj. Gen.
Polignac."

United States Army History Institute, Carlisle Barracks, Pennsylvania.
John G. Walker, "The War of Secession West of the Mississippi
River during the Years 1863–4–&5" (typescript).

GOVERNMENT DOCUMENTS

Journal of the Congress of the Confederate States of America, 1861–1865.
7 vols. Washington, D.C.: Government Printing Office, 1904–1905.

U.S. Congress. *Report of the Joint Committee on the Conduct of the War, at
the Second Session, Thirty-Eighth Congress.* Vol. 2, *Red River Expedition.*
Washington, D.C., 1865

U.S. House. *Captured and Forfeited Cotton.* 39th Cong., 2nd sess. H. Doc.
97. Serial 1293.

U.S. Navy Department. *Official Records of the Union and Confederate
Navies in the War of the Rebellion.* 31 vols. Washington, D.C.: Government Printing Office, 1890–1901.

U.S. Senate. *Captured and Abandoned Cotton.* 40th Cong., 2nd sess. S.
Doc. 56. Serial 1317.

U.S. War Department. *The War of the Rebellion: A Compilation of the Official Records of the Union and Confederate Armies.* 128 vols. Washington, D.C.: Government Printing Office, 1890–1901.

BOOKS AND ARTICLES

Anderson, John Q. *Campaigning with Parson's Texas Cavalry Brigade,
C.S.A.* Hillsboro, Tex.: Hill Junior College Press, 1957.
———. *A Texas Surgeon in the C.S.A.* Tuscaloosa, Ala.: Confederate Pub-
lishing Company, 1957.

Andrews, J. Cutler. *The North Reports the Civil War*. Pittsburgh: University of Pittsburgh Press, 1955.

Arceneaux, William. *Acadian General: Alfred Mouton and the Civil War*. Lafayette: University of Southwestern Louisiana Press, 1981.

Artz, Frederick B. *France under the Bourbon Restoration*. Cambridge, Mass.: Harvard University Press, 1931.

————. *Reaction and Revolution*. New York: Harper Torchbooks, 1963.

Ashcraft, Allan C. *Texas in the Civil War: A Resume History*. Austin: Texas Civil War Centennial Commission, 1962.

Bankston, Mary L. B. *Camp-Fire Stories of the Mississippi Valley Campaign*. New Orleans: L. Graham Company, 1914.

Barkley, A. J. "The Battle of Pleasant Hill, Louisiana: Recollections of a Private Soldier." *Annals of Iowa* 3 (April, 1897): 23–31.

Barr, Alwyn. *Polignac's Texas Brigade*. Houston: Texas Gulf Coast Historical Association, 1964.

————. "Texas Losses in the Red River Campaign, 1864." *Texas Military History* 3, no. 2 (summer, 1963): 103–10.

————, ed. "William T. Mechling's Journal of the Red River Campaign, April 7–May 10, 1864." *Texana* 1 (fall, 1963): 363–79.

Bartlett, Napier. *Military Record of Louisiana; Including Biographical and Historical Papers Relating to the Military Organization of the State*. New Orleans: L. Graham and Company, 1875. Reprint, Baton Rouge: Louisiana State University Press, 1964.

Battine, Cecil. *The Crisis of the Confederacy*. New York: Longmans, Green, and Company, 1905.

"The Battle of Mansfield." *Southern Bivouac* 3 (April, 1885): 412–15.

Bearss, Edwin C., ed. *A Louisiana Confederate—Diary of Felix Pierre Poché*. Natchitoches: Northwestern Louisiana State University Press, 1972.

Bee, Hamilton P. "Battle of Pleasant Hill—An Error Corrected." *Southern Historical Society Papers* 8 (1880; reprint, Wilmington, N.C.: Broadfoot Publishing, 1990).

Bell, Alfred Hoyt. *The Beleaguered City: Richmond, 1861–1865*. New York: Alfred A. Knopf, 1946.

Bergeron, Arthur W., Jr. *Guide to Louisiana Confederate Military Units, 1861–1865*. Baton Rouge: Louisiana State University Press, 1989.

————, ed. *The Civil War Reminiscences of Major Silas T. Grisamore, C.S.A.* Baton Rouge: Louisiana State University Press, 1993.

Biegel, Peter. *History of the Second Battalion Duryee Zouaves, 65th Regiment New York Volunteer Infantry*. Rev. ed. New York: n.p., 1903.

Blessington, Joseph Palmer. *The Campaigns of Walker's Texas Division.* New York: Lange, Little and Co., 1875.

Boatner, Mark Mayo, III. *The Civil War Dictionary.* New York: David McKay Company, 1987.

Bonner, Thomas Reuben. "Sketches of the Campaign of 1864." *The Land We Love* 5:459–66, 6:7–12.

Bowman, John S., gen. ed. *Who Was Who in the Civil War.* New York: Crescent Books, 1994.

Boyd, William K., ed. *Military Reminiscences of Gen. Wm. R. Boggs, C.S.A.* Durham, N.C.: Seeman Printery, 1913.

Boynton, Charles B. *The History of the Navy during the Rebellion.* 2 vols. New York: D. Appleton and Company, 1867.

Bragg, Jefferson Davis. *Louisiana in the Confederacy.* Baton Rouge: Louisiana State University Press, 1941.

Bridgers, Roger S., ed. *Confederate Military History: A Library of Confederate States History, in Seventeen Volumes.* Extended edition. 1899. Reprint, Wilmington, N.C.: Broadfoot Publishing Company, 1988.

Bringhurst, Thomas H., and Frank Swigart. *History of the Forty-sixth Regiment Indiana Volunteer Infantry.* Logansport, Ind.: Wilson Humphreys and Company, 1888.

Brock, Miss Sally. *Richmond during the War: Four Years of Personal Observation.* New York: G. W. Carleton and Company, 1867.

Brown, Norman D., ed. *Journey to Pleasant Hill: The Civil War Letters of Captain Elijah P. Petty, Walker's Texas Division, C.S.A.* San Antonio: University of Texas Institute of Texan Cultures, 1982.

Bryner, Cloyd. The *Story of the Illinois 47th.* Springfield, Ill.: Phillip Brothers Printers, 1905.

Byam, W. W. "Swapping Stories in Texas." *Blue and Gray* 4 (November, 1894): 313–15.

Campbell, J. I. "Reminiscences of a Private Soldier." *Confederate Veteran* 21, no. 2 (February, 1913): 67.

Caskey, W. M. *Secession and Restoration of Louisiana.* Baton Rouge: Louisiana State University Press, 1964.

Chaiten, Peter M., and the editors of Time-Life Books. *The Coastal War: Chesapeake Bay to Rio Grande.* Alexandria, Va.: Time-Life Books, 1984.

Clark, Orton S. *The One Hundred and Sixteenth Regiment of York State Volunteers.* Buffalo: Printing House of Mathews and Warren, 1868.

Combs, D. S. "Texas Boys in the War." *Confederate Veteran* 35 (July, 1925): 265.

Connelly, Thomas Lawrence. *Army of the Heartland: The Army of Ten-*

nessee, 1861–1862. Baton Rouge: Louisiana State University Press, 1967.

Crist, Lynda Lasswell, ed. *The Papers of Jefferson Davis: Vol. 8, 1862*. Baton Rouge: Louisiana State University Press, 1995.

Crute, Joseph, Jr. *Units of the Confederate States Army*. Midlothian, Va.: Derwent Books, 1987.

Daniel, Larry J. *Soldiering in the Army of Tennessee: A Portrait of Life in the Confederate Army*. Chapel Hill: University of North Carolina Press, 1991.

Davis, J. B. "The Life of Richard Taylor." *Louisiana Historical Quarterly* 24 (January, 1941): 40–126.

Davis, Varina Howell. *Jefferson Davis*. New York: Belford Company, 1890.

DeBray, Xavier Blanchard. "A Sketch of DeBray's 26th Regiment of Texas Cavalry." *Southern Historical Society Papers* 12 (January–December, 1885; reprint, Wilmington, N.C.: Broadfoot Publishing, 1990): 547–54.

DeLeon, Thomas Cooper. *Belles, Beaux and Brains of the 60's*. New York: W. D. Dillingham, 1907.

———. *Four Years in the Rebel Capitals*. New York: Collier Books, 1962.

Dickey, Thomas S., and Peter C. George. *Field Artillery Projectiles of the American Civil War*. Rev. ed. Mechanicsville, Va.: Arsenal Publications II, 1993.

Dorsey, Sarah A., ed. *Recollections of Henry Watkins Allen, Brigadier General, Confederate States Army, Ex-Governor of Louisiana*. New York: M. Doolady, 1866.

Duaine, Carl L. *The Dead Men Wore Boots: An Account of the 32nd Texas Volunteer Cavalry, CSA*. Austin, Tex.: San Felipe Press, 1966.

Duke, B. W. "Bragg's Campaign in Kentucky, 1862." *Southern Bivouac* 4 (June, 1885–May, 1886): 232–40.

Duncan, Merle Mears. "David Richard Wallace." *Texana* 1 (fall, 1963): 341–62.

Eaton, Clement. *A History of the Southern Confederacy*. New York: Free Press, 1988.

Erath, Lucy A., ed. *The Memoirs of Major George B. Erath, 1813–1891*. Waco, Tex.: Heritage Society of Waco, 1956.

Evans, Clement A., ed. *Confederate Military History: A Library of the Confederate States in Seventeen Volumes: Written by Distinguished Men of the South*. Wilmington, N.C.: Confederate Publishing Company, 1899.

Evans, Eli N. *Judah P. Benjamin, The Jewish Confederate*. New York: Free Press, 1988.

Ewer, James K. *The Third Massachusetts Cavalry in the War for the Union.* Maplewood, Mass.: Wm. G. J. Perry Press, 1903.

Fitzhugh, Lester N. *Texas Batteries, Battalions, Regiments, Commanders, and Field Officers: Confederate States Army, 1861–1865.* Midlothian, Tex.: Mirror Press, 1959.

———. "Texas Forces in the Red River Campaign, March–May, 1864." *Southwestern Historical Quarterly* 61, no. 1 (July, 1957): 15–22.

Flinn, Frank M. *Campaigning with Banks in Louisiana.* Lynn, Mass.: Thos. P. Nichols, 1887.

Folliot, Denise. *Queen of France.* Translated by Andre Castelot. New York: Harper and Bros., 1957.

Fortier, Alcee. *A History of Louisiana.* 4 vols. New York: Joyant and Company, 1904.

Frankignoul, Daniel J. *Prince Camille de Polignac, Major General, C.S.A. "The Lafayette of the South."* Brussels: Confederate Historical Association of Belgium, 1996.

Gallaway, B. P. *The Ragged Rebel: A Common Soldier in W. H. Parson's Texas Cavalry, 1861–1865.* Austin: University of Texas Press, 1988.

Gibbons, Tony. *Warships and Naval Battles of the U.S. Civil War.* London: Dragons World, 1989.

Gibbs, Phillip. *Men and Women of the French Revolution.* London: Kegan Paul, Trench, Trukner, and Company, 1906.

Goodloe, P. H. "Service in the Trans-Mississippi." *Confederate Veteran* 23 (January, 1915): 31–32.

Goodrich, B. G. "Batile [*sic*] of Mansfield, LA." *Confederate Veteran* 8 (August, 1900): 103.

Goyne, Minetta Altgelt. *Lone Star and Double Eagle.* Fort Worth: Texas Christian University Press, 1982.

Hagy, P. S. "Military Operations of the Lower Trans-Mississippi Department, 1863–64." *Confederate Veteran* 12 (December, 1916): 545.

Hammond, Paul F. "General Kirby Smith's Campaign in Kentucky in 1862." *Southern Historical Society Papers* 9 (July–August, 1881; reprint, Wilmington, N.C.: Broadfoot Publishing, 1990): 246–553.

Hanaburgh, D. H. *History of the One Hundred and Twenty-eighth Regiment, New York Volunteers.* Po[ugh]keepsie, N.Y.: Press of the Enterprise Publishing Company, 1894.

Hardin, J. Fair. *Northwest Louisiana: A History of the Watershed of the Red River, 1714–1939.* Shreveport, La.: Historical Record Association, 1939.

Harrington, Fred H. *Fighting Politician: Major General N. P. Banks.* Philadelphia: University of Pennsylvania Press, 1948.

Hatton, Roy O. "Prince Camille de Polignac and the American Civil War, 1863–1865." *Louisiana Studies* 3 (summer, 1868): 65–74.

Heartsill, William W. *Fourteen Hundred and 91 Days in the Confederate Army.* Edited by Bell I. Wiley. Jackson, Tex.: McCowat-Mercer Press, 1954.

Henderson, Harry McCorry. *Texas in the Confederacy.* San Antonio, Tex.: Naylor Company, 1955.

Hewitt, J. E. *1864 Battle of Mansfield, Mansfield, Louisiana.* 1925. Reprint, Mansfield, La.: Kate Beard Chapter No. 397, Daughters of the Confederacy, 1949.

———. "The Battle of Mansfield, Louisiana." *Confederate Veteran* 33 (May, 1925): 172–73, 198.

Hoffman, Wickham. *Camp, Court, and Siege, a Narrative of Personal Adventure and Observation during Two Wars 1861–1865, 1870–1871.* New York: Harper and Bros., 1877.

Hoole, William Stanley, ed., and Charles Girard, trans. *A Visit to the Confederate States of America in 1863, Memoir to His Majesty Napoleon III.* Tuscaloosa, Ala.: Confederate Publishing Company, 1962.

Irwin, Richard B. *History of the Nineteenth Army Corps.* New York: G. P. Putnam's Sons, 1892.

———. "The Red River Campaign." In *Battles and Leaders of the Civil War*, eds. Robert Johnson and Clarence Buel. New York: Century Company, 1887–88. 4:345–68.

Johnson, Ludwell H. *Red River Campaign: Politics and Cotton in the Civil War.* 1958. Reprint, Kent, Ohio: Kent State University Press, 1993.

Johnson, Robert Underwood, and Clarence Clough Buel, eds. *Battles and Leaders of the Civil War.* 4 Vols. 1887–88. Reprint, Secaucus, N.J.: Booksales, 1984.

Jones, Allen W. "Military events in Texas During the Civil War, 1861–1865." *Southwestern Historical Quarterly* 34 (1930–31): 203–30.

Jones, John B. *A Rebel War Clerk's Diary.* Edited by Earl Schenck Miers. New York: A. S. Barnes and Company, 1961.

Jones, S. C. *Reminiscences of the Twenty-second Iowa Volunteer Infantry.* Iowa City: n.p., 1907.

Josephy, Alvin M., Jr. *The Civil War in the American West.* New York: Vintage Books, 1991.

Kerby, Robert L. *Kirby Smith's Confederacy: The Trans-Mississippi South, 1863–1865.* New York: Columbia University Press, 1972.

Kimball, William J., ed. *Richmond in Time of War.* Boston: Houghton Mifflin, 1960.

Landon, Melville D. *The Franco-Prussian War in a Nutshell.* New York: G. W. Carleton and Company, 1962.

Lemay, Judge Harry J. "General de Polignac." *United Daughters of the Confederacy Magazine* 34 (January, 1968): 12.

Livermore, Thomas L. *Numbers and Losses in the Civil War in America: 1861–65.* Bloomington: Indiana University Press, 1957.

Lonn, Ella. *Desertion during the Civil War.* Gloucester, Mass.: Peter Smith, 1966.

———. *Foreigners in the Confederacy.* Chapel Hill: University of North Carolina Press, 1940.

———. *Foreigners in the Union Army and Navy.* Baton Rouge: Louisiana State University Press, 1951.

Lord, Walter, ed. *The Fremantle Diary: Being the Journal of Lieutenant Colonel James Arthur Lyon Fremantle, Coldstream Guards, on his Three Months in the Southern States.* Boston: Little, Brown and Company, 1954.

Lufkin, Edwin B. *History of the Thirteenth Maine Regiment.* Bridgton, Maine: H. A. Shorey and Son, 1898.

Luvaas, Jay. *The Military Legacy of the Civil War.* Chicago: University of Chicago Press, 1957.

Mahan, A. T. *The Gulf and Inland Waters.* New York: Charles Scribner's Sons, 1901.

McDonough, James Lee. *War in Kentucky: From Shiloh to Perryville.* Knoxville: University of Tennessee Press, 1994.

McWhiney, Grady. *Braxton Bragg and Confederate Defeat.* New York: Columbia University Press, 1969.

———. *Cracker Culture: Celtic Way in the Old South.* Tuscaloosa: University of Alabama Press, 1988.

McWhiney, Grady, and Perry Jamieson. *Attack and Die: Civil War Military Tactics and the Southern Heritage.* Tuscaloosa: University of Alabama Press, 1982.

"Major General Prince Camille de Polignac, C.S.A." *United Daughters of the Confederacy Magazine* 20 (January, 1957): 14, 15, 19, 22.

Marshall, T. B. *History of the Eighty-third Ohio Volunteer Infantry.* Cincinnati: Eighty-third Ohio Volunteer Infantry Association, 1913.

Maury, Dabney H. "Sketch of General Richard Taylor." *Southern Historical Society Papers* 7 (July, 1879): 343–45.

Merrick, Caroline. *Old Times in Dixieland: A Southern Matron's Recollections.* New York: Grafton Press, 1941.

Miller, Francis T., ed. *The Photographic History of the Civil War.* 10 vols. New York: Review of Reviews, 1911.

Moneyhon, Carl, and Bobby Roberts. *Portraits of Conflict: A Photographic History of Louisiana in the Civil War.* Fayetteville: University of Arkansas Press, 1990.

Moore, Frank, ed. *The Rebellion Record: A Diary of American Events.* 12 vols. New York: D. Van Nostrand, 1862–71.

Norris, L. David, ed. *With the 18th Texas Infantry: The Autobiography of Wilburn Hill King.* Hillsboro, Tex.: Hill College Press, 1996.

Oates, Stephen B. *Confederate Cavalry West of the River.* Austin: University of Texas Press, 1961.

Olmsted, Frederick Law. *A Journey Through Texas; or, A Saddletrip on the Southwestern Frontier: with a Statistical Appendix.* New York: Dix, Edwards & Company, 1857.

Owsley, Frank. *King Cotton Diplomacy.* Chicago: University of Chicago Press, 1931.

Paris, Comte de (Louis Philippe Albert d'Orléans). *History of the Civil War in America.* 4 vols. Philadelphia: Porter and Coates, 1875–88.

Parks, Joseph Howard. *General Edmund Kirby Smith, C.S.A.* Baton Rouge: Louisiana State University Press, 1954.

———. *General Leonidas Polk, C.S.A.: The Fighting Bishop.* Baton Rouge: Louisiana State University Press, 1962.

Parrish, T. Michael. *Richard Taylor: Soldier Prince of Dixie.* Chapel Hill: University of North Carolina Press, 1992.

Pellet, Elias P. *History of the 114th Regiment. New York State Volunteers.* Norwich, N.Y.: Telegraphic and Chronicle Press Print, 1866.

Pierredon, Count Michel de. "Major General C. J. Polignac, C.S.A." *Confederate-Veteran* 22 (September, 1914): 389.

Polignac, Camille de. *L'Union Americaine apres la guerre.* Paris: E. Dentu, 1866.

———. "Polignac's Mission." *Southern Historical Society Papers* 32 (January–December, 1904): 365–71.

———. "Ulster and the Confederate States." *Nineteenth Century Review* 33 (June, 1893): 927–31.

Polignac, Hedwige de. *Les Polignac.* Paris: Fasquelle Additions, 1960.

Porter, David D. *Incidents and Anecdotes of the Civil War.* New York: D. Appleton and Company, 1891.

———. *The Naval History of the Civil War.* New York: Sherman Publishing Company and J. Dewing Company, 1887.

Powers, George W. *The Story of the Thirty-Eighth Regiment of Massachusetts Volunteers.* Cambridge, Mass.: Dakin and Metcalf, 1866.

Pratt, Fletcher. *Civil War on Western Waters.* New York: Henry Holt and Company, 1956.

Ragan, Cooper K., ed. "The Diary of Captain George W. O'Brien, 1863." *Southwestern Historical Quarterly* 67 (January, 1964): 364–66.

Roman, Alfred. The *Military-Operations of General Beauregard in the War between the States, 1861–1865.* 2 vols. New York: Harper and Bros., 1884.

Sawyer, William E., and Neal. A. Baker, Jr., eds. "A Texan in the Civil War." *Texas Military History* 2:275–78.

Scott, John. *Story of the Thirty Second Iowa Infantry Volunteers.* Nevada, Iowa: privately printed, 1896.

Scott, R. B. *The History of the 67th Regiment Indiana Infantry.* Bedford, Ind.: Herald Book and Job Print, 1892.

Sherman, William Tecumseh. *Memoirs of General W. T. Sherman.* New York: Library of America, 1990.

Shorey, Henry A. *The Story of the Maine Fifteenth.* Bridgton, Maine: Press of the Bridgton News, 1890.

Sifakis, Stewart. *Compendium of the Confederate Armies: Louisiana.* New York: Facts on File, 1995.

———. *Compendium of the Confederate Armies: Texas.* New York: Facts on File, 1995.

Smith, Page. *Trial by Fire, A Peoples' History of the Civil War and Reconstruction.* Vol. 5. New York: McGraw-Hill Book, 1982.

Smith, Rebecca, and Marion Mullins, eds. "The Diary of H. C. Medford, Confederate Soldier, 1864." *Southwestern Historical Quarterly* 34 (January, 1931): 203–30.

Smith, Walter G., ed. *Life and Letters of Thomas Kilby Smith.* New York: G. P. Putnam's Sons, 1898.

Sperry, A. F. *History of the 33d Iowa Volunteer Regiment.* Des Moines, Iowa: Mills and Company, 1866.

Sprague, Homer B. *History of the 13th Infantry Regiment of Connecticut Volunteers.* Hartford, Conn.: Case, Lockwood and Company, 1867.

Stanyan, John M. *A History of the Eighth Regiment of New Hampshire Volunteers.* Concord, N.H.: Ira C. Evans, Printer, 1892.

Taylor, Richard. *Destruction and Reconstruction: Personal Experiences of the Late War.* Edited by Richard B. Harwell. New York: Longmans, Green and Company, 1955.

Thomas, Emory M. *The Confederate State of Richmond, A Biography of the Capital.* Austin: University of Texas Press, 1971.

Tiemann, William F. *The 159th Regiment Infantry, New York State Volunteers.* Brooklyn: privately printed, 1896.

Tyler, Lyon Gardner. *Encyclopedia of Virginia Biography II*. New York: Lewis Historical Publishing, 1951.

Tyson, Carl Newton. *The Red River in Southwestern History*. Norman: University of Oklahoma Press, 1981.

Waitt, Robert W., Jr. *Confederate Military Hospitals in Richmond*. Richmond, Va.: Richmond Civil War Centennial Committee, 1964.

Warner, Ezra J. *Generals in Blue: Lives of the Union Commanders*. Baton Rouge: Louisiana State University Press, 1964.

———. *Generals in Gray: Lives of the Confederate Commanders*. Baton Rouge: Louisiana State University Press, 1987.

Watkins, Sam R. *"Co. Aytch" A Side Show of the Big Show*. Edited by Bell I. Wiley. Wilmington, N.C.: Broadfoot Publishing Company, 1990.

Weddle, Robert S. *Plow-Horse Cavalry: The Caney Creek Boys in the Thirty-fourth Texas*. Austin, Tex.: Madrona Press, 1974.

Wiley, Bell Irvin. *Confederate Women*. Westport, Conn.: Greenwood Press, 1975.

———. *The Life of Johnny Reb: The Common Soldier of the Confederacy*. Baton Rouge: Louisiana State University Press, 1981.

Williams, J. M. *"The Eagle Regiment": 8th Wis. Inf'ty Vols*. Belleville, Wisc.: Recorder Print, 1890.

Williams, T. Harry. *Hayes of the Twenty-Third*. New York: Alfred A. Knopf, 1965.

———. *P. G. T. Beauregard: Napoleon in Gray*. Baton Rouge: Louisiana State University Press, 1955.

Wilson, James Grant, and John Fiske, eds. *Appleton's Cyclopaedia of American Biography*. New York: D. Appleton and Company, 1888.

Winters, John D. *The Civil War in Louisiana*. Baton Rouge: Louisiana State University Press, 1963.

Wolf, John B. *France: 1814–1919*. New York: Harper Torchbooks, 1963.

Woods, J. T. *Services in the Ninety-sixth Ohio Volunteers*. Toledo, Ohio: Blade Printing and Papers, 1874.

Woodward, C. Vann. *Mary Chesnut's Civil War*. New Haven, Conn.: Yale University Press, 1981.

Wooster, Ralph A. *Texas and Texans in the Civil War*. Austin, Tex.: Eakin Press, 1995.

———, ed. *Lone Star Blue and Gray: Essays on Texas in the Civil War*. Austin: Texas State Historical Association, 1995.

Wright, Mrs. D. Giraud. *A Southern Girl in '61: The War-Time Memories of a Confederate Senator's Daughter*. New York: Doubleday, Page and Company, 1959.

Wright, Gordon. *France in Modern Times.* Chicago: Rand McNally and Company, 1960.

Wright, Marcus J., comp. *Texas in the War, 1861–1865.* Hillsboro, Tex.: Hill Junior College Press, 1965.

Wright, Mike. *City under Siege: Richmond in the Civil War.* Lanham, Md.: Madison Books, 1995.

Yeary, Mamie, comp. *Reminiscences of the Boys in Gray, 1861–1865.* Dallas: Smith and Lamar, 1912.

DISSERTATIONS AND THESES

Ashcraft, Allan Coleman. "Texas: 1860–1866. The Lone Star State in the Civil War." Ph.D. diss., Columbia University, 1960.

Felgar, Robert Pattison. "Texas in the War for Southern Independence, 1861–1865." M.A. thesis, University of Texas, 1935.

Hatton, Roy O. "A Soldier's Life." Ph.D. diss., Louisiana State University, 1970.

———. "Prince de Polignac and the American Civil War, 1863–1865." M.A. thesis, Northwestern State College, 1963.

Index

Pages containing illustrations appear in *italics*.

Index